2.2.

Rugby in Focus

By the same Author

THE AVENGING ALL BLACKS (1972–73)
THE ROARING LIONS
THE MEN IN SCARLET
THE GREATEST LIONS (SOUTH AFRICA 1974)
GREAT MOMENTS IN SPORT: RUGBY FOOTBALL
WALLABIES' WALKABOUT
TRIAL OF STRENGTH (1977 LIONS IN NEW ZEALAND)

Rugby in Focus

A Review of Rugby Union Football 1978

J. B. G. Thomas

PELHAM BOOKS · LONDON

To those who really love the game

First published in Great Britain by
Pelham Books Ltd
52 Bedford Square
London WC1
1979

ISBN 0 7207 1137 1

Printed in Great Britain by Hollen Street Press, Slough
and bound by G. & J. Kitcat Ltd, London

Contents

Illustrations

Photographic Credits

BBC: 27-31
Mike Brett: 16-19
Peter Bush, Auckland: 7, 14
Colorsport: 33, 36, 37
Cork Examiner: 1, 32
D. Fullager: 8
The Irish Times: 35
The Scotsman Publications: 6
Topix: 20, 21
Western Mail and Echo, Cardiff: 2-5, 9, 11, 22, 24-6, 34

Foreword

When a son produces a Foreword to one of his father's books, the event requires a declaration of interest on his part. Therefore, I confess I have always considered most writing about rugby football to catch, in monochrome, only the muddy boots and smells of sweat and wintergreen and the steam from the bath left behind in the dressing-room after the game, but I believe Bryn Thomas's writing, on the contrary, is in Kodachrome and captures the period between first and final whistle, the glamour, brilliance and struggle of the game itself.

Rugby in Focus is a book in which there is violence. My own books are often violent, but with the violence of extreme situations and of lives led in fashions totally other than our own. My books are fiction – *Rugby in Focus* is fact. The violent incidents it documents did happen, and they are a matter of disgrace. To cry that 'It is only a game' is no longer a denigration of the passions in the grandstands and on the terraces; it is, and should be, a statement of affirmation. Rugby *is* only a game, and in that sense it is an artificiality, a confection, an illusion. So why does the oppressive, violent reality of the way we settle international disputes or call attention to our political aspirations, have to become an ingredient in such a confection? Violence in a sport is like artificial colouring in cake decoration: one drop too much (one drop, indeed might be too much) stains the whole of the icing a colour that is wrong and which cannot be ameliorated.

Rugby is a game of physical contact. I believe love is also largely about physical contact, at least on occasions. I do not understand why 'physical contact' has suffered a semantic shift, so that it now means 'raking with studs', 'punching when the referee is unsighted', 'straight-arm tackling' and 'deliberate injury'. Most of us do not beat our wives or lovers, and most rugby players are not sadists or on the kind of ego-trip that needs to leave marks on other human physiques; but some are, and for some coaches (at *all* levels), for some referees and for some law-makers, anything goes .

Rugby in Focus is in respects a harsher book than many that have preceded it in my father's output. His enviable enthusiasm has in no way dimmed, and it is not an old man's book carping of golden ages and Arcadian times and how everything has gone bad. It is a passionate book, but passionate in the cause of the game he has loved and studied for fifty years. If *he*, with his close knowledge of the game, is worried that it may cease to be amateur, perhaps we should all vie for commercial contracts, create Packer-style circuses, or go into the rugby helmet business. We could thereby make a great deal of money. It is an *amateur* game my father has loved. His book records a year in which the game has broken out with the myriad symptoms of 'the modern disease'. But in curing the patient, the doctors must also provide for the patient's future health. Sponsorship is not of necessity unpalatable, nor is remuneration; touch judges might be allowed to be responsible adults, like soccer's linesmen; someone is going to have to decide just what rugby players are allowed to wear; and someone is going to have to develop soft boot-studs.

I have a vision of sitting beside my father at the National Ground at Cardiff (even legends are mutable – whatever happened to the mystic 'Arms Park' where I spent my boyhood, perpetually freezing in the wait for the great autograph dash across a muddy sea?), and both of us are there to report a match, the first international Wales *v.* USSR. Fifteen men in scarlet jerseys are lined up against fifteen T-72 tanks. When the first ruck forms, more than split heads may result from this apotheosis of what is, after all, only a game – isn't it?

CRAIG THOMAS
Lichfield, January 1979

Preface

Rugby Union Football is at the crossroads in a changing world. It is the time when all those who love the game should stand up and be counted.

The remarkable growth of the game throughout the world in the last twenty-five years has been accompanied by 'over-sophistication', and a touch of violence, commercialism, and a possible threat of 'professionalism' at top level. If not checked or guided, these developments could see the great game move away from what it has been since its official launching in 1823, a game played by amateurs for enjoyment.

This book aims to look at the world game, its players, its matches, and controversies, during 1978. Rugby administrators, players old and young, critics and followers said and wrote much during the year. I have tried to combine some of this with my own comment and narrative of events. My thanks are due to all those who entertained me and talked to me at home and round the world.

There are many words of hard criticism in this book; my intent is to encourage protection of the game. I am confident that such words will not diminish in the least my host of friends in the game. It is a great game, and those who love it must protect it and help it as it continues to grow.

J. B. G. THOMAS
Cardiff, January 1979

I

This Is The Year
That Was!

The year 1978 in Rugby Union Football will be remembered as one of both success and failure by all countries, one of excitement, disappointment, changes and criticism, of development in new countries and of the retirement of world figures in the game. It was the year in which New Zealand sent a workmanlike side to the British Isles and returned home with the Grand Slam because opposing sides were timid in attack and referees were over-kind to the All Blacks. It was the year in which, at long last, France was made a member of the International Board, and in which Russia entered the European scene as a new potential rugby power. It was a year in which Australia adopted a win-at-all-costs attitude against Wales, and then almost overcame New Zealand at home. It was the year in which the first reactions to possible over-coaching were sounded, and a cry from the heart given, for more flair. It was a year when all four home countries demanded cleaner play and sterner action from referees, but at international level it was as though all was sweetness and light (the tourists were allowed so much more latitude than club players).

It was a year in which leading players attacked the establishment for greater consideration, and a share of the profits, in one way or another, as well as for better conditions, and in which South Africa were refused a tour at top level at home or away, and in which it was realized that tours, long and short, were too frequent, bringing leading players under too much pressure. It was a year of too much rugby, too much competition, and possibly one of too much sponsorship and commercialism, with the almighty dollar receiving greater consideration than the players. It was also a year in which a new form of rugby violence, spearheaded by the stud, must have caught the attention of the International Board's Laws sub-committee, as it reviewed the Laws of the Game for adoption in 1980.

So, 1978 was a busy year, but not one in which the game made any great progress. It saw the end of a successful decade enjoyed by Wales, in circumstances that were neither happy nor satisfactory. For Gareth Edwards, it was a decisive year after a period of indecision – he retired, to earn more money as an author in six months than he ever thought about while playing!

Television, radio, and sponsorship moved into the British game; accusations were made from time to time that leading players were receiving liberal expenses beyond the intention of the Regulations relating to Amateurism. The BBC paid large amounts to the four Home Unions for television rights and, often, kick-off times were adjusted to meet the needs of the all-powerful box. In New Zealand, a young showbiz whizz-kid suggested a professional rugby union circus of leading players to tour the world playing exhibition matches. The alarm bells sounded, although outwardly officials dismissed it casually. They were more worried than they were ready to admit; several British players were approached by 'middle men' to test their readiness to join the circus. Some said they were interested if the money was right. For a few months in 1978, the shadow of a rugby 'Packer' loomed over the essentially amateur game. It is estimated that ninety-five per cent of rugby players enjoy the game while playing it, essentially, for fun, without glory or fringe benefits, without big matches and tours. It is they who will keep the game amateur, as long as they are not forgotten by the governing body.

By now, the reader may feel that it was all darkness in 1978; however, there were certainly moments of delight and enjoyment, though perhaps less in number than usual. Many will say that after 1978 the Game will never be quite the same again. That is true, but it has been said of many sports at the end of a year of transition!

The year began with the Championship of the Five Nations, and the genuine hope of a full revival by England, and the prospect of

14

a possible decline by Wales, coming to the end of a successful era. But Wales did achieve the Grand Slam for the eighth time and the Triple Crown for the fifteenth time (the third successive), taking the lead in both records.

Gareth Edwards, most-capped of Welsh players, and possibly the greatest player in the scrum-half position of this and any other era; Phil Bennett, the Grand Slam leader and record point-scorer at outside half; Gerald Davies, possibly one of the greatest wings in the game; and fiery pack leader, Terry Cobner, all retired from the international scene, as did superb all-rounder Mike Gibson of Ireland. The absence of Edwards and Bennett may well have cost Wales the Test series in Australia, despite unbelievably bad refereeing in that country.

The absence of the four swung the balance in favour of New Zealand at Cardiff in November. Yet Wales played well enough to have beaten the All Blacks, and should have overcome the unprecedented lineout incident (which will be remembered more than the result, as the New Zealand forwards produced the most blatant 'con trick' in the history of the game). Wales should have been well ahead by the final minute, so that the disputed penalty which enabled New Zealand to win 13–12 would not have mattered. Wales did not take their chances in attack; this was the story of the New Zealand tour: few sides ran at the All Blacks, who defended sternly, spoiled, and pounced on opposing errors.

Throughout this book, I have attempted to highlight the penalty goal and its exaggerated importance and influence upon the game at all levels. Particularly at top level, referees, by awarding penalty kicks, can change the course of a match, and even occasionally provide a result that is entirely contrary to the course of play. In 1978 there were many instances of this; in some cases there was sympathy for referees and players; in others there was poor refereeing and poor sportsmanship. The most frequent score in the game was the penalty goal. The recent changes in the laws, with the award of the indirect penalty for certain infringements, had little if any effect: there was no reduction in the number of goals kicked. While attacking play and midfield flair declined, the penalty goal grew in importance and frequency. In the Wales–New Zealand match, there were 7 penalty goals and 1 try; in the four international matches played by New Zealand on tour, the tally was 7 tries (6 by NZ) and 15 penalty goals (9 to New Zealand). I believe the All Blacks could have had several more penalties given against them, but referees appeared more intent upon watching the home sides. During the tour there were 34 penalty goals for New Zealand and 30 against.

Looking back to 1935–36 and summarizing the four international matches of that New Zealand tour of that season, I find that there were 18 tries scored and 4 penalty goals kicked, with New Zealand collecting 9 tries and 2 penalties of these totals. It could be argued that the game has changed, not for the better in the attacking and try-scoring sense.

The 1978 All Blacks proved one of the best defensive sides to visit these islands, but how often did opposing sides run at them? The All Blacks scored many breakaway tries from opposing attacking errors, as the final try against Scotland indicates (dare one suggest an offside infringement?).

In 1935–36 there was either greater scoring power on the part of the All Blacks and the opposing four home union sides, or poorer defences. But the late 1930s are remembered as 'the defensive years'; I feel the conclusion that the game has changed is a fair one. Players were more attack-conscious in those days; the try was the ultimate. In 1978 there were more opportunities to kick penalty goals – far more. That is why individual goal-kickers amassed such imposing totals of points. It can be argued that defensive play is sharper, and re-grouping quicker, but I remain convinced that attacking rugby throughout the world has fallen away in quantity and quality, that defences have become all-embracing, and that the penalty goal the dominant method of scoring and winning.

I have tried in this book to bring into focus the modern game as it is played in many countries, highlighting trends in attack and defence and strengths and weaknesses on and off the field. As in every sport, rugby men seek perfection; as an amateur game, it has at present to fight off the threat of professionalism, and seek to beat off the innuendos that suggest all is not well within its ranks.

In 1978 the Championship of the Five Nations was hard, as the leaders, France and Wales, fought for supremacy. Wales succeeded in the end, but the 1979 series could be different, with the greater resources in skilled players of the French ensuring (with better selection and coaching) continued dominance of the game by Europe. In 1978, the French selectors often committed the side to play at a disadvantage: never was this point better illustrated than in the match against Wales at Cardiff, where the absence of a reliable place kicker reduced the side's effectiveness.

For Wales to maintain its remarkable run of success, particularly that against the other home countries, it will be necessary for the young talent available to blossom quickly: there is no great strength in depth at international level.

England cannot seem to make full use of the resources available; the mood of the country is one of impatience and destructive criticism, rather than patience and constructive help and advice. In the last ten years many good players have lost heart through being chopped and changed. I do not accept the idea that England cannot be strong in the game. The fact that England made the poorest showing of the four home countries against the All Blacks was one of the tragedies of 1978; the wound was deep and embarrassing. English rugby is much stronger than the International revealed.

Ireland achieved the long-awaited victory against a visiting New Zealand side through the mighty Men of Munster. No praise can be too high for former Lions captain, Tom Kiernan, for his coaching. The achievement of defeating the All Blacks 12–0 reflected the spirit of Munster as a team, the dedication and discipline of each individual player, and a referee who allowed the All Blacks no latitude.

The Munster achievement presented a new side of Irish rugby. The national XV went reasonably close, being denied a draw in injury time. Ireland, with never many outstanding players available for selection, possesses remarkable spirit; the country need not worry unduly about its forthcoming visit to Australia.

Scotland, after a dreadful first six months in 1978, came back fighting-fit in December, and gave the All Blacks a real run for their money. A few defensive lapses prevented a drawn match which many would say they deserved. New national coach Nairn MacEwan did not allow early defeats to subdue his energy, enthusiasm and optimism, and he possesses the qualities that make for a good coach.

The problem of violence in the game received more publicity in 1978 than in any previous year and the media, especially the BBC, would not let the matter rest. The drama of Chris Ralston's head and J. P. R. Williams's face held the headlines for longer than any other incidents I can recall of a similar nature and were not really settled by the end of the year.

However sad they may have been, the incidents brought to attention two important points that need the fullest and frankest investigation and discussion by the International Board: the vital question of the ruck as a phase in the game, and the use and nature of studs or sprigs. One could almost call it the year of the sprig: more players suffered sprig cuts than for many a season. Some of them, as in the case of Ralston and Williams, were serious. There was no doubt, at the end of 1978, that the ruck was dangerous and will remain dangerous unless the laws are amended. The greatest care must be taken over the maintenance and inspection of sprigs, or the injuries will continue and maybe increase. In New Zealand, 'raking' is called a 'sprig massage'.

The medical officers of the International Board member-countries are engaged in a survey into the cause and nature of injuries. This decision, taken in 1978, is a worthy one and its importance cannot be over-emphasized. I hope that the medical officers will press for a change in the laws to minimize the danger. New Zealand may oppose any change, bitterly, but the Board is leglislating for all players, the world over. It is the duty of the Board to make the game as safe as possible without eliminating its character and enjoyment.

There may still be objection from some quarters to playing the ball with hands off the ground after a tackle and in the ruck or pile-up, but it is better than broken bones, gashed heads and deep cuts. There may not be many, but all countries have violent rugby players, and there is urgent need to rid the game of these rogue players who use their boots as offensive weapons.

If one should be tempted to regard Chris Ralston and J. P. R. Williams as the unluckiest players of the year at top level, then the luckiest must be the intinerant Andy Haden (he started the tour as an unemployed man) who executed his 'fall-out' at Cardiff, and k.o. punch at Murrayfield. In the first instance he contravened the whole spirit of the game, and in the second he took the law into his own hands, flattening McHarg. The fact that he was 'hidden' from the media after the Cardiff incident, and no official comment was made, was not good PR work.

The quote of the year came from cheerful Russell Thomas, the All Blacks manager: 'I think your British referees are wonderful!'

As players of the year, I choose Gareth Edwards, ending his magnificent career at scrum-half; Phil Bennett, the world's leading representative-match scorer; Graham Mourie, the effective captain of the All Blacks; Brian McKechnie, who became the side's chief goal-kicking match-winner; and Jerome Gallion, who could become the number one pin-up of French rugby, if he blends his individualism with cohesive team play.

The scoop (or 'leak') of the year was provided by *The Daily Telegraph*, when it announced the England XV to meet New Zealand before the selectors. The most challenging statement of the year came from Wilfred Wooller in the *Sunday Telegraph*: 'If I was a member of the International Board, I would be most anxious to know how much further professionalism is to be allowed to dominate an amateur rugby game.' The most sensational comment came from Doug Ibbotson in the *Evening News*: 'Today, rugby players in certain senior clubs are being paid.' Whether true or false – and concrete evidence would be needed if it were to be followed up – it caused a stir in the rugby establishment.

There was a call in 1978 for touch judges to be neutral and have powers to assist the referee in representative matches, particularly concerning dirty play and continual infringement. This followed the incredible scenes at Sydney, where Welsh prop Graham Price was punched in the open, after play had moved on, by Australian prop Steve Finnane (a lawyer by profession), and by the injury to J. P. R. Williams at Bridgend. Neither was seen by the referees, and many ugly off-the-ball incidents are missed, but touch judges could well have seen them!

If touch judges were authorized to help and advise referees in representative rugby as, strangely enough, the Australian Rugby Union will recommend to the IB in 1979, supported by New Zealand, it would help. Yet referee John West saw Andy Haden flatten Alistair McHarg at Murrayfield but did not send him off, and Cholley flattened a Scot in Paris before the eyes of Referee Meirion Joseph. Both acts were deserving of the ultimate penalty if the recommendation of the four Home Unions had been observed. Both players were penalized, but no more. Only lip service seems to be paid to some Laws, regulations and recommendations.

Nineteen seventy-eight saw the increasing encroachment of sponsorship in greater waves; individual matches were sponsored by companies, and manufacturers gave sports equipment to leading clubs in return for display of company motifs. One club had all its financial affairs sponsored by a company. Finally, it was alleged that senior players were being tempted to wear certain firm's equipment in big matches for payment. How far can sponsorship go in the game? Subsidy is growing in importance when the prices of international tickets rocket.

The game went through 1978 as it will go through future years, in spite of the bad things that may exist and hit the headlines. The grass roots of the game is the ninety-five per cent of rugby throughout the world for which unknown officials give hours of their time to run their clubs, and for which players pay their own travel and hotel expenses. Rugby will survive. Despite all the criticism, I believe it was as healthy overall on 1 January 1979 as it was on 1 January 1978.

2

'They're Off!'

The year 1977 left an adverse legacy for 1978. The Lions returned from New Zealand having lost the Test series by three matches to one, leaving the management and players (not to mention camp followers) sad, weary and concerned as to the future of British Rugby. There was stern criticism, some fair and some biased, on television and radio, and, particularly, in the Press of both countries. Yet, as Willie John McBride would remark in good times or bad, 'It is history now, lads!'

The end of 1977 saw North Midlands winning the RFU County Championship for the first time. The match was virtually a club affair between Moseley, an outstanding club playing attractive football, and Gloucester. In the previous six seasons, Gloucestershire had won the title four times and Lancashire twice, and the achievement of North Midlands gave a great deal of pleasure to followers at The Reddings. Shortly after this victory, Gloucester, as a club, defeated Moseley, so satisfying the knowledgeable but partisan followers at Kingsholm!

The 'Club' and 'County' Systems
Also for the first time, the RFU's County Championship had been completed in the first half of the season. This was due in no small measure to the fiery enthusiasm of R. E. G. 'Dick' Jeeps and his attempt while President during the 1976-77 season to streamline RFU administration and control of the game. It allowed the John Player Challenge Cup to be competed for in the second half of the season.

The first round proper of the Cup was staged on 28 January,

and the competition carried on until 15 April when the final was played at Twickenham. The new arrangement was less demanding upon the leading players, and clubs were better able to field their strongest sides in the Cup competition. However, there remain two schools of thought in English rugby; both have support for their beliefs. Those who favour the county system feel that it gives greater opportunity for more players to develop and be recognized, while those for the club system favour its more compact, competitive nature.

It would be unwise for a Welshman to sit in judgement upon the two systems as the Welsh have a closely-knit club system. Eighteen leading clubs are in an area seventy miles by thirty, from Llanelli to Ebbw Vale; distances are nothing compared with that from the Northern Club to Penzance and Newlyn. The county system does give the lesser players a chance to impress, but the high standard of competition for the select group of leading players remains within the top clubs. It is a problem not easily solved. Whatever changes are made in the future, the county system will not die easily.

Sandy Sanders, Chairman of selectors (a good, cheerful one) and his five associates travel many thousands of miles each season. One can be assured of their deep interest in both systems and their willingness to watch both clubs and counties, but it is competitive rugby between top clubs that produces international players. The weekly diet in Wales allows for two or three matches of near-international standard each week.

The Final Trial Matches
On 7 January, England, Scotland and Ireland staged their final trial matches, searching for sides good enough to wrest the Grand Slam from France and the Triple Crown from Wales. At Twickenham the selectors were not amused by a final score of England 15 points, The Rest 15. It was worse at Lansdowne Road, where the Probables lost to the Possibles 21–13, and at Murrayfield, where the favoured Blues were beaten 20–18 by the Whites.

Alan Old, a favourite of mine as a classic kicker and smooth outside half, still appeared to be the steadiest of players in the position for England; Mick Quinn and Tony Ward were the rivals for the position for Ireland. Douglas Morgan (a Lions Test player) was still the dominant scrum-half and match-winner in Scotland, with thirteen trial points, but he could not prevent the Blues from losing; this added to the worry of the selectors. After these three matches it would appear that the challengers were still far away from being in a position to challenge the top two countries, even though the French were unhappy with their halves and the 'Little Napoleon', Jacques Fouroux, had further disturbed them by retiring from the captaincy and representative rugby. Also, the Welsh were said to be 'too old' and Bennett, as leader, was said to be tired by his traumatic New Zealand tour experience. England, of the other three countries, was expected to make the strongest challenge upon the Franco-Welsh citadel. Scotland would rise like a phoenix from the ashes of defeat, and Ireland would burn with raw Celtic fire under inspiration and coaching from the former warrior in green of many seasons, Noel Murphy.

The Proposed South African Tour
Meanwhile from the South Africans came the announcement that they could fulfil the conditions for a Springboks tour to the British Isles in the winter of 1978-79. It was made with deep sincerity by their veteran President, world rugby figure Dr Danie Craven; it was factual and realistic. A brave flame of hope flickered for a few weeks before, deeply concerned, the four Home Unions met and decided to postpone the tour (although the decision at first was far from unanimous) with the 'mutual consent' of both countries. The hopes of true rugby men were thus dashed, and when I sat with Dr Craven after the March meeting of the International Board, he had tears in his eyes as he said, 'What more can we rugby men of South Africa do? We have organized multi-racial rugby and it will develop. We will bring a multi-racial side to the British Isles selected by a multi-racial committee. What more must we do in sport to regain the brotherhood of sports-men?' His plea came from the heart, and he was as sincere as an administrator in 1978 as he was as a young player at Neath in 1931, when the referee accused him of not putting the ball in straight after the giant Springbok scrum effected a sharp 'first shove'! It was the memory of the 1969-70 non-rugby 'activists' that disturbed the four Home Unions. This very small minority would not allow the majority to enjoy what they desired. Rugby

union football had finally fallen victim of the threat of political terrorism, in this, the world's most democratic country. How then can the majority have its way? It may only be the beginning of the denial of individual freedom to Britons who are not prepared to fight to maintain it. It is the rule of the minority, bad for sport.

This unfortunate decision came as an even bigger disappointment to rugby men of all races in South Africa. While there was some danger from the political 'activists' for Springboks travelling as a team, there was no genuine rugby reason why Scotland should not visit South Africa, and I believe the decision surprised the other three Home Unions. The South African invitation to Scotland was withdrawn because the SRU refused to approve such a tour, despite encouragement from some quarters. It was a sad decision, and it was little wonder that Dr Craven cried out in the rugby wilderness, 'Who is going to help us?' Fortunately, there were rugby friends working behind the scenes to help South African rugby; the near future could bring happier news for them.

Here is the press statement issued by the Committee of Home Unions relating to the postponement of the Springboks tour.

'A meeting was held in London today, 18 December, between Representatives of the South African Rugby Board and the Committee of Home Unions of England, Scotland, Ireland and Wales. The Representatives of the SARB requested the Committee to agree to a postponement of their tour of Great Britain and Ireland which was scheduled to take place in the season 1978/79. The Home Unions have agreed to this request and no date has yet been considered for the re-arrangement of this tour.

The Committee of Home Unions regret the circumstances which have caused this decision to be made; they have acknowledged for some time both from information supplied by the Representative of South Africa on the International Board and by their personal examination of the situation in South Africa, the major steps that have already been taken by the rugby authorities in that country to remove any form of racial discrimination from the Game. Springbok teams are now selected on merit by a multi-racial selection committee after multi-racial trials. The game is now open to sportsmen of any colour to participate at all levels.

The Committee believes that the South African Rugby authorities have already done more in that direction than the Committee at one time believed possible and thinks it unfortunate that the progress already achieved is not more widely understood.

The Representatives of the SARB stated that they would use the interval arising from the postponement of the tour to consolidate the very considerable advances already made and thus avoid the danger of halting progress towards the establishment of good relationships and understanding in their country.

The Committee welcomes the resolve of their colleagues in South Africa to continue their efforts and thus make possible the resumption of international fixtures at an early date.'

Here is the Press Statement of January 1978 issued by the Scottish Rugby Union:

'The South African Rugby Board have decided not to invite the Scottish Rugby Union to play in South Africa in May and June of this year. The Scottish Rugby Union very much regret the circumstances behind this decision, and they greatly hope that conditions will permit the visit to take place in the near future.

The SRU are conscious of the determined efforts made by the SARB to remove any form of racial discrimination from the game in South Africa and they recognise the success that has been achieved with the game now being open to sportsmen of any colour at all levels.'

Selection for the Ireland–Scotland Match

Ireland announced their first international side of the season, that to meet Scotland on 21 January at Dublin; they awarded four new caps as well as appointing a new captain in Lions scrum-half, John Moloney. The new caps were centre Paul McNaughton, outside half Tony Ward, and forwards Donald Spring and John O'Driscoll. Mike Gibson was unfit and could not be considered; Stewart McKinney failed to win a place.

The selectors again refused the temptation to recall Willie John McBride, the most popular of Irish players in their long history and certainly the most modest. No player has ever given more on the field to Irish rugby – and, indeed, to British rugby as a Lion:

he enjoyed the supreme success of being the only captain to lead an unbeaten British side in this century. Throughout 1978, I never ceased to wonder at the reluctance of certain critics and officials to give the 1974 Lions side the praise it deserved. Far too often their judgement was clouded by an over-emphasis of the 'ninety-nine' business, when the Lions meted out punishment themselves when they considered the referee had failed to do so. For those not with the team, there was the tendency to presume that it happened all the time; in fact, it was only applied when necessary. The 1974 side was the most efficient British rugby machine produced this century; it had no weaknesses. It scored 107 tries in twenty-two matches, against 14, and was only the third side to remain unbeaten on a long tour. Every back in the side scored a try and the total of 729 points was the largest achieved by a British side abroad. It possessed a magnificent pack, superb controlling halves and try-scoring three-quarters, and two brilliant full-backs. It produced rugby of a quality and effectiveness that could not be countered, and if I were a coach of any side, in any grade, the approach and technique of the 1974 side would be my ideal. The side contained many great players, and received good management. Other sides have been blessed with the same attributes, but have never had the same togetherness; for much of this the credit must go to captain Willie John McBride. He is a big man in every way, a captain the players were 'prepared to die for' – and he for them. It will be many years before his like is seen again, and he had been hardened in the cauldron of four previous Lions tours. He was modest; he was natural; he had a big heart, and he knew how to get the very best out of players who loved him. He was an outstanding British leader, as have been so many Irishmen, and he was still playing in 1978! But like most of his friends and followers, I was glad that the Irish selectors resisted the temptation to recall him to the national XV at the age of 37, as had been Tony O'Reilly at Twickenham and Brian Lochore of New Zealand at Wellington. It is grossly unfair to great players to make them suffer such punishment: the sad memory of the recall of the once brilliant Albert Jenkins to the Welsh side for the match against Ireland in 1928, and that of Gwyn Nicholls in 1906-07, remains. It is said that the champions never make a come back, and in the main this is true. It was just that Willie John McBride was

26

allowed the comfort of his memories and triumphs, even though he was ready and willing for action. The event of his non-selection may have passed unnoticed in many countries but for those who played with him and those who travelled with him, it was a happy decision. The 'big, happy fella' remains an idol for the young to follow. For Irish players of the future, he will remain the man to follow: strong, friendly, generous and modest.

The All Black Tour Proposed
The news that the New Zealand All Blacks would substitute for the South African Springboks during the winter of 1978-79, with a medium-length sixteen-match tour meant that the All Blacks would be in some part of the British Isles in four successive winters. This could prove as much of an embarrassment for them as for their hosts, as they would be put in the grave danger of wearing out their welcome. Yet the four Home Unions were glad to have them agree to this tour, as it would provide much useful cash for them. Long tours remain the most lucrative form of money-taking in the modern game, far beyond that of the present returns from (modest) sponsorship. The 1974 Lions tour in South Africa produced receipts of three-and-a-half million Rand – almost two million sterling. In 1977, the Lions produced receipts of two million New Zealand dollars, (more than one-and-a-quarter million sterling). These figures represent enormous profits from amateur sport, since players receive no bonus for their hard work. At the end of the 1977 tour, and throughout 1978, the problem of rewards for players at the top in rugby union football has continued to rear its ugly head. It is discussed in detail in the final chapter of this book, that dealing with the future of rugby. For the leading players in all countries, participation has become more demanding. Although the glamour of fame and success may see players drive themselves to the top, it becomes all the harder to remain there where the rewards are nil, financially. In 1977 in New Zealand outside organizations made so much on the 'backs' of the Lions that it was the turning point in the attitude of many leading players.

Selection for the England–France Match
England capped two new players for their first match against France in Paris; full-back David Caplan because Alistair Hignell

was unfit, and John Scott at number eight as the experienced and unfortunate Roger Uttley could not play with his recurring back injury. The Lions of 1977 missed the presence of Uttley, who is a splendid forward, team man, tourist and leader; England missed him even more, although Billy Beaumont (who substituted for him most ably on tour in 1977) did a noble job as the new captain of England. Despite criticism from certain quarters, Beaumont was a popular and effective captain. He was a players' man, and his forwards, especially, gave him everything. Under his command the side improved and he refuted all criticism.

The loss of Hignell and Uttley was not the only problem for the England selectors, since their leading prop, Fran Cotton, was forced to retire through injury before the match against France was played. This let in Mike Burton of Gloucester, ahead of his friend and rival, Barry Nelmes of Cardiff. Cotton suffered a torn ligament of his right knee, which was to keep him out of the England side until the match against Scotland. Burton gained his sixteenth cap, while Nelmes had to wait until the next match (against Wales) to make his first appearance for his country at home, after winning two caps on tour in Australia. In the third match, against Scotland, Cotton returned, at the expense of Burton. Burton promptly refused to sit on the reserves' bench at Murrayfield, preferring to play for his clubs; this decision has probably ended his international career.

Norman Sanson of Scotland was a happy choice of referee for the France–England match in Paris and the Wales–England one at Twickenham. He had made history in 1977, by sending off Irish number eight Willie Duggan, and Welsh lock Geoffrey Wheel, in the Wales–Ireland match at Cardiff. Having been rejected by France for the England–France match in 1977, he was now fully restored to his original status and was extremely happy about it. The Welsh had previously invited him to take charge of the Wales–Australia Schools match held in December 1977.

Sanson had been wrongly condemned by many for sending off Duggan and Wheel, and Scotland were annoyed that Ireland saw fit to suspend Duggan for no more than two weeks while their own Gordon Brown, after being sent off in an inter-region match, was given three months. The fact is that Sanson was not to blame for sending off the two players in the Cardiff international; they struck blows in front of him. However, they were not the leading law breakers and during the first twenty-five minutes of play he had been lax in his control of the lineout, which is where the trouble started that led to the fracas. The Irish Union thought that Duggan had not been to blame (although he had struck a retaliatory punch), and there were at least three others punching rapidly. It had been a difficult situation and, as these two players were the first to be sent off in an International Championship match, the sending-off became headline news. Sanson had to suffer in silence, and even be attacked by the French Federation. His restoration was just and popular, and he had a good season.

Violent Play
The question of rough and dirty play was raised at the time of Sanson's timely 'restoration' by the court case at Lyons which involved the French international lock forward, Michel Palmie of the Beziers Club, a 27-year-old, six-foot-four-and-a-half, sixteen-stone-seven-pound heavyweight and pharmacist, who is easily distinguished on the field by the amount of surgical plaster and bandaging worn. He was charged by an opposing player who suffered severe eye damage in a club match, and Palmie was fined £160 and ordered to pay £7000 damages.

However, as Palmie appealed against the decision of the court, the French selectors continued to include him in the national XV; this came as a considerable surprise to the four Home Unions, who were determined to stamp out rough play. They believed that the French selectors would recognize the court decision, as Palmie had been over-vigorous in several international matches, especially in the France–Wales match of 1977. It was no special advert for French club rugby and did not comply with the new practice of the Federation in its attempt to eliminate rough play in its club championship. In many ways Palmie was fortunate to be selected, and Scotland, after the suspension of Gordon Brown and the rough play of French prop Cholley against them in 1977, were not at all happy. However, as is their habit, they maintained a strong silence. Fortunately, Palmie was to curb his vigour considerably during the international season and one believes that the forceful French President Albert Fourasse issued a stern warning to all players before accepting later in the year, on behalf of his Federation, the invitation to join the International Board.

Selection of the French Team

When the French selectors announced the side for their first match against England in Paris, it contained seven changes from that defeated by New Zealand in the second Test in Paris in the early part of the season. They never do things by halves, oh no, and had summarily dismissed five of the original seven backs, leaving only full-back Jean-Michel Aguirre, and centre Roland Bertranne. Two forwards were also dropped in favour of returning heroes Bastiat and Rives, who had been unable to play against New Zealand through injury. Their absence had weakened the French pack considerably.

Jacques Fouroux had announced his retirement. Most critics, including myself, had expected to see Richard Astre recalled to the colours. Instead, the French launched a new player into the position, Jerome Gallion, a 23-year-old 'B' cap, a dental surgeon. He was to become one of the discoveries of the season, a try-scoring individualist rather than a smooth worker. With the changes one had anticipated a return to the traditional French approach of running and handling, since the (expert) goal-kicking tactical punter at outside half, Romeu, had been dropped in favour of another 'B' international, Bernard Vivies. In fact, in the end the French approach was neither one thing or the other, and at the end of the season the selectors must have regretted their premature discarding of such a fine and experienced player as Romeu who might have worked well with the ebullient Gallion. Gallion appealed to the masses, but whether he and Vivies were the best halves for the French cause was a matter for debate.

Vivies did not engage in the running play for which he was selected, and the failure to kick goals cost France dearly against Ireland and in the final match against Wales. I should think that the Welsh selectors held a private cheering session when they heard the news that Romeu, who always did well at Cardiff, was not recalled! The captaincy went to Bastiat and he (like many other great forwards, including Colin Meads of New Zealand) was never really happy when shouldering the responsibility of captaincy. Bastiat was worried about his team, and I believe this

30

did affect his general play, especially at the lineout and in the loose, where he previously used, in the eyes of opponents, to operate as a one-man danger outfit.

The return of Bastiat and the blond-haired attacker Rives brought the French pack up to full strength, and it was upon a hard, tried and trusted pack that the hope of France was placed. As the side never really decided between the choice of an open or tight approach, the folly of omitting Romeu as a tactical kicker and pack supporter became more obvious, perhaps more so to the opponents of France than to France itself!

Selection of the Scottish Team
Scotland did not award any new caps when they announced their first side, but they did change their captain, and also revealed they could not make up their minds as to the respective qualities of Andy Irvine and Bruce Hay at full-back. Both were experienced internationals and all-round players, Irvine being in world class as an attacking footballer, having played in two Tests on the wing in the unbeaten 1974 side. Hay could also play on the wing, and for this match Hay was at full-back and Irvine on the wing. In truth, they are both better full-backs than wings. One has to go back to 1937 to find a similar case of an international side fielding two fullbacks-cum-wings. They were the legendary Gerry Brand of South Africa and his young rival Freddie Turner, both outstanding players . After the team was announced *The Scotsman* headed its report on the selection 'The Day of the Old Faces': the side contained some very senior players who had been ever-present, with distinction, for many years. Prop Sandy Carmichael was making his 50th appearance, Alistair McHarg had appeared 39 times, Ian McLaughlan 34, Andy Irvine and Ian McGeechan 25, Jim Renwick 22, and the new captain, Lion Douglas Morgan, 18. Morgan took over the leadership from McGeechan; although he worked hard, he was no more successful. A new coach, no longer festooned with the title 'Adviser to the Captain', took command of the team's preparations, although he was not made a selector until the summer, in readiness for the next season. He was the fine flank forward, Nairn MacEwan, of the Gala and Highland Clubs, who had played in twenty international matches and taken the Highland Club from the fourth to the

31

first division of the Scottish Club Championship.

It was never as easy a season for MacEwan as it was for John Dawes of Wales with his ready-made side, although the task confronting Dawes before the start of the Championship season was not that of proving himself but of reminding the critics that he and his team were not quite finished, even though it was true that the traumatic experience in Australia must have re-created some doubts. These were due almost entirely to matters beyond his control – too much rugby, and indifferent refereeing.

Selection of the Welsh Team

When the Welsh selectors eventually announced their side to meet England it contained no new caps, and was particularly experienced, much as were the English sides of the early 1920s under W. J. A. Davies.

Of the fifteen players, thirteen were 1977 Lions. These were rejoined by Gareth Edwards, honoured for the fiftieth successive occasion by the selectors, and Geoffrey Wheel, withdrawn on medical grounds from the tour. Obviously, Edwards would have been first choice, enough in himself to have tipped the controversial tour in the favour of the Lions. Records proved it to be the most experienced side ever fielded by Wales, and it would have remained unchanged through the Championship but for unfortunate injury to Gerald Davies before the French match.

The Australian Schoolboys Tour

Before the Championship season started, the touring Australian Schoolboys team ended its delightful romp through the British Isles in a blaze of rugby glory, despite the dense fog at Twickenham where they met England in the final game of their fourteen-match tour. They hammered a good England side 31–9, and provided those who were close enough to observe through fog reminiscent of Sherlock Holmes' adventures a remarkable display of cohesive, accurate, fast-moving rugby.

Throughout their tour they produced perfect text-book rugby in an attractive manner, and delighted their hosts while mesmerizing their opponents. It was the strict emphasis upon doing the basic things well that was an object lesson to players of all ages. One could not be other than deeply impressed by these boys who

32

were, in every way, a credit to their country. How Adrian Stoop and Gwyn Nicholls would have applauded them!

Their record, played 14 and won 14, with 479 points for and only 93 against, is improved by the fact that they scored 103 tries with only 5 against; ample proof of their ability as attackers and defenders. When in Australia with Wales, I was confronted with the contrast between Junior and Senior Wallabies, both in attitude of mind and approach in play, and how much more pleasure was obtained in watching the Juniors, even though they blasted the Welsh Schools on the Cardiff Arms Park! One does not mind defeat when beaten by quality rugby and good sportsmanship.

In the Australian Schools team there were three outstanding players. These were the Ella brothers, Glen, Gary and Mark, three young Aborigines from Matraville High School who on their return home were subject to much publicity. Only one appeared in a match the Welsh team were able to watch, at a curtain-raiser before the New South Wales game at Sydney. Wisely, I feel, these three brilliant young players were being held back, and allowed to bridge the gap gradually between school and senior rugby; the major rugby league clubs in Sydney closely followed their career with cheque books at the ready. One hopes that they would remain amateur but would certainly understand any decision made to turn professional, remembering how it would help their family.

RFU former president and the present Hon. Treasurer of the Home Unions Tours Committee, Douglas Harrison, was full of admiration for the Australian Schoolboys and, as President of the RFU's Schools Union, he was unstinted in his praise, since the young tourists retaught the lesson that there is no substitute for team work and accuracy to provide match-winning, open rugby. The maxim that tries are more important than penalty goals remains unchanged even if there are, rather unfortunately, more opportunities provided per match to kick penalty goals than score tries. Little wonder, then, that no less a world rugby figure than Dr Danie Craven of South Africa should put before the International Board at its March meeting in London, that the penalty goal value should be reduced from three to two points.

Pontypool v. *Cardiff*
A match was played in Wales in January and tele-recorded for the

33

BBC2 'Rugby Special' programme that emphasized to the full the value of try-scoring. It was a WRU/Schweppes Cup Third Round match at Pontypool Park, between Pontypool and Cardiff on 7 January. Cardiff won in an exciting finish, and it was a personal triumph for the club captain, the world acclaimed wing-three-quarter, Gerald Davies. He scored four tries from his side's five attacking movements. It was, in every way, a tremendous match. Pontypool, much maligned by critics and opponents down through the years for their hard rugby, emerged from this match with credit, having shared in a rugby occasion.

As for the 34-year-old Gerald Davies, he revealed that touch of greatness that is enjoyed by few, in any sport, and, in the midst of their extreme disappointment at losing such a match, Pontypool followers were full of praise for Davies, who had, in his own special way, added something that will be remembered for many a year on the classic slopes of Pontypool Park. He had waved his magic wand of pace and elusiveness, and the quickness of thought and ease of action that makes for watchers' delight. Davies, a modest, likeable player, is unique. If only the Welsh centres had done more for him over the years, how many more tries he would have scored than his collection of 20 in 46 appearances? Possibly, he is the greatest of wings in the history of the game. Certainly, there have been few better.

Professional Rugby Union?
In January, a new code, professional rugby union, reared its ugly head, setting alarm bells ringing through the rugby union head-quarters of member countries of the International Board. The threat was launched in, of all places, Auckland, New Zealand: a young entertainment impressario, Russell Clarke, was audacious enough to issue a warning challenge. Perhaps encouraged by the success of a certain Mr Packer in Australian television and cricket, Mr Clarke warned the world that he was to stage professional rugby union with leading players from many countries, and that he was proceeding to South Africa in the near future to talk to players and arrange venues.

This statement, following upon the refusal of the four Home Unions and Scotland to play against the Springboks, produced rumours of a 'take-over bid' for the South African union game.

At first, one believed that Mr Clarke would be received with open arms even by some of the more august members of the SA governing body. These fears were soon dispelled, however when Dr Craven, as President, told the world that his Union would survive, come what may. Hence, Mr Clarke's trip to SA did not prove as fruitful as had been anticipated.

Some leading British players were approached discreetly, but no details were available as to what form the new code would eventually take and everyone had to imagine what would happen. Carwyn James, at his continental 'hideaway' in Rivigo, Italy was approached as one of the world's leading union coaches, and tempted with £20,000 to coach the professional World XV. James promptly rejected the offer, saying that, 'Contracts are not part of the union code, which should remain amateur.'

It was well past mid-summer before the date of the first professional exhibition match reached the British Isles, given as 8 October. The match was to be at Whangarei in the North Island of New Zealand, the city where Sid Going and his North Auckland side had proved so difficult to overcome. At that stage in the preparations, there was much speculation as to which former great players would join the new rugby circus. There was also much speculation at the time as to when Gareth Edwards would publish his autobiography, and thus retire from the union code. It had been completed with the help of Tony Lewis, the sports feature writer of the *Sunday Telegraph*, and was said at the time to contain little or nothing sensational. His agent had visited the main houses in Fleet Street, offering the serial rights of the book, an 'exclusive' on the Edwards retirement, and the player as a rugby columnist.

Then the publishers, Stanley Paul (an imprint of the Hutchinson group), issued to the trade a brochure announcing the publication date of the book as October. *The Bookseller* gave the date as 5 October. Edwards was thus going to find himself 'retiring' before the All Blacks' matches against Cardiff and Wales, as the publication of the book for' gain or the promise of payment', as laid down in the International Board's regulations relating to amateur status, prevented him from playing once the book was published. Obviously, after his long service to the game as an amateur, Edwards was entitled to 'cash in' on his fame and world-name in the game. The advance against royalties was reported as 'high' for such a book, although it was some time before the first serial rights were sold.

Whatever fee was paid to Edwards for his retirement story, it would have been more, I feel, had it been paid after the 1978 French match, or at the end of the 1977-78 season, or after his playing for Wales against New Zealand; the book would have to be published later. Having paid quite a large amount for the book, Stanley Paul quite rightly wanted to capture the Christmas market, the best for rugby books. Had I had the opportunity to advise Edwards in this, I would have opted for the end of the season, or after the Wales *v.* New Zealand match. During the close season, Edwards made frequent 'personal appearances' (as did several other leading players), especially in Wales. This brought the matter of 'gain' into the headlines, setting further problems for the International Board, although in rugby it is the responsibility of the player's club to see that he does not opt out of the amateur regulations while, at the same time, not restricting individual freedom.

The player has first to decide what he wishes to do; make money out of his fame as a rugby player, or continue playing without any financial gain apart from the normal expenses paid for travel and subsistence. However, as the member countries of the International Board agree to enforce the amateur regulations rigidly, there has been growing for some time a feeling of unrest among the top players in all countries. They argue that as they attract large crowds and produce handsome profits for the Unions, especially so while on tour, they should receive some extra award.

There is no 'grey' area between amateur and professional in rugby football, despite alarming rumours, greatly exaggerated, that clubs have been 'paying over the odds' or 'putting money in the boot' for certain players. Again, there have been rumours that some players have been 'cared for' while speaking at dinners. As an after-dinner speaker who has never been offered a fee and would never take one, I cannot vouch for any of this. One enjoys the stories of alleged 'activities' with the 'greenbacks', but has to admit that I have never seen any transaction, or been told of any by a player.

The member countries of the International Board face a challenge that will not go away if one pretends it is not there! The

Rugby Unions receive considerable sums of money from sponsors, which is ploughed back into the game and its clubs. Two things encourage sponsorship; the plugging of the firm's name on television and in the Press, and the association of leading players' names with the firm, with specially designed playing kit with motifs.

Yet while one has sympathy for several leading players in many countries because of their time-consuming dedication to the game in order to remain at the top, I cannot see any way in which the International Board can arrive at a compromise without breaking the game's strictly amateur code. The leading players are the very tip of the rugby iceberg, and a small percentage of the number of union players throughout the world. The Board regulates for *all* players and it cannot opt out of its responsibility. Come what may it is not going to do so!

3
The Championship of Five Nations

The 1978 Championship of the Five Nations was won deservedly by Wales in a season of play that was interesting, if not always marked by high skills. Wales remained unbeaten and achieved the Grand Slam to prove themselves the best side, a conclusion not unexpected or surprising in view of the side's talent and the highly developed sense of team work and cohesion possessed by the Welshmen. At the end of the season, the side, virtually unchanged, could look back upon three extremely successful years in which three Triple Crowns and two Grand Slams were achieved. The successive Triple Crowns created a new record for the Championship and were the cause of much rejoicing throughout the Principality although the future suggested a possible break up of one of the most consistently successful of all Welsh teams. In three seasons, twelve matches were played with only one defeat, a record that emulated the great England side of the early 1920s.

Yet it was not an easy passage for Wales, since all except two members of the side had been busily engaged with the British Lions in New Zealand during the summer of 1977. Having to enter a new season immediately following an arduous tour was exacting and demanding in the extreme, upon both the physical and mental capacity of the players concerned. That they were equal to these excessive demands, and achieved the Grand Slam, was a tribute to their enthusiasm, technical skill, and love of the game.

The Lions returned from New Zealand in an atmosphere of criticism, especially the Welsh section of the party and, of them, particularly coach John Dawes and captain Philip Bennett. Certain members of the Fleet Street and New Zealand Press were extremely harsh in their criticisms and it was obvious at the start of the representative season that the Sword of Damocles was hanging over the Welsh side. If some of the criticism lacked the quality of sensitive appreciation and was more personal than realistic, it still demanded much of the side.

The criticism was answered most ably by the Welshmen, who won back most of the original critics to their side even if one Australian writer watching them play France wrote them off as indeed fortunate, and ageing! The players were growing older, inevitably, and the selectors appreciated to the full that at the end of the season they would have to rebuild. Two outstanding members of the side declined the invitation to tour in Australia, Gareth Edwards and Phil Bennett, and this allowed for the inclusion in the touring team of several younger, uncapped players. The four halves chosen for the tour were all uncapped, and in all eleven members set out in an attempt to win their first international caps.

As expected, France proved the major rival to Wales, and when the two countries met at Cardiff on 18 March, both unbeaten, it was for the Championship and the Grand Slam. Victory carried with it the title of 'leading country in Europe'; for several years this envied position had been held in turn by France and Wales.

In 1978 the countries contrasted in style and approach. Wales were firmly established from 1977, whereas the French made an unspectacular start to their representative season by sharing a two-match Test series with a touring New Zealand side and then narrowly avoiding defeat by Romania. At the end of this third match, the team captain Jacques Fouroux, known as 'Little Napoleon', informed the selectors that he was retiring from representative football.

It is true that he was not playing particularly well at the time, rather disenchanted with the French selectorial set-up and his position as captain. While some critics expected his departure to herald a return to the traditional free-running style of French play, they were to regret it before the end of the season, since the giant number eight forward Jean-Pierre Bastiat, worried by having the responsibility of captaincy thrust upon him, did not lead well or produce his traditional form. Fouroux's replacement at scrum-half, Jerome Gallion, proved himself something of a discovery and a possible successor to Gareth Edwards in Europe; he played with the spirit of adventure to collect three tries in three successive matches, although he did reveal a tendency to selfishness rather than complete co-ordination with his back row, one rated as one of the best fielded by France.

The French did not find it easy against England in Paris until England suffered unfortunate injuries to flank forward Peter Dixon and centre Andy Maxwell, and their departure assisted the French recovery sparked off by full-back Aguirre and scrum-half Gallion. Against Scotland they were again in trouble, until an injury to Scotland's key player, Andy Irvine, made life easier for them.

Against Ireland, the score difference of a mere point suggests that the French were rather fortunate to survive, but this is not strictly true. They could have succeeded by a bigger margin in normal conditions. Yet this match revealed that as a result of a desperate and often homeric Irish defence, the French were not as cohesive or quite as dangerous as in previous seasons, and were especially lacking in direction at outside half, (technically termed 'move calling' in modern rugby terminology) and in the accuracy of their place kicking. These weaknesses persisted throughout the season and were evident at times against Wales. Followers could not comprehend the continued omission of the experienced Jean-Pierre Romeu at outside half, a selectorial failure that considerably reduced the side's potential.

England, as inevitably in recent years, enjoyed little, if any, good fortune. Injuries during the Paris match had a disturbing influence, spoiled any chance of a possible victory over the French, and left the selectors with a changed side to face Wales. With half the matches played, England had no victory, but they fielded their best side of the season against Scotland and it was unchanged against Ireland. It played well enough, particularly at forward, to deserve the two victories and suggest better play in future behind the scrum. Such an improvement, plus the determination revealed in overcoming the injury handicap, was encouraging after an unhappy first half to the season in which protracted trial matches solved little and merely disturbed the even and competitive tenor of club rugby.

England well deserved third place in the final Championship

table and one would not support the theory that the Championship is in two divisions, with Wales and France in Division One and England, Ireland and Scotland in Division Two. The results were often close enough to suggest that all five countries were in contention, even although Scotland lost all four matches. Wales fielded the best balanced and, possibly the most gifted side, with six or more world-class players who were able to lift the side whenever the effort was needed. Incidentally, one believes that more than four Welshmen would have won places in the French side at the end of the season!

France, although passing through a temporary transitional period, might have proved more impressive with better and less parochial selection; complete unity never appears to be achieved between selectors, players, coaches and leading critics. The history of modern French rugby is linked, inevitably, with these unhappy but very real differences which erupt in public from time to time like a volcano with indigestion – as when Fouroux retired in January. The Gallic temperament, and the fact that so many good players are spread over a wide area and possess slightly varying approaches to the game, are additional handicaps to the selection of the national XV, a task observed by followers with even greater passion and partisanship than in Wales.

Ireland, although winning only one of four matches, revealed signs of having turned the corner, at least at home at Lansdowne Road, and showed a prospect of better times ahead even if the final performance against England was rather less impressive than that of the previous three matches. Much of the good work at forward in earlier matches was not repeated due to a lack of direction and control in the art of ball-winning, while the whole side's lack of cohesion and attacking flair was due, mainly, to the inexperience of Tony Ward at outside half in only his first season of representative rugby. However, he proved himself a highly successful and match-winning place kicker.

Ireland have something to build upon in 1979, despite the shortage of key players indicated by the continued selection of the 36-year-old Michael Gibson as a wing, and the fact that half a dozen members of the side will be thirty-plus in 1979. Coach Noel Murphy, with his fire-and-brimstone approach plus 'a dash of holy water', got the Irish players to believe in themselves again and fanned the embers of traditional enthusiasm into flames; when he is able to harness the revived fires, the energy output will be put to better use and the younger players will be able to play their part in what is hoped will be a continued revival. Enough was revealed against France and Wales to suggest better days ahead if there is a more subtle direction of the energy generated. If players like Phillip Orr and Moss Keane can give so much without over-stepping the mark, it should be easier for the other experienced forwards to do so.

Scotland did not get off the ground as a match-winning team or do real justice to themselves in a season which, with four defeats, was a blow to the rugby prestige of the country. The reasons were many and varied, but more a reflection upon the approach of the past decade and a hang-over from a period of too rigid coaching methods and, to a lesser degree, the selections of recent seasons. Scotland could have achieved much more had they had greater flexibility on and off the field, and allowed rein to a spirit of adventure behind, rather than emphasized action by the front row of the scrum.

The observant Scottish critic Norman Mair wrote in *The Scotsman* after the England match a sentence that could well reflect the opinion of many devoted followers – and there are many in the land; 'No one in his right senses would suggest that the Scottish selectors at present are diving into a bottomless pool of talent, but a heart-broken borderer expressed his own view perfectly when he said that while any country may have a few lean years or even a barren decade in terms of (in officialdom's phrase) quality players, the fact that it is forty years since we won either the Triple Crown or the Championship outright would hardly suggest that we have been making exactly inspired use of our resources.'

Yet there were periods when they proved superior to the French and the equal of Wales and had something in their make-up that deserved better. Their new coach, Nairn MacEwan, needs a few years to regenerate the spirit of the 1930s; he may well do it with help, encouragement and a readiness to take a gamble with younger players.

Scottish club rugby is not as bad as to suggest they be permanent holders of a wooden spoon: the feared 'Greens' of Hawick are as good as any leading club side in the other three home countries. Yet no country in Europe, or indeed the rugby world, has the number of really good players enjoyed by France, or the small group of exceptionally talented performers possessed by Wales. The natural ability of the French for the game is often harnessed and moulded, be it sometimes crudely and over-vigorously, by the intensity of their club championship, which develops a dramatic sense of competition. Wales enjoys the pleasure and privilege of having its eighteen leading clubs situated in a compact area. Thus it is easy to develop cohesion and understanding with the competitive spirit and initiative for success.

Outstanding players are encouraged by the personality cult which is very real and demanding, and the players are challenged constantly by younger players eager to achieve similar fame. Even a player of the calibre and quality of Gareth Edwards, an automatic choice for any team anywhere, and quite the most effective director of operations in any of the five sides in the Championship in 1978, has always been challenged in club football by four or five inside halves. Not one of them, obviously, was as good as Edwards, but they could well have played for one of the other countries. The Welsh side had experience and character, a sort of charisma surrounding it that saw it flash into action with controlled panache whenever the situation demanded it, and this was really due to its confidence and belief in its own ability.

It was not arrogance, as some critics misread it, but a feeling that often permeates through a highly successful club side, and much of this was inspired by the senior players. Finally, the Welsh side had something to prove, not to itself but to its critics, and this was a basic incentive for success.

The next few years may not produce three Triple Crowns or two Grand Slams, as the senior players will gradually slip from the scene they have adorned so colourfully, but Wales will always have a good side in the field, and be challenging because of its splendid squad system and the geographical setting of its club rugby.

The season may not have been truly great, but it was a good one, and in almost every match the spirit of the play was good. No country can afford to sit back and rest upon success achieved, since the game is constantly changing and there are always new challenges to face. The game is growing rapidly across the globe; westward one can see the Americas increasing their enthusiasm and application. Thus it was a long overdue and necessary action to encompass France in the select and important International Board. Membership of that august body will give France increased dignity to match their enthusiasm, and will ensure that the control of the game in Europe will be in wise hands.

The traditional ten matches of the Five Nations Championship were played on five Saturdays between 21 January and 18 March and the reports that follow highlight the play of all five countries.

France v. England

Saturday 21 January   Parc des Princes, Paris
France 15 points (2 tries, 1 penalty, 2 conversions)
England 6 points (2 dropped goals)

This proved to be a sad and unlucky day for English rugby, and added no cheer to the *entente cordiale*. England played so well for half an hour as to appear likely to win the match; their forwards had slightly the better of the exchanges with the Grand Slam French pack, allowing outside half Alan Old carefully to control events with accurate tactical kicking. To English eyes, everything appeared to be proceeding according to plan, when suddenly two key English players were injured and forced to leave the field; as one was the superb and experienced flanker Peter Dixon, and the other the sturdy centre Andy Maxwell, this was a crisis. Both were badly injured; Maxwell was forced to retire from rugby altogether with badly torn knee ligaments; Dixon was out of the England side until the Scottish match. The crisis was completely unexpected, and a dramatically underserved blow to England. From the replacement bench came Charles Kent for the centre and Tony Neary for the flank. At this stage, England were leading, 6-3. Old had dropped two goals, against a penalty by French full-back, Aguirre.

The Parc des Princes is one of the world's noisiest rugby grounds. Despite its comparatively short career in its new form it produces a constant cacophony of sounds that harrass and jar the minds of visiting players and spectators. It is almost bizarre, with numerous bands sounding off martial music, fireworks exploding as if in *Star Wars*, and cockerels running loose in the goal areas. At the same time, the mainly Parisian crowd (in traditional continental style) maintains a whistling symphony, as though one hundred Marilyn Monroes were parading the pitch in the manner of *The Seven Year Itch*. Yet the French are now a true rugby nation, accepting the game as the second national sport. They have enough good players available almost to guarantee the constant leadership of the Championship of the Five Nations.

At this stage of the match, this reputation and prestige in the Championship was being seriously challenged by an England side which was determined, if not audacious, in its efforts. This state of affairs just would not do for the French supporters, who wanted action and victory.

The French team, led by Bastiat in the number eight position (he is a giant of a man from Dax), welcomed the arrival of the three-minute interval, and addressed his men with the earnestness of a colonel before Verdun. Indeed, one even thought of him speaking to them as if they were members of the Queen's Guard, harrassed by Cardinal Richelieu. 'To arms, to arms!' was his cry, and the tide that had hitherto run strongly from Dover to Calais turned again; fiery French waves of light blue crashed against the white cliffs of England. Two splendid tries were scored by wing Averous and scrum-half Gallion. Cockerels crowed, bands boomed and fireworks flashed as Jerome Gallion, 23-year-old dentist in his first big match, dashed and weaved his way through the English forwards to dive over for his spectacular try.

England fought bravely, but the French, through these two tries, had recovered their poise, and now remained dominant. England, however, despite their several injuries (Cowling played on as prop in excruciating pain with a dislocated shoulder), did not submit. The critics, alas so keen to hail and applaud an English victory on foreign soil, foreseeing perhaps an England revival in the Championship, were forced to fall back upon time-honoured clichés. *The Sunday Times* said, 'Gallion the Great!', *The Observer*, 'French make a meal of snail pace English!', and the *Sunday Express*, 'French maul Billy's boys'.

Peter Robbins in *The Financial Times* was cruelly honest in

45

writing, 'There was a bitter familiarity about England's game against France both in pattern and in certainty in the result. However, the England side showed tremendous spirit, and it says much that they did not cave in before the pace and power of this good French side.'

TEAMS
France: J. M. Aguirre; J. F. Gourdon, C. Belascain, R. Bertranne, J-L. Averous; B. Vivies, J. Gallion; J-P. Bastiat (capt.), J-C. Skrela, M. Palmie, J-F. Imbernon, J-P. Rives; R. Paparemborde, A. Paco, G. Cholley
England: W. H. Hare; P. J. Squires, B. Corless, A. Maxwell (sub: C. P. Kent), M. A. C. Slemen; A. G. B. Old, M. Young; J. P. Scott, P. J. Dixon, N. E. Horton, W. B. Beaumont (capt.), M. J. Rafter; M. A. Burton, P. J. Wheeler, R. Cowling

REFEREE: N. R. Sanson (Scotland)

SCORERS
France: Gallion, Averous, tries; Aguirre, 1 penalty, 2 conversions
England: Old, 2 dropped goals

Ireland v. Scotland

Saturday 21 January   Lansdowne Road, Dublin
Ireland 12 points (1 try, 2 penalties, 1 conversion)
Scotland 9 points (3 penalties)

This match was hard, exciting, and produced a thriller finish, yet it remained notable only for the traditional fire of the Irish forward play, which had been revived by the no-nonsense appeal of Ireland's new coach, Noel Murphy of Cork, a vigorous Lion of the 1950s and 60s. Under his guidance and motivation, Ireland employed straightforward methods to harrass the Scots at forward and provide new and promising outside half Tony Ward with the opportunity of proving his worth as a tactical and place kicker.

The ageing Scottish pack (Sandy Carmichael making his fiftieth appearance), did provide however enough possession – perhaps not always good possession – for the backs; the unimaginative backs just did not make enough use of it. Scotland thus lost, despite a desperate rally in the closing stages. Scotland lost partly because of basic weaknesses, while Ron Wilson at outside half had an uninspired day, and Andy Irvine's transfer to the wing did not produce the attacking power anticipated. But Scotland also lost because of an error of judgement: the side's new captain, 1977 Lions scrum-half Douglas Morgan, refused the chance to achieve a draw. In the closing minutes, with the score at 12–9 in Ireland's favour, a penalty was awarded in the Irish '25' to Scotland. Morgan behaved more like John Buchan's Richard Hannay than a Championship captain, although whether his action can be criticized in the highest ideals of the game is arguable. Instead of taking the kick at goal which he would have converted, making the score 12–12, he went for the short penalty and the try. (Judging from the television action-replay, he appeared to be influenced in his judgement by a senior forward, Ian McLauchlan, who should have known better!) At the time, a draw would have kept Scotland in the running for the Championship; later events, with defeats by France and Wales, meant that it did not matter in retrospect. The Scottish Rugby Union supported the 'sporting' action of Morgan; all other countries in the Championship of Five Nations and the International Board would have gone for the draw. Modern sport, whether we like it or not, is based on the maxim, 'If you cannot win, at least try not to lose!' This is not unreasonable.

The tapped penalty was the kiss of death, as Scotland never appeared likely to score a try against an heroic and desperate Irish defence. Alas, the movement broke down, and the unashamed delight of the Irish supporters had no time to subside before the final whistle sounded. Ireland thus celebrated their first victory at Lansdowne Road for two years, whilst the Scots trooped off the field bitterly disappointed. Irishmen everywhere drank deeply of the porter; Murphy's 'Marauders' had won, and for Irish rugby it was a few steps along the road back to success after years of disappointment.

The Irish XV was a young one with five new caps, but its foundation was the five Lions in the pack (one a replacement, McKinney). After-match discussion in the many Dublin bars could now turn towards hope of the Triple Crown, last won in 1949. In contrast, Scotland had but one option ahead of them in preparation for their next match with France: to make changes.

A lack of decisiveness in midfield, the waste of Irvine's potential on the wing, and forward play that was erratic, had all proved Scotland's undoing; Ireland, with their Lions Orr, Keane, Duggan, Slattery and now McKinney (who scored the only try of the match two minutes after taking the field), were in splendid form. Moloney their captain for the first time, and new cap Tony Ward proved sound half-backs. Ward converted McKinney's try and kicked two penalties against three for Scotland by Morgan.

TEAMS

Ireland: A. H. Ensor (sub: L. A. Maloney); T. O. Grace, A. R. McKibbin, P. P. McNaughton, A. C. McLennan; A. J. P. Ward, J. J. Moloney (capt.); W. P. Duggan, J. O'Driscoll (sub: S. McKinney), M. Keane, D. E. Spring, J. F. Slattery; M. P. Fitzpatrick, P. C. Whelan, P. A. Orr

Scotland: B. H. Hay; A. R. Irvine, J. M. Renwick, I. R. Mc-Geechan, D. Shedden; R. Wilson, D. W. Morgan (capt.); D. S. M. MacDonald, M. A. Biggar, A. J. Tomes. A. F. McHarg, C. B. Hegarty; A. B. Carmichael, D. F. Madsen, J. McLauchlan

REFEREE: P. E. Hughes (England)

SCORERS
Ireland: McKinney, 1 try; Ward, 2 penalties, 1 conversion
Scotland: Morgan, 3 penalties

Wales v. England

Saturday 4 February   Twickenham, London
England 6 points (2 penalties)
Wales 9 points (3 penalties)

When England announced their side for this important match, they had to do so without being able to include Dixon, Cowling or Maxwell (all casualties from Paris), and Fran Cotton (labelled by the popular press as the 'Iron Man' of English rugby) was originally nominated for the side but had to withdraw immediately after the announcement when a fitness test was unsuccessful. This was a sad blow for both the player and his country. Even so the side appeared quite strong on paper, with an obvious inclination towards attack through the inclusion of two new backs, John Horton of Bath at outside half, and Paul Dodge, a 19-year-old from Leicester, at centre. Hignell returned to the full-back position, although not really match fit; Nelmes of Cardiff came in as loose head prop; Mordell, a new cap, was selected on the flank in preference to Tony Neary.

Wales selected one of the most experienced teams in its colourful history, with the 15 players providing a total of 308 caps. Bennett led, as he had done Wales and the Lions in 1977.

For Gareth Edwards at scrum-half, it was a special selection. He was awarded his fiftieth consecutive cap, creating a spectacular new record for both Wales and the scrum-half position throughout the world. Tributes reached his home at Porthcawl from officials, players, friends and admirers. The *Western Mail* commented, 'Thank you, Gareth, for the pleasure you have given to those who have watched you in action, young and old, and good luck from those who are privileged to have you as a friend in the game. Fifty not out – what a splendid innings!'

For all members of the Welsh team (only two of them were not Lions, and those, Gravell and Wheel, might well have made the tour had they been fit), this was an important match. Critics had been severe in their comments on the 1977 tour, especially of John Dawes as coach and Phil Bennett as captain; here these two were together again, 'seeking the blood of the Englishmen'. Wales had four outstanding backs in J. P. R. Williams, Gerald Davies, Phil Bennett and Gareth Edwards; their supporters believed that if the Welsh forwards did well enough, Wales would carry the day and continue the run of success against their nearest and greatest rivals, England. Talk of Welsh hatred for the English was so much rubbish. Although Wales did win again, by three penalty goals to two (9–6), and the English were bitterly disappointed, there remained between the two teams and their Unions an atmosphere of good feeling. At the after-match dinner President Sir Anthony Wharton of the RFU presented Gareth Edwards with a beautiful china fruit bowl on behalf of the Union, commemorating the player's fiftieth appearance. This gesture was much appreciated, and significant because it was rare and unusual.

Interest in the match proved greater than ever: the 69,000 admission tickets could have been sold five times (the RFU returned £200,000 in cash). In all this, secretary Air Commodore Bob Weighill had a difficult role to play, since no Union secretary enjoys refusing admission to genuine followers. There were enough Welshmen to crowd the M4 even though hundreds of thousands of supporters remained behind in the Principality, glued to their television sets. Representative rugby football has become the 'in thing' with sports followers, but despite the serious rivalry and intensely physical approach on the field, the terraces remain safe for the *aficionados* of all ages.

Unfortunately, the day was wet and cold, and the Twickenham pitch, the pride and joy of the RFU caretakers, was heavy, greasy and shrouded in driving rain that made running and handling and, indeed, combined play hazardous exercises. England set about achieving control at forward, and worked exceedingly hard in the first half with the wind and rain at their backs to achieve dominance. However, they changed ends no more than three points in the lead (6–3) through two penalties by Alistair Hignell against one by Phil Bennett. This was not a large enough lead to prevent Wales winning. The Welsh decided at the interval to keep play as tight as possible, aiming to make no errors and provide enough ball for Edwards to kick tactically, turning the England forwards and putting pressure on defenders (especially on Hignell, who was desperately short of match practice).

Edwards was the key player, and his tactical control ensured victory as well as highlighting the basic weakness of the 1977 Lions. His kicking penned England in their own half during the final twenty minutes of play, preventing them from breaking out in a bid to score and win the match. Towards the end, under the severe strain of such continuous pressure, England conceded a penalty at a ruck; Bennett kicked a straight goal, and it was 9–6. Even so, Hignell just failed to level the scores with a final penalty attempt before the final whistle. The balance of the match was slight in points, if not in respective quality; penalty goals remain a constant source of argument and the match was decided by the accuracy of the two main kickers. Hignell landed two goals for England in six attempts (some were near misses), against Bennett's three goals in four attempts for Wales. Had the penalty goal value been reduced to two points (as in Rugby League), or even one, the final score would still have been in favour of Wales.

The Welsh forwards, by their excellent second-half display, surprised even the most faithful of their many supporters who argued that age could not reduce the players' spirit and skill. Gareth Edwards did enough in his own special way to indicate yet again his mastery of all the skills, especially those of scrum-half. The best scrum-half in the world at present, and one of the greatest of all times, it is little wonder that the RFU saw fit to present him with the bowl to honour his fiftieth appearance. The narrowly beaten English were understandably disappointed because they could not see how victory was to come in future matches and what more they had to do to achieve it. But for coach John Dawes and captain Phil Bennett of the 1977 Lions it was a satisfying triumph, and they remained content and silent in victory.

TEAMS

England: A. J. Hignell; P. J. Squires, B. J. Corless, P. Dodge, M. A. C. Slemen; J. P. Horton, M. Young; J. P. Scott, R. J. Mordell, N. E. Horton, W. B. Beaumont (capt.), M. J. Rafter; M. A. Burton, P. J. Wheeler, B. G. Nelmes

Wales: J. P. R. Williams; T. G. R. Davies, W. R. Gravell, S. P. Fenwick, J. J. Williams; P. Bennett (capt.), G. O. Edwards; D. L. Quinnell, J. Squire, A. J. Martin, G. A. D. Wheel, T. J. Cobner; G. Price, R. W. Windsor, A. G. Faulkner

REFEREE: N. R. Sanson (Scotland)

SCORERS

England: Hignell, 2 penalties
Wales: Bennett, 3 penalties

France v. Scotland

Saturday 4 February   Murrayfield, Edinburgh
Scotland 16 points (2 tries, 2 penalties, 1 conversion)
France 19 points (2 tries, 3 penalties, 1 conversion)

Following their defeat in Dublin by Ireland through a lack of imagination, the Scots viewed this match with genuine apprehension, hoping their backs would perform with greater skill and enterprise. The restoration of the exciting Andy Irvine to the full-back position suggested greater possibilities in attack, even though there was no optimism abroad in Edinburgh that Wilson and Morgan at half-back would set the Forth alight: their play was by no means complementary in the representative sense. In defence the Scots had the task of containing the new French discovery at scrum-half, Gallion; it was thought that the forwards would find it difficult dealing with the new French captain at number eight, the giant Bastiat.

All appeared set for a comfortable French victory, but whilst France did succeed in the end, their passage through an exciting match was anything but comfortable. In the course of rapidly changing fortunes, the match was one of lost opportunity; a vital blow was suffered by Scotland in the injury to Irvine when the match was half over. The match turned on this unhappy event, as Irvine was the brilliant and effective counter-attacker both feared and respected by the French for his flair; they experienced considerable difficulty in containing him. Without him Scotland were like a blunted sword, a hammer without a handle, and they could not maintain their magnificent attacking play of the first thirty-six minutes. At the end of that time, they had led by thirteen points, with every thought of achieving a convincing and notable victory against the Champions of the Five Nations.

Douglas Morgan, captain at scrum-half, put Scotland into the lead with a penalty goal, and towards the interval there came two tries originated by Morgan. First he kicked to the left corner, where David Sheddon scored after charging down a clearance kick by Gourdon; then he kicked upfield for Irvine to chase after the ball. When the full-back set off there appeared little or no chance of a try, but Irvine is no ordinary player . . . . He hacked on past Averous and then, although then blatantly obstructed by Gourdon, got clear and dived heavily on the ball after it had crossed the French goal line. It was an opportunist try but the heavy dive was unfortunately to prove the undoing of a brave Scottish team.

Irvine badly damaged the ligaments in his shoulder, and as Morgan struck a beautiful conversion to make it 13–0 to Scotland, there was genuine concern for the full-back as he left the field for treatment. While he was off, Gallion scored a try for France, his second in successive matches, and confirmed the good impression he had created against England. This was just before the interval.

In the first twenty minutes of the second half, France rampaged as they did in the same period against England in Paris. The Scottish forwards faded for a while, and the French regained their poise and enthusiasm. Irvine had to be replaced by Cranston, and later Sheddon by Hogg, with Hay dropping back to the vacant full-back position. Scotland thus finished the match with four centres at three-quarter. France collected a penalty goal kicked by full-back Aguirre, and he also converted a try by the powerful lock Haget. The giant score board read 'Scotland 13, France 13'. The tension mounted. The crowd erupted when Morgan quickly dropped a goal from an indirect penalty award without first tapping forward, catching Welsh Referee Cenydd Thomas and the annoyed French side unaware. The French quickly demonstrated their displeasure, but the goal had to stand, and Scotland were in the lead. Could they hold on to the lead and, despite their earlier misfortunes, achieve a very special victory? Alas, no, for Aguirre landed his second penalty goal to level the scores, and then kicked a third to win the match 19–16.

This ending was a particularly sad one for the Scots, who deserved better. Yet it was significant that their weakness in scrummaging and in certain aspects of tight play during the first twenty minutes of the second half was to appear again in their next match, that against Wales at Cardiff.

TEAMS

Scotland: A. R. Irvine (sub: A. G. Cranston); B. H. Hay, J. M. Renwick, I. R. McGeechan, D. Shedden (sub: G. Hogg); R. Wilson, D. W. Morgan (capt.); G. Y. Mackie, C. B. Hegarty, A. F. McHarg, A. J. Tomes, M. A. Biggar; J. McLauchlan, C. T. Deans, N. E. K. Pender

France: J. M. Aguirre; J. F. Gourdon, R. Bertranne, C. Belascain, J-L. Averous; B. Vivies, J. Gallion; J-P. Bastiat (capt.), J-C. Skrela, F. Haget, M. Palmie, J-P. Rives; R. Paparemborde, A. Paco, G. Cholley

REFEREE: C. G. P. Thomas (Wales)

SCORERS

Scotland: Shedden, Irvine, tries; Morgan, 2 penalties, 1 con.
France: Gallion, Haget, tries; Aguirre, 3 penalties, 1 conversion

Wales v. Scotland

Saturday 18 February   Cardiff Arms Park
Wales 22 points (4 tries, 1 dropped goal, 1 penalty)
Scotland 14 points (2 tries, 2 penalties)

After their French defeat, Scotland made changes; their misfortunes continued. Andy Irvine failed to get fit in time, and Bruce Hay moved to full-back from the wing once more, playing 'general post' in the side with admirable enthusiasm. Wales, having beaten England, fielded the same XV, but ever mindful of the sensational and unexpected defeat of 1951 at Murrayfield, when as Champions Wales were humbled 19–0 by one of the youngest of Scottish sides, John Dawes as Welsh coach was extremely cautious. He told his side that the match would be hard, and that Scotland, inspired by a heartening display against France believed they could surprise the Welsh, even although, as they had not won at Cardiff since 1962, there were considerable odds against a Scottish victory. During the week of the match the weather grew colder; about the time the Scottish party flew into Cardiff Airport, the temperature dropped dramatically.

Fortunately, groundsman Bill Hardiman had his well-nursed pitch protected by a cover of polythene; it remained firm and dry. Tickets of admission were almost impossible to obtain: they had been distributed to clubs long before (the black marketeers had a poor day). This was a feature of the Championship season in the British Isles and France. Few (if any) tickets were on sale outside the grounds on the morning of the ten matches played. This highlighted the growing interest in top level rugby football. As if a new cult has been launched, it now appears to be the 'in thing' among sports followers to be present at representative rugby matches and, if possible, to support one's country in away matches. One well-known dental surgeon, a player in his youth, told me he was rather proud of the fact that he and his wife had watched Wales play all four matches in the Championship. As an active administrator in an amateur game, he felt that it was a reward for his annual labours on behalf of the game, and to hell with the expense! I wonder how many followers watch their country play all four times in a season? Certainly more than did so twenty years ago, although the invading Welsh 'armies' of the 1950s are

54

much reduced in size since all international matches are now all-ticket affairs. Those thousands of Welshmen who travelled to Murrayfield or Lansdowne Road for 'club outings' in the 1950s now have to obtain tickets before contemplating the journey – although many in Dublin in 1978 said they had made the trip to recapture the memories of the past. One suspects that national grounds accommodating 100,000 spectators will not meet the growing demands of the new rugby cult.

The Welsh Rugby Union opened its new West stand at a cost of one-and-a-quarter million pounds; this figure would have met the needs of rebuilding the entire ground some twenty years ago. The additional construction added to the impressive appearance of the historic ground, and indeed to its comfort and safety. The new Act concerning the safety of major sporting arenas has cut the total accommodation by several thousands, however, and the ground's capacity for this match was forty-five thousand. At one time its accommodation was almost sixty thousand, but the changeover from standing places to seating has played no small part in the reduction. To provide seating instead of standing places is the advice given by the experts to all developers of major stadia, as seating plays an important part in curtailing crowd misbehaviour. Even at Cardiff, when Scotland and France played at the Arms Park in 1976, there were a few ugly crowd scenes. The changing situation needed the immediate attention of the ground controllers and their architects.

In this match the crowd behaved well, but perhaps it was too cold for anything other than good behaviour! The East wind blew down the ground from the Westgate Street end and rebounded from the new West stand. It swirled round the North stand, virtually freezing all the seated spectators, making place kicking something of a hazard, and heralding one of the worst blizzards to hit South Wales since the storm of 1962/3. The blizzard was to maroon the Welsh team and officials in their hotel headquarters until Monday morning, causing more than one player to comment, 'It was the best week-end of an international match ever enjoyed in Cardiff!'

The critics expected Welsh experience to overcome a strong Scottish challenge, although *The Scotsman* suggested that the Scots would exploit the lack of pace in the Welsh back row, a misjudgement that was to confuse other opponents, even the French; *The Guardian* believed Scotland were out to surprise Wales; *The Daily Telegraph* warned that the hungry Scots could give Wales a fright.

Wales, facing a biting wind in the first half, proved themselves to be a side of lasting quality and purpose as Scotland strove to gain a comfortable lead. They had to do so if they were to stand any chance of surviving the second half, which they would play against the cold, biting wind that made handling and kicking unusually hazardous. On winning the toss, Wales wisely chose to play into the wind, believing they would be able to make more use of it after the interval. They defended most ably against a variation of Scottish attacks as well as counter-attacking with panache.

Scotland collected a penalty goal through Douglas Morgan and an excellent try through Jim Renwick, one of their best at Cardiff for many years; Wales scored two tries. Gareth Edwards collected his twentieth with a clever twenty-yard dash from a scrum; Ray Gravell scored his first for his country. Wales thus enjoyed an interval lead of one point. Basically, this lead was achieved through superior scrummaging (in which the Welsh front row did a splendid job): the eight-man shove on the Scottish put-in was often devastating. Thus after the change of ends the result was inevitable, although there was still much good football to come from both sides.

The match was often remarkable, considering the conditions. In the first fourteen minutes of the second half, Wales moved with crushing efficiency and natural skill from 8–7 to 22–7 to make sure of victory; they then appeared to relax, as if riding the wind. First Bennett dropped a goal with nonchalant ease, then there was a Fenwick try that was to cause much discussion upon the existing tackle law; Bennett eased over a long penalty, and then the powerful Derek Quinnell thundered up the left touch-line to crash over for a try. That appeared to be enough for the Welshmen, and Scotland fought back with enthusiasm, eager to restore the balance and share in the wintry festivities. Morgan kicked a penalty goal and Alan Tomes got a try after a Morgan dash from a short penalty. At the close it was 22–14 to Wales, left with only Ireland to overcome in Dublin for a third successive Triple Crown.

It had proved an enjoyable match and *The Daily Telegraph*

summed it up fairly in stating 'Welsh flair versus Scottish dogged-ness made for a happy occasion.' Wales had made better use of the wind, kicked more accurately and proved far more cohesive at forward. The back row of Terry Cobner, Derek Quinnell and Jeff Squire had lacked for nothing; Scotland never stopped fighting back, however, with Bruce Hay immensely brave in defence at full-back. Renwick was sharp in attack and Mike Biggar tireless in the loose, with the three tall men, MacDonald McHarg and Tomes dominating the lineout. Yet, Bennett and Edwards, traditionally cool and playing almost as one, controlled events as they saw fit; it was all good, clean fun. A most enjoyable match!

TEAMS

Wales: J. P. R. Williams; T. G. R. Davies, R. W. R. Gravell, S. P. Fenwick, J. J. Williams; P. Bennett (capt.), G. O. Edwards; D. L. Quinnell, T. J. Cobner, A. J. Martin, G. A. D. Wheel, J. Squire, G. Price, R. W. Windsor, A. G. Faulkner

Scotland: B. H. Hay; W. B. B. Gammell, J. M. Renwick, A. G. Cranston, D. Shedden (sub: G. Hogg); I. R. McGeechan, D. W. Morgan (capt.); D. S. M. MacDonald, C. B. Hegarty, A. F. McHarg, A. J. Tomes, M. A. Biggar, N. E. K. Pender, C. T. Deans, J. L. McLauchlan

REFEREE: J. R. West (Ireland)

SCORERS

Wales: Edwards, Gravell, Fenwick, Quinnell, tries; Bennett, 1 dropped goal, 1 penalty

Scotland: Renwick, Tomes, tries; Morgan, 2 penalties

France v. Ireland

Saturday 18 February   Parc des Princes, Paris
France 10 points (1 try, 2 penalties)
Ireland 9 points (3 penalties)

This match had promised much to critics and spectators alike, but neither expected quite as much pre-match drama as that which charged the atmosphere of the day with an air of unreality. The Irish party flew into Paris determined to upset the French (who has only just survived their visit to Murrayfield), but on arrival they found the pitch covered with several inches of snow. Both teams trained on snow-covered pitches in Paris, the French work-out being conducted *in camera*. (This has always appeared to me as a somewhat ridiculous exercise: what is there really new in rugby? It is a game of variations on the basic principles of winning the ball and using it wisely, and preventing the other side scoring when they have it.)

The conditions at lunchtime at the Parc des Princes were grim. The Irish regarded them as unplayable and the Referee, Cenydd Thomas of Wales, agreed. The French too were unhappy, with the pitch frozen hard and the temperature low. However, specta-tors were admitted at the normal time despite thoughts of cracked heads and broken limbs, and the real tragedy was that the Referee could not refuse to start the match since he had no powers to do so! In accordance with Championship regulations, it was the responsibility of the host Union. Thus only the French Rugby Federation could make the vital decision before the match; only once it had been started was it the responsibility of the referee.

Two members of the Irish Union, former President Harry McKibbin and coach Noel Murphy, inspected the pitch on their bare knees with their trousers rolled up, (making one of the best rugby pictures of the year), and they joined the Referee in saying, 'The pitch is dangerous and unfit for play.' The French Federa-tion, having allowed the crowd into the stands, were put in a spot; concerned at the thought of a possible continental style sporting riot if the match was suddenly postponed (apart from any financial loss), the Federation waived aside all objections, and said, 'Play ball!' Once the match had started, the decision would be up to the referee. The crowd could not reasonably complain if the match had to be abandoned after a broken limb or two.

Cenydd Thomas is a worthy member of the South Wales Constabulary. For him it was a case of almost Gilbertian con-stabulary duties. His lot was not a happy one. He admitted afterwards, 'I made a decision before I took the field to bring the players off the moment an injury occured that was attributable to the hard pitch, even if it happened immediately after the start. By some miracle, the match was played without any player suffering serious injury.'

France won by a mere point in the end, and they were given a real run for their money by a lively Irish side motivated by Noel Murphy, who encouraged the side to forget the hard ground and remain on their feet whenever possible. France scored a try and two penalties (against Ireland's three penalties) but the match did not have the full-bloodedness of a normal international. Naturally the players remained apprehensive of the conditions; this demonstrated quite clearly that the match should not have been played.

Conditions favoured the spoiling, disruptive, chance-taking Irishmen who did well at the set scrum and the lineout, although they were subjected to severe pressure for long periods in their own '25' during the second half. It was quite amazing how they kept the French out with a particularly brave defence. In sum, the French deserved their win, although it was right that it was a narrow margin.

Before the start, the lighter Harry Steel (normally at number eight) replaced the injured O'Rafferty at lock. He played well enough, although not quite able to match the bigger Frenchmen Haget and Bastiat at the lineout, which made it harder for Keane and Duggan. Yet Steele did his work in the scrum, the maul and about the field. Ensor played soundly at full-back; Gibson did his share in defence, and young Ward was almost a match-winner at outside half kicking his side's three penalties for nine points, all superb kicks.

For France, flanker Jean-Pierre Rives was outstanding in this match. (His form fell away considerably before the end of the season, probably due to the hard knocks he suffered in stern tackling when he became a closely marked member of the French XV – opponents ensured that Gallion, an individualist at scrum-half, was cut off from his support.) Unfortunately, Aguirre at full-back was less accurate as the side's place kicker, succeeding with only two attempts in seven; this suggests that Ireland could have been beaten by a bigger margin; poor place kicking remained France's major problem through the season. Gallion scored his third successive try to continue his promise but still appeared to be more of an individual than a linking team player.

The try came through number eight Bastiat moving to the blind side of a scrum, committing the Irish back row, and then feeding

Gallion, who ran clear and scored. This move was not lost upon the Welsh when they later studied the video recording of the try. France, with three victories in three matches, became favourites to retain the Grand Slam, although there were yet four weeks before their visit to the Cardiff Arms Park to meet Wales. Even the continued success did not appear to please the more discerning of French critics, however, who longed to see more traditional French play from the side with continuous running. Rumours indicated that the French selectors (all thirteen of them) were divided in their approach to the pattern of play; while some appeared to want to leave everything to Bastiat and his pack, the others desired more direction behind from outside half Vivies, claiming that there was little unison in combined play as the team was at present. This became more evident in the final match against Wales.

TEAMS

France: J. M. Aguirre; L. Bilbas, R. Bertranne, C. Belascain, J. L. Averous; B. Vivies, J. Gallion; J-P. Bastiat (capt.), J-P. Rives, M. Palmie, F. Haget, J-C. Skrela, R. Paparemborde, A. Paco, G. Cholley

Ireland: A. H. Ensor; C. M. H. Gibson, P. McNaughton, A. McKibbin, A. McLennan; A. Ward, J. J. Moloney (capt.); W. P. Duggan, J. F. Slattery, M. I. Keane, H. Steele, S. A. McKinney, N. Byrne, P. Whelan, P. Orr

REFEREE: C. G. P. Thomas (Wales)

SCORERS
France: Gallion, 1 try; Aguirre, 2 penalties
Ireland: Ward, 3 penalties

England v. Scotland

Saturday 4 March   Murrayfield, Edinburgh
Scotland 0 points
England 15 points (2 tries, 1 penalty, 2 conversions)

For Scots and Englishmen, the Calcutta Cup has a special meaning; its appeal cannot be enjoyed by others with the same intensity of affection or purpose. An additional but important factor is that the annual meeting of England and Scotland represents the oldest international match in world rugby, the series having started with the meeting at the Raeburn Place Ground, Edinburgh in 1871; for the players of both countries, their participation in the Calcutta Cup match is the high point of their rugby ambition.

Wilson Shaw, the brilliant Scottish outside half and utility player of the 1930s (later an able president of the Scottish Rugby Union as well as a hard-working International Board member), readily confessed in many happy discussions that to lead Scotland to victory and the Triple Crown at Twickenham in the outstanding 1938 match was the most wonderful experience of his colourful career. On that day he was truly brilliant, scoring a remarkable and decisive try. (The final score, 21–16, after the lead had constantly changed hands, suggests a match to remember.)

In March 1978, the Calcutta Cup was 99 years old; there is thus good reason to envisage a match of special significance in 1979 at Twickenham when the magnificent trophy celebrates its century. Tribute will certainly be paid in full to the members of the Calcutta Rugby Club, who disbanded because of a lack of fixtures in 1877, ordering that the Club's assets in silver rupees be melted down and moulded into a cup. The attractive trophy was presented to the Rugby Football Union; it was offered for an annual competition between England and Scotland. It was first played for at Raeburn Place, but as the match was drawn it could not be held by either country until the following year when England beat Scotland at the Whally Range Ground in Manchester. Scotland proved far superior in the clashes of the 1890s; then England did, from 1913 to 1925 when they handed over the Cup after the first international match at Murrayfield. (What a magnificent match it was. Any reader in doubt of this should ask Barbarian President Herbert Waddell to relate the progress, movement by movement, of a match in which a younger and inspired Scottish team defeated an older but magnificent England side that ran out of steam!) England held it again from 1951 to 1964 in a run.

England were also holders when they took the field at Murrayfield for the 1978 match. Scotland were hampered by late injuries. England nominated their side dropping Gloucester prop Mike Burton, relegating him to reserve; they found the lively forward unable to accept the position of a replacement, forced to watch

c

play from the touch line: 'I would rather play and keep fit for my Club in a bid to win the John Player Cup, than act as a reserve. (This is not a complaint because I have been dropped from the side.)' Fran Cotton, having recovered from injury, replaced Burton; Cardiff's Barry Nelmes held his place because of his additional mobility which was much in evidence in this match. One has to acknowledge the point made by Burton.

Ten years previously there were no substitutes in European rugby (certain dispensations were allowed to Australia and New Zealand, who always believed them necessary). It happened once during a match in a French tour of South Africa during 1958, when full-back Michel Vannier broke a leg and was replaced without creating an international incident.

Pressure upon the International Board had first arisen after Reg Higgins was injured in the first Test of the Lions' 1955 tour in South Africa; the seven Lions forwards just managed to survive for a magnificent 23–22 victory. Continual injuries suffered to key players on tours eventually convinced the Board of the need of allowing replacements, and while at first they were limited to representative matches, the law is now applied to all grades of the game. This, however, has produced a new problem as a number of players (six in representative and two in club matches) have to sit in the stand and miss playing, while still remaining committed to their team. At international level reserves had always been sitting in the stand with never a chance of taking the field, but now there is more chance, since injuries appear to be frequent, and the replacement system prevents a player from continuing when really not fit to do so: many a player has ended a successful career prematurely by remaining on the field after injury for the sake of his side. So one should welcome this change in the Laws of the Game. Individual players still have the choice of opting out of being replacements, as did Alan Lawson of Scotland in 1977 and Geoffrey Evans and Alan Old of England in 1978.

This England–Scotland match was deservedly won by England as a result of better controlled and more effective forward play and more decisive back play. Scotland, did not succeed, despite having many chances, because they could not pierce an eminently sound and well-organized English defence; they suffered their fourth defeat of the season and were forced to accept the wooden

62

spoon. The England victory, their first at Murrayfield for ten years, brought happiness to players, selectors and supporters alike, and the proving of players like David Caplan at full-back, Paul Dodge in the centre, and Mike Colclough and John Scott in the pack, suggested that England may have turned the corner at long last.

It was the general wish of rugby men everywhere that the tide should turn. English clubs continued to do well against their Welsh rivals, and the question seemed to be that of assessing the available playing talent and blending it, a task which is always more difficult in England than the other three home countries. For Scotland and Ireland, there remained the ever-present handicap of having fewer players from which to select sides, compared with Wales, bubbling with a national fervour and intensity of purpose, or with France with more good players available than almost all four home countries together (even if she is hampered by parochial regional prejudices: these used to exist in Wales quite dramatically between East and West, and have only been eliminated by wiser selection and the squad system).

The English forwards blended well from the start, and their close driving was admirable: it had a considerable effect upon the stamina of the Scottish pack, who could not match the English in expertise or mobility. In the set scrums, Wheeler won four tightheads against two and Beaumont led with admirable enthusiasm; England's possession could have been still greater had their throwing-in to the end of the lineout been more accurate. However (as David Irvine wisely pointed out in the *Guardian*), England learned before the end, and young John Scott got the better of Donald MacDonald.

England scored first, with a good try by Peter Squires which followed a sharp blindside dash by Mike Slemen. He sent a pass inside, expecting support, and the forwards were there. Wheeler, Nelmes, Dixon and Beaumont handled accurately, and then a long pass to Squires saw him deceive several would-be tacklers and score at the posts for Malcolm Young to convert. This was followed by a powerful kick by the 19-year-old centre, Paul Dodge, which, from inside his own half, landed a penalty goal. Scotland continued to waste what chances they received (some of them quite reasonable), and it was well into the second half before the next and final score was achieved. Scott won lineout possession near to the front of the line, and Corless moved right and worked a scissors move with Dodge. Corless ran hard, but was stopped by Renwick; Nelmes was on hand to pick up and charge over, taking a few defenders with him. Young kicked an easy goal, and England were home and dry, leaving a disappointed Scotland whitewashed at the end.

TEAMS
Scotland: A. R. Irvine; W. B. B. Gammell, J. M. Renwick, A. G. Cranston, B. H. Hay; R. W. Breakey*, D. W. Morgan (capt.); D. S. M. MacDonald, C. B. Hegarty, A. J. Tomes, D. Gray*, M. A. Biggar, N. E. K. Pender, C. T. Deans, J. L. McLauchlan
England: D. W. N. Caplan*; P. J. Squires, P. W. Dodge, B. J. Corless, M. A. C. Slemen; J. P. Horton, M. Young; J. P. Scott, M. Rafter, M. Colclough*, W. B. Beaumont (capt.), P. J. Dixon, F. E. Cotton, P. J. Wheeler, B. G. Nelmes
*Denotes new cap

REFEREE: J. R. West (Ireland)

SCORERS
England: Squires, Nelmes, tries; Dodge, penalty; Young, 2 conversions

Wales v. Ireland

Saturday 4 March   Lansdowne Road, Dublin
Ireland 16 points (1 try, 3 penalties, 1 dropped goal)
Wales 20 points (2 tries, 4 penalties)

Some of the previous Championship matches had been hard and exciting, but this meeting between Ireland and Wales, for the Triple Crown, was expected to prove harder than any of them. From the very moment that the Welsh XV to meet Ireland was announced as unchanged from that which defeated Scotland, forecasts were issued fast and furiously from the pens of critics in both participating countries and in England. All regarded it as a major challenge for Wales; the memorable occasions of the past were recalled in which Wales had faltered in Ireland in search of

64

the Triple Crown. In contrast, Ireland were encouraged by the fact that they had beaten Scotland and almost France. There was the distinct possibility that the tearaway Irish forwards, inspired by coach Noel Murphy and pack leader Fergus Slattery, would disturb the talented Welsh out of their normal rhythm.

In themselves, the Irish were confident, rather than hopeful: there is considerable difference between these terms. The discovery of a goal-kicking outside half (Tony Ward) was a bonus that could produce points when the Welsh forwards made errors. Colm Smith, rugby writer of the *Irish Independent*, in a rather provocative article, suggested that it was 'Irish grit versus Welsh arrogance'; I felt, however, that the Welsh were far from arrogant and would be well satisfied with a point lead at the end of the match. Yet Smith did emphasize that in the previous three matches, all won by Wales, they had scored 92 points, with 22 against them.

Edmund Van Esbeck in *The Irish Times* argued that Ireland possessed the ability to blunt Wales, and that the major responsibility rested upon the forwards, to upset Gareth Edwards, the key Welsh player appearing in his fifty-second consecutive match. The message to the Welsh players was to remain cool and unruffled in the heat of battle; concern was expressed on both sides that the French referee, Georges Domercq, would not enjoy a heated match, much preferring the open approach of Barbarian encounters. As was to be proved, he had not been made aware of the new regulations regarding the 'pile-up', as distinct from the ruck and maul, and this was only to add fuel to the flames that sometimes burned brightly with scorched vigour at the rucks and mauls!

Of special importance was the fact that the season marked the hundredth anniversary of rugby football at the Lansdowne Road Ground; this made it the oldest active international rugby arena in the world, and the Irish were keen to celebrate the occasion with a Triple Crown victory. If they could beat Wales, their hopes of defeating England at Twickenham would be considerably improved.

Michael Gibson, appearing on the wing for Ireland, was winning his 64th cap, creating a new record by passing that of the 63 caps won by his former captain, Willie John McBride; although 34 years old, Gibson was still as sprightly as any of his younger colleagues. There was a division of opinion within the Irish Union as to whether he should have been recalled, but for the followers of the game it was another enjoyable record to discuss!

The interest in the match produced a great demand for tickets, and the 'sold out' notices were soon posted. Even so, thousands of Welshmen made the journey to Dublin in the hope of obtaining tickets in the City on Saturday morning near the ground before kick off; a few were fortunate. The ground was full to capacity when the teams took the field, in perfect conditions, to start the match.

Steve Fenwick, who was to enjoy a special match, put Wales in the lead with an early penalty goal from sixty yards and followed with a second from forty-seven yards before Tony Ward countered for Ireland with a penalty to make it 6–3. Fenwick then landed his third from forty yards and a little later scored a fine try. Derek Quinnell and Ray Gravell drove through strongly, and then Gareth Price did well to send Fenwick running diagonally to the right and through the Irish cover to cross the line for a try, although it was not converted. A second penalty from Ward made it 13–6 to Wales at the interval; Ward had failed with three of his five attempts at goal. He made amends, however, early in the second half, dropping a sharp goal from a tapped penalty.

Shortly after, Ireland drew level with a controversial try. Ward punted high into the Welsh '25' area, where J. P. R. Williams for once miscued his clearance; the ball flew back over his own goal line. Gerald Davies was covering, and he thought he had grounded the ball before it went loose for John Moloney to dive on it and claim a try; Referee Domercq was some distance away.

The try was awarded. No one in the Press box was able to argue with the decision; even the television replay did not provide any further light upon the problem. However, the score was a real challenge to the Welsh, and the decisive period of the whole tournament. Success for them depended upon their ability to recover and stand firm in the face of a most formidable challenge. It may be trite to suggest that it revealed the real 'character and strength of the side', but this is true in the sense that the greatness of this Welsh team revealed itself more clearly when the side was under severe pressure.

As he revealed later, Irish coach Noel Murphy believed at this stage that his side would win the match; however, the Welsh forwards, led by Terry Cobner, remained cool and determined under pressure, and made no mistakes as they battled away to win possession. Behind them, Edwards and Bennett were especially cool, and Edwards was increasingly aware of the need for Wales to score. It was during this vital period that the experience, confidence, ability, coolness and character shone through, like a beacon highlighting the right of the team to be Champions. All great sides in the past have had that 'something' which enabled them to raise their game to meet the demands of the occasion; it is this indefinable quality which won this match for Wales.

Edwards, receiving from his forwards on the right, moved across field to his left, dummying as he went (this opened up the defence, eventually producing the overlap for left wing J. J. Williams), and sent a lofted pass to Fenwick, who passed on to Williams, who stretched for it and went over in the corner. It was decisive.

Fenwick kicked another penalty for Wales, increasing his tally of points to sixteen (Wales were now leading 20–13); however, the promising Ward, so sure of foot and full of quiet confidence, then landed the fourth goal for Ireland when Wales were penalized. The match retained its atmosphere of tension and excitement to the very end, although the lead never changed hands, of course. For Fenwick, the match was a triumph (with his sixteen points); his contribution highlighted the vital necessity of any successful side, that of having more than one match-winning place kicker. Fenwick's strange calm is unusual, and his ability to be in the right place at the right time highlights his usefulness to any side. Terry Cobner, pack leader, was in tremendous form, and the whole eight, regarded earlier in the season of being suspect in certain phases, mantained a steady, determined, unflurried effort that was a winning one.

The relief for the Welsh XV in winning this vital match was remarkable, and it was some time before they realized the historic value of their achievement; many of them were so drained of evergy, mental and physical, that it took them much longer than normal to shower and change.

Noel Murphy and his Irishmen were bitterly disappointed. They had come so near to achieving the almost impossible; the beating of Wales would have been something much more than a shining emerald in the Triple Crown. Murphy had, however achieved much in restoring the fighting spirit of Ireland on the rugby field (even if a couple of forwards had carried the instructions slightly beyond the letter of the law). In particular, the gallant lock, Moss Keane, who had returned from New Zealand with hepatitis and been out of the game for several months, produced the best performance of his career in this match.

Richard Streeton, in *The Times*, looked forward with some perception in his report of the match: Phil Bennett, who uncharacteristically did not score in this match, still needed three points to pass the Championship individual scoring record of T. J. Kiernan of Ireland; Streeton wrote, 'Thus his chance to pass the British Isles individual record is preserved until Cardiff. It will only add to the emotion and drama of what could be the farewell performance of a remarkable Welsh team.'

John Dawes smiled with much inward satisfaction at the victory, and commented, 'It was a team effort in a match charged with emotion. Wales revealed, especially at forward, the control necessary for victory.'

In the midst of the atmosphere of triumph, there was one slightly discordant note. The intensely competitive Welsh full-back, J. P. R. Williams, was guilty of a late charge on Mike Gibson, after that player had kicked ahead during the second half. The charge was not sighted by Referee Domercq. It was seen by a large section of the capacity crowd and by some occupants of the Press box; Williams was subject to a barrage of booing whenever in the play until the end of the match. Gibson was shaken by the charge but said afterwards that he did not believe it was all that intentional.

Williams admitted that it was late, but said that he had been committed, and that it was an instinctive reaction. He suffered much criticism for his action; one would not suggest that he was in any way happy about it. Williams, although totally committed on the field, is not a dirty player. He has received his fair share of knocks and bruises as a charging full-back. The next day he expressed the opinion: 'At times, this match came as near to warfare as sport can get. It was very vicious.' However, apart from his lapse, and the 'fancy footwork' of two Irish forwards, much of it was sheer physical endeavour that occasionally got out of hand.

The match was never easy for Referee Domercq; the discussion highlighted the need for the appointment of referees suitable to the demands of 'needle' matches – this was in every sense of the word. The fact that France and Wales would be playing as unbeaten sides for the Grand Slam two weeks later caused some concern among those close to the game; they feared lest that match should develop into a brawl, with the prize taking precedence over good rugby.

TEAMS
Ireland: A. H. Ensor; C. M. H. Gibson, P. McNaughton, A. A. McKibbin, A. McLennan; A. Ward, J. J. Moloney (capt.) W. P. Duggan, J. F. Slattery, M. I. Keane, H. Steele, S. A. McKinney, N. Byrne, P. Whelan, P. A. Orr
Wales: J. P. R. Williams; T. G. R. Davies, R. W. R. Gravell, S. P. Fenwick, J. J. Williams; P. Bennett (capt.), G. O. Edwards; D. L. Quinnell, T. J. Cobner, A. J. Martin, G. A. D. Wheel, J. Squire, G. Price, R. W. Windsor, A. G. Faulkner

REFEREE: G. Domercq (France)

SCORERS
Ireland: Moloney, 1 try; Ward, 3 penalties, 1 dropped goal
Wales: Fenwick, J. J. Williams, tries; Fenwick, 4 penalties

England v. Ireland

Saturday 18 March   Twickenham, London
England 15 points (2 tries, 1 penalty, 2 conversions)
Ireland 9 points (2 penalties, 2 dropped goals)

Ireland were confident that their splendid record at Twickenham would continue, whilst England nominated the same team and replacements who had beaten Scotland; this act of leaving the team unchanged was a pleasant and refreshing change from the years of variation (particularly at half-back). In the previous seven matches between the countries at Twickenham, England had succeeded only once, in 1970, through the kicking of their best post-war match-winner, full-back Bob Hiller. In the Scottish match the new full-back David Caplan revealed enough skill and enthusiasm to deserve the retention of his place, and so scrum-half Malcolm Young became the first-choice place kicker. (No side –

club or representative – should ever take the field without a reliable and accurate place kicker with a range of forty yards.) One feels that the England players were much encouraged by being selected unchanged; they felt there was light at last at the end of the long dark tunnel of misfortune and defeat.

Ireland, too, selected the same side that had played with such enthusiasm against Wales, confident that these would be able to harrass England out of their new-found composure. Gibson remained on the wing for his sixty-fifth cap at the age of thirty-four; it suggests that famous rugby players carry on for ever and never fade away! Before the match, however, injuries to number eight Willie Duggan, and the young outside half Tony Ward were to cause the Irish coach Noel Murphy and his fellow selectors some concern. Wing Michael Slemen of Liverpool was a doubtful starter for England. Fortunately, all three players recovered in time to take their place at Twickenham (Duggan's decision was made on the eve of the match). As Gerald Davies was also a doubtful starter at Cardiff for the Wales–France match, and was eventually forced to withdraw, the series of injuries gave support to the belief that contemporary players are more susceptible to injury than those of twenty-five years ago – at least at top level, where, like thoroughbred racehorses, they are more highly trained and more easily bruised; they are built for speed, wear lighter equipment, and are often subject to 'fancy footwork' in the rucks. Whatever the reasons, though, I am inclined to agree, after fifty years of keen observation, that injuries are more frequent. The majority cannot be attributed to rough play, however, and this is an important point. Muscle injuries, especially the 'demon' hamstring, are by far the most prevalent; head injuries are a close second. The replacement law helps matters, but far too many injured players refuse to take a long enough rest after injury. I would like to see a compulsory three-week rest after concussion.

The pre-Twickenham match preparations were hard and thorough. Noel Murphy, on the eve of the match, still maintained his side was capable of beating England. England remained quietly confident, although one of the selectors did admit privately, 'If we lose this one, we are all for the axe. You are only as good as your last match, but, after Scotland, we feel we will not be beaten easily!'

The player whom England followers wanted to see was young Tony Ward, a convert from Association football regarded as a 'discovery', much as was Jerome Gallion in France. The two players were destined to challenge as successors to Phil Bennett and Gareth Edwards as kings in the half-back positions. However, their experiences on 18 March revealed to them that the road to the top is never wide and straight, and that there is no real substitute for match experience. But they impressed in their first seasons of representative rugby, and that is important.

On the eve of the match, the Rugby Football Union re-elected their Chairman of Selectors, Sandy Sanders, a notable former prop forward and an extremely knowledgeable and popular administrator, for a third successive year. This was a tribute to the chairman and also a token of appreciation on the part of the Union of the selectors' energy and the side's fight-back during the season. Again, the side could only have been encouraged by the re-election of Mr Sanders: he is popular with the players, and has always been a players' man, a quality which is required for success as a selector since a major part of the task is the ability both to listen to and understand the player's point of view, and to realize that each player's approach will be slightly different. Indeed, one believes that selectors in rugby football, and club managers in Association football, would benefit considerably from courses in man-management! The men in charge who succeed are those who are (1) born lucky, (2) have enough good players to select from and (3) can communicate easily with each player.

One thing that disturbed both countries before this match was the suggestion that they, plus Scotland, were in the second division of the Five Nations Championship, France and Wales forming the first. Michael Green was quick to answer this the next day in *The Sunday Times* writing, 'If this was second-division international rugby then let us have some more of it. It might be an exaggeration to say that the match had everything, but it did have tension, lots of running with the ball, a super-human effort to come back by the Irish, and, what is more, two rare birds these days, two English tries on their own ground.'

Ireland began with a fierce foray, and ended with a desperate bid for victory. England won by two goals and a penalty to a dropped goal and two penalties. With only fifteen minutes of play remaining the score was level at 9–9; Slemen than scored a very good try which Young converted, giving England a 15–9 lead. Ireland attacked with great enthusiasm; Gibson was prominent in the forays, but his side could not achieve the equalizing score against a stable and well-knit English defence.

England's back row, Slemen on the wing, and Caplan at full-back, were decisive players, and while young Ward collected another 9 points to make his total for the season 38, he revealed that he still has much to learn, tactically, as a pivot player. Former England outside half, Richard Sharp, writing in the *Sunday Telegraph*, criticized him for holding on too long under pressure instead of getting in his clearing kick quickly.

Only time will tell if Ward is capable of matching his kicking skills with tactical skills. He scored his side's nine points in the second half with a penalty, a dropped goal and another penalty, after England had achieved a first-half lead through a try by Peter Dixon; that came at the end of a movement by Barry Nelmes from a ruck after Ward had been caught in possession (hence the criticism by Sharp); John Horton broke the defence, and Young converted the try with a fine kick. Young also kicked a penalty in the second half before converting the winning try and enjoyed a sound and successful afternoon.

Once again Ireland experienced problems at the rucks and mauls, perhaps due to the fact that in the match against Wales, French Referee Georges Domercq did not apply the new interpretation of the 'pile-up', as differing from the ruck and maul; afterwards, he and his touch judge, Francois Palmade, were told of the change. In the England–Ireland match, Palmade was in charge and applied the new interpretation, of which England were aware; thereby he confused the Irish, unintentionally.

Later in the season, the International Board representative and former New Zealand captain Bob Stuart was to complain about the new interpretation, and suggested that trouble might occur later in the year when New Zealand toured in the British Isles.

TEAMS
England: D. W. N. Caplan; P. J. Squires, B. J. Corless, P. W. Dodge, M. A. C. Slemen; J. P. Horton, M. Young; J. P.

Scott, R. J. Dixon, M. Colclough, W. B. Beaumont, M. J. Rafter, F. E. Cotton, P. J. Wheeler, B. G. Nelmes
Ireland: A. H. Ensor; C. M. H. Gibson, A. R. McKibbin, P. P. McNaughton, A. C. McLennan; A. J. Ward, J. J. Moloney (capt.); W. P. Duggan, S. A. McKinney, M. I. Keane, H. W. Steele, J. F. Slattery, N. Byrne, P. C. Whelan, P. A. Orr

REFEREE: F. Palmade (France)

SCORERS
England: Dixon, Slemen, tries; Young, 1 penalty, 2 conversions
Ireland: Ward, 2 penalties, 1 dropped goal

Wales v. France

Saturday 18 March   Cardiff Arms Park
Wales 16 points (2 tries, 2 dropped goals, 1 conversion)
France 7 points (1 try, 1 dropped goal)

The meeting of the 1976 and 1977 Grand Slam sides in the final and decisive match of the Championship was the most important match of the year, since it would reveal which was the top country in Europe, and possibly whether there was truth in the suggestion that both countries were as good as one another, and that they just managed to win on their own grounds, but if their meeting could take place in mid-Channel, the match would end in a draw!

The suggestion, or at least part of it, was proved true, since Wales won at Cardiff, after France won in Paris in 1977, and Wales at Cardiff in 1976; however, Wales had won in Paris in 1975 and the match of 1974 at Cardiff was drawn! The French were bitterly disappointed in defeat. They did not play as well as they had hoped to do; the Welsh were delighted, ending the season as undisputed champions of Europe.

Wales had employed only sixteen players throughout the season, and almost achieved their ambition to field the same side in four matches. Unfortunately, Gerald Davies, although selected, withdrew through injury on the eve of the match rather than let his country down; it meant his missing his record breaking forty-fifth appearance as a three-quarter for Wales. He was replaced by Gareth Evans, who thus received his first full cap,

73

having made a replacement appearance for Davies in Paris in 1977.

The ambition of the Welshmen was considerable, and their achievement was splendidly described by David Frost in the *Guardian*. He wrote in his match report, 'Eighteen of the thirty-three Lions in New Zealand in 1977 were Welshmen, yet here is the 1978 Welsh team winning everything in sight. What a feat of survival against fatigue, what a triumph over the underminding influence of insidious staleness.'

The staleness and fatigue did, eventually, overtake them, at least mentally during their nine-match tour of Australia, when so many of the 'few' were in action having played through 1975, 1976 and 1977, and into 1978, without a break. No country's leading players, in the history of the game, have ever been subjected to such continuous demands at top level. They had played themselves into the ground, yet as tried and frustrated as they were in the second Test at Sydney in June 1978, they played their hearts out in the cause of rugby and victory.

It was this spirit that enabled them to overcome the very real challenge of France, although it would be wrong and unsporting not to mention the fact that the French, with true Gallic cussedness, aided the Welsh cause by refusing to play Jean-Pierre Romeu at outside half. France thus took the field without an accurate place kicker or a shrewd tactical kicker. His opposite number in the Welsh team, Phil Bennett, was the man of the match; he scored two tries and kicked a conversion to finish as the world's leading big-match points scorer. It was his big day! Bennett, more than any other player on the field, wanted victory in this match because it was his own rugby redemption; it was to answer his many critics at home and abroad, who never believed he had the toughness, aided the Welsh cause by refusing to play Jean-Pierre Romeu New Zealand. Thus he gave the match everything he had, after a late fitness decision had allowed him to take the field. He was suffering from a badly bruised foot (especially, a bad toe) and the selectors did not wish the news to reach the French until after the match: a small pad was made to protect his toe.

When the match was all over, and Wales had won, he uttered the words, 'I am delighted for the team which played so well. We have all received a great deal of stick this season and we have been classed as a side past its best. I believe the team gave the answer to this criticism today. However, it was a hard match and the French made us fight all the way!' It was his last match for Wales.

When Bennett scored his first try, he passed Tom Kiernan's previous record of 158 points in the Five Nations Championship. He finished the match with ten points, and a total of 166. This, when added to his points in Lions Test matches, put him ahead of Don Clarke as the world-record representative-match individual points scorer. At the end of the match (which incidentally was to be Gareth Edwards' last appearance in the Welsh jersey), he and Bennett had scored between them 254 points. It was a remarkable record of match-winning, and highlights Edwards and Barry John, and Edwards and Bennett, as the two of the greatest match-winning pairs and points scorers in representative rugby.

The match was played in perfect, sunny Spring weather before a happy crowd, and was extremely well refereed by Alan Welsby of England. Play was slightly in favour of the French at first, and their forwards drove well. After eighteen minutes they got down to the Welsh '25' area; from a lineout five yards short of the Welsh goal line, the giant French number eight and captain Bastiat tapped down smartly from the middle of the line, and Skrela, the tall energetic flanker (playing his last match for France), gathered to burrow his way over the line for a try. Full-back Aguirre failed to convert. In all, the French missed five kicks at goal. Had they succeeded with some of these, as the absent Romeu might have done, the match could have been a much closer affair.

Five minutes after this score, France received an indirect penalty thirty yards out. Outside half Vivies employed a tapped penalty kick, and then dropped a smart goal to give France a seven-point lead. The French forwards appeared to have an edge over their rivals, and with better place kicking and surer handling behind, the lead could have been larger.

It must be said, however, that Gallion and Vivies were somehow not an ideal combination, as Gallion attempted rather too much on his own, and Vivies was neither as good a tactical kicker or runner as Romeu; the centres handled badly mainly through the basic fault of taking their eyes off the ball or passing wildly.

Wales defended well, tackled hard and covered ably. They were eventually able to turn the tide before the interval. To achieve this, Bennett punted high downfield with most of the Welsh in hot pursuit. This turned the French, who knocked-on in their own '25', giving a scrum. Another scrum followed; Wales heeled at the French put-in, and Allan Martin broke away to gather and feed Bennett; he darted left and then jinked inside, over the French line as he was tackled. He then kicked an excellent goal. Wales soon scored again; this time it was Edwards. He kicked his side down into the French '25', where Wales won the ball at the lineout. Price collected and moved away, but then checked wisely, and sent the ball on to Edwards on the run; Edwards dropped a lovely high goal, and put Wales in the lead.

Two minutes later Wales scored again. They went away from a lineout. Although the vigorous charge of centre Gravell was checked, he got the ball away to Fenwick, his fellow centre; Fenwick then switched the attack to the right. Edwards got outside him and managed a low pass to J. J. Williams on the right wing near the touch-line. Williams was challenged and forced to send a lobbed ball inside to someone. The someone was Bennett, who was really running hard. With the ball safely pouched, Bennett was over the French line to score a try that Martin just failed to convert.

At the interval Wales led 13–7. They were not going to concede, even through a long and hard second half. The only score of the second half was a high dropped goal by Fenwick, after an Edwards pass had sailed wide of Bennett. It was enough for the day. The Grand Slam was back in Wales. The International Championship was complete.

TEAMS
Wales: J. P. R. Williams; J. J. Williams, R. W. R. Gravell, S. P. Fenwick, G. L. Evans; P. Bennett (capt.), G. O. Edwards; D. L. Quinnell, J. Squire, A. J. Martin, G. A. D. Wheel, T. J. Cobner, G. Price, R. W. Windsor, A. G. Faulkner
France: J. M. Aguirre; G. Noves, C. Belascain, R. Bertranne, D. Bustaffa; B. Vivies, J. Gallion; J-P. Bastiat (capt.), J-C. Skrela, F. Haget, M. Palmie, J-P. Rives, R. Paparemborde, A. Paco, G. Cholley

SCORERS
Wales: Bennett, 2 tries; Edwards, Fenwick, dropped goals;
Bennett, 1 conversion
France: Skrela 1 try, Vivies 1 dropped goal

4

Odds and Ends

The International Board met in London on 13–17 March, at the East India Sports Club in St James's Square. This was in the week before the last international matches of the season, and the two most important points agreed upon by representatives of the seven member countries were the admission of France as a full member of the Board, and a reduction in the length of Lions tours, to eighteen matches. The former decision was one which stemmed from many years of discussion; the latter was the result of growing uninterest by senior players in long tours, the matter being brought to a head by the Lions 1977 tour of New Zealand. It seems that players are becoming less and less attracted by the 'pleasures' of touring. A third decision was that announced by Australia, that they had cancelled their 1979 tour to South Africa for political reasons. This was another blow to the hopes of South African rugby men of all races.

The Board also decided to raise the daily expense allowance for touring players from £3.00 to £3.50: a magnificent sum indeed; it should be £5.00 without question. Why do amateur bodies, when confronted with the very real challenge of 'professionalism', fail to adjust, to make the necessary amendments within the amateur regulations? £35.00 a week out-of-pocket expenses would not turn an amateur rugby player into a professional.

It was also agreed to allow an 'honorary medical officer' to accompany a team on tour. This was long overdue. Each doctor may be accompanied by a physiotherapist. If Rugby Unions are concerned about amateur status, they could well study the various teams participating in the Commonwealth Games, and check on the number of advisers and medical experts attached to them. Rugby Union is still in the dark ages compared with their brothers in athletics. Until recently, only two persons have been sent overseas with a party of thirty players on a tour of three months (compare, for example, the party which goes to a Commonwealth Games of less than three weeks). It makes one wonder how much the various rugby countries are prepared to spend to ensure that a touring team is properly prepared and cared for in all respects. One is tempted to think that most host unions are more concerned with tour profits.

There is much that can be done by the International Board, through its member countries, to bring rugby into line with other major amateur sports, and at the same time kill off the trend of leading players to seek loopholes in the amateur regulations. Tours have become fast-moving affairs, with players earning big cash sums for host unions. Those players are not always being housed or cared for in a manner befitting their status. No wonder amateur rugby players at representative level compare their lot with that of their professional colleagues in other sports. How can we best reward those amateurs from New Zealand who fill Twickenham and the Cardiff Arms Park, and those Lions who fill the grounds at Wellington, Auckland and Christchurch? As I point out in the final chapter of this book, much can be done without infringing the amateur regulations.

John Dawes keeps saying, 'Rugby is only a game!'. But it is a game the whole world wants to play. Russia has recognized its potential and got itself elected a full member of the European Rugby Association. (The delegates then immediately asked that all business be conducted in Russian, thereby launching a rugby 'cold war' with France, the senior Western European rugby nation.) This move put the International Board into something of dilemma, since they had to aim to preserve the game as an amateur and non-political one, yet recognize the world-wide growth of the game. They are uncertain of Russia's motives and intentions in the sport. The lessons to be learnt from FIFA have been studied closely by the Board; the decision to invite France to become a full member has ensured a firm foothold for the Board in Europe. France, with the Board's backing, will be allowed to control affairs.

Long tours are a thing of the past: players are simply not interested in being away for three-and-a-half months, subjected to a life of training and playing, with very little spare time. (Less partisan refereeing, and less Press abuse in the Southern Hemisphere would have made the experience of recent British teams more enjoyable, but the last long New Zealand tour to Europe, in 1972–73, was not one marked for friendliness, either.) It was agreed that tours to the British Isles should be limited to a maximum of twenty-five matches. This does go part-way to meeting the problem. Since the Board is a most conservative body, the decision was particularly well received.

Rough play and consequent injury concerned the Board (and rightly so), and it announced the setting up of an advisory medical committee, to be comprised of the honorary medical officers of the member country's Unions, and headed by Roger Vanderfield, an up-and-coming Australian official and former referee. He has considerable influence in his country in the matter of law interpretation and refereeing appointments. His work on the medical side of the game has been considerable (as also has been that of his brother), and the medical officers of the member Unions give of their time freely and with considerable enthusiasm. In Wales in particular, under the guidance of Gordon Rowley and Jack Matthews, there has been good progress; the practical advice and help of these two officials has encouraged the coaching committee to work in close laision with both club doctors and what were once known as the 'bottle-and-sponge-men'. These gallant camp-followers, who used to believe that a cold sponge would cure all injuries, are now well organized, fully instructed, and given the status they deserve.

Many stories have been told about their activities, and many a player has related how he has waited in fear and trembling of the arrival of the 'magic sponge'. There was the case of Gareth Edwards, found 'exhausted' at the bottom of a ruck in a test at Loftus Versveld, Pretoria, asking the ambulance man to 'dig a hole and bury him' as the ground was so hard. Another player, having suffered a groin injury in a particularly tough club match in Wales, is reported as saying to the sponge-man, 'Don't touch 'em; count 'em'!

One spectator was heard to shout, as the sponge-man ran onto the field to attend an injured member of a visiting touring side, 'Nothing trivial, I hope?'

The stories are many, but the final recognition of those who undertake the rather thankless task is important, as is the fact that the sponge-men are now being taught to recognize rugby injuries, and not disturb injured players if the injuries are serious. It complements the wise decision of a few years ago to allow substitutes for injured players.

It also raises the point that there appear to be more injuries in modern rugby. There are many possible causes for this. Since figures have not been kept over the years, it is impossible to clearly define any theory. However, cases of muscle bruising and injury are more prevalent, because the muscles have to cope with a faster overall game and are, perhaps, finer, sharper and less robust than previously. Clothing on the field has changed. Rugby boots are now more akin to old-fashioned running shoes than the rugby boots of the 1920s. Old-time props look askance at their modern counterparts, who take the field with boots that do not provide full ankle-cover!

'Professionalism' in coaching is also a sensitive problem with the Board. The case of a former League player now engaged in amateur rugby activities was raised: Malcolm Reid, a PE lecturer, had been coaching the Scottish Universities team, but was thought to be ineligible to coach a rugby Union side. As a lecturer at a college, he is directly involved with education, and, since rugby football is a genuine part of university life, almost a section of the extra mural studies, rugby coaching could be considered part of his job. Scotland had brought the matter before the Board when Reid was appointed to act as coach to the Scottish Universities on a short tour.

It was reported, after the Board's discussion of the case in March, that the matter had been discussed at length, but that they would rather Reid did not coach the Scottish Universities side. This was only to be expected, as the Board, through its member countries, has always held that former League players should never be allowed back into positions of authority in the Union code. At the same time the Board could do no more than turn a blind eye to the number of former League players teaching in schools in England and Wales, who must be coaching schoolboys in the finer arts of the Union game. For that matter, one knows of many former League players who would offer their services readily to clubs as coaches, just for the honour and pleasure it would give them.

The chairman of the Board's March meeting was its junior member, Bob Stuart of New Zealand, (who was captain of the 1953–54 All Blacks in the British Isles, and is one of the more progressive of New Zealand's administrators, destined to become, one expects, chairman of the NZRU rugby council). He did not say a great deal at the Board's Press conference, but he made it known on his return that he did not admire the new tackle law and thought it would fail. He thus broke the Board's 'rule' that no member would speak independently once a decision has been taken. The law had come into force on 1 September 1977, but even before the end of 1977, the All Blacks team in France had taken a dislike to it, believing it would reduce the effect of their expertise in the art of rucking.

Stuart's comment was quickly taken up by Jack Gleeson, coach with the All Blacks in France, and other leading figures, including that astute coach and judge of a player, J. J. Stewart. In New Zealand, J. J. is respected and admired, and for the main part followed in his beliefs; British experts, however, disagree with the New Zealand viewpoint. There is little doubt that Stuart will raise it again in March, 1979. He suggested to delegates at the AGM of the NZRU that they should campaign and make a case to put before the Board that the tackle law was wrong. One must appreciate that although Bob Stuart was honest in his opinion, he was campaigning outside the Board, against the Board's decision. Even Dr Craven of South Africa, another progressive, does not air his disagreement with Board decisions publicly, although he has put the case for a reduction in the value of a penalty goal from three points to two.

The bone of contention is Law 18, 'Tackle'. It reads; 'A tackle occurs when a player carrying the ball in the field of play is held by one or more opponents so that while he is held the ball touches the ground.' This means it is *not* a tackle *if the ball does not touch the ground*. Previously, under the old Law, it was stated, 'When a player is tackled but not brought to ground, he must *immediately* release the ball. Another player may play the ball before it has

82

touched the ground.' The old Law did not allow a prolonged struggle for the ball between two players; the new Law implies that a 'standing tackle' (which generally leads to a maul) is not a proper tackle in the sense that the ball must be released immediately.

The new Law is helpful to those sides and countries better at the maul than at the ruck – Lions compared with All Blacks, for example. New Zealand wish the ball to be released at all times, immediately, once the player with the ball is held, even if the ball does not touch the ground so that the ruck can be started.

In the revised code, Law 22, 'Maul', states; 'A maul is formed by one or more players from each team on their feet and in physical contact closing round a player who is carrying the ball. A maul ends when the ball is on the ground, or when the ball or a player carrying the ball emerges from the maul, or when a scrummage is ordered.' New Zealand argue that this will see an end to the popularity and effectiveness of the ruck, the basis of their ball-winning ability at forward.

One of the delights of living in Wales and following rugby football is the annual Easter Tour to South Wales by the illustrious Barbarians Club. (It is more than a club: it is an institution.)

The Barbarians were formed in 1890 at an oyster supper in Bradford. It was the brain child of W. P. Carpmael, who became the first Captain, and later President of the club. The present President of the Barbarians, Herbert Waddell, writes of him in a foreword to Nigel Starmer-Smith's third history of the club; 'Those invited to join him on the short tours that he arranged had not only to share his enthusiasm for hard, clean, attacking rugby, but also be good company on and off the field.' This applies as much to the Barbarian Club today. Those who have followed Carpmael in high office down through the years (Emile de Lissa, Jack Haig Smith, Glyn Hughes and Herbert Waddell) have insisted that the idea and ideals of Carpmael are honoured. The Club has played many matches in Wales, and its present four-match Easter Tour became established in 1901 (although Cardiff were first met in 1891). The four clubs played, Penarth, Cardiff, Swansea and Newport, are the envy of other Welsh clubs. In addition, the Barbarians play annual matches against Leicester,

83

and against the East Midlands with equal enthusiasm. All six matches are important fixtures on the rugby calendar.

In 1948, the Barbarians were honoured by being invited to play a special end-of-tour match against the Wallabies at the Cardiff Arms Park. Such was the quality and spectacle of this event that it became a regular part of future tours. This event began because the Wallabies team, managed by Arnold Tancred and captained by W. M. 'Bill' McLean (uncle of the present Paul and a distinguished member of the famous Queensland McLean family) desired to return home via Canada and the States but had no cash for the trip. The four Home Unions asked the Barbarians to raise a suitable side to oppose the tourists, with Cardiff Arms Park named as the venue. I followed the negotiations at the time, while helping Arthur Cornish to stage the match and compile the special programme that was to become the first of many: one Friday afternoon, Cornish had invited me to his school in Cardiff, where he was headmaster, and said, 'I have some special news, J. B. The Wallabies want to play the Barbarians at Cardiff on January 31st. It could be a great match. Will you help?'

My association with the Barbarians became close from that moment onwards – though I had watched them play from the late 'twenties (especially at their four Welsh venues), and had grown to admire them, their alickadoos (officials), and their approach. They represent the real spirit of rugby. Following the success of the 1948 match, they have played every touring team visiting Britain since.

The first 1978 tour match, against Penarth on Good Friday, was won comfortably by 84 points to 12. This was the highest total ever achieved by the Club, passing the 76 scored in Canada in 1976 and the 73 against Penarth in 1974. In 67 matches, Penarth has been successful on only ten occasions. Other major clubs in Wales are keen to take over the fixture, especially Llanelli, who can offer a much more impressive guarantee. However, one would not want to see Penarth lose this historic fixture for two reasons. First, the gate receipts help enormously to balance the Penarth Club's budget each year and the match is always thoroughly enjoyed – whatever the weather – by holiday spectators. Secondly, from 1901 until, quite recently, the Esplanade Hotel was burned down, Penarth was the 'home' of the Barbarians. The new home is

84

at the Royal Hotel, Cardiff, but I feel that the Barbarians, despite the fact that they have to be concerned with money nowadays, will not release the Penarth Good Friday fixture after seventy-seven years of happy association.

After this 1978 match, following a brilliant display in which he scored twenty points, Phil Bennett told me in the Club's dressing room that he and Gareth Edwards would not be touring with Wales in Australia. 'We both need a rest after so much football at home and overseas,' he said. Of course, he was right, but what a blow to the hopes of Wales! Without them, the side could never hope to be quite as efficient or as dangerous. They were the established, point-scoring Triple Crown leaders.

The next day, the 95th match against Cardiff was played at the Arms Park, and the delighted Barbarians won for the thirty-first time, by 20 points to 8; Gareth Edwards was not available to play what would otherwise have been his last match against the tourists for whom he had appeared often with distinction. Billy Beaumont led the Barbarians with pride before a record Easter Saturday crowd at the new Club ground.

There were then bold hopes of an Easter 'Grand Slam' by the Barbarians. But Swansea (yet again), upset them with a splendid display of aggressive, attacking, match-winning rugby. So many times in previous seasons, has the Easter Monday fixture proved a stumbling block to the Barbarians' ambition (they have won all four on eight occasions since 1901: 1931/32/33/34/35 – a marvellous run of success against good Welsh sides, 1949, 1970 and 1973). Swansea had won 34-18 in 1977, and in 1978 they won 36-15 as they prepared themselves for the WRU/Schweppes Cup semi-final a week later. Full-back Roger Blyth, sadly neglected by the Welsh tour selectors, scored 13 points for Swansea, achieving 200 points for the season. Swansea scored six tries, and outside half David Richards played well: he enjoys himself in open, running rugby.

The final match of the tour was against Newport at Rodney Parade. While Swansea have played 65 matches against the Barbarians and won 31, Newport have now played 71 and won 45. They won the 1978 match 13-0 on a field of mud. (Referee Jeff Kelleher blew for 'no side' thirteen minutes early.)

During the Easter week-end, the Welsh touring party for

Australia was announced, without Bennett and Edwards. Terry Cobner, touring with the Barbarians, was announced as the Welsh captain. (I felt at the time, that we had seen the last of the renowned half-back pair in action – the belief was that Edwards, if not both, would retire. Edwards did, and Bennett went on to lead Llanelli for yet another season.) The party included eleven uncapped players; seven of these were to be honoured during the two Tests in Australia. Also included was Geoffrey Wheel, declared fit to travel with Wales again after his disappointment of 1977, when he was withdrawn from the Lions side. Although he possessed an absolute loathing of flying, on the tour he was to play well and hard despite injury. Selector Clive Rowlands was the honorary manager, and selector John Dawes, assistant and coach.

In the English John Player Cup, the Harlequins lost to firm favourites Gloucester 6–12, and 'dark horses' Leicester beat Coventry 25–16; this left Gloucester and Leicester in the final at Twickenham on 15 April. Full-back Peter Butler kicked Gloucester to victory by a goal and two penalties to two penalties, revealing yet again the power of the penalty goal against the try. (No changes in the Laws appear to amend this worrying trend in all grades, because players continue to infringe, and the sanction of a penalty goal must be a deterrent.) Leicester managed two tries in a total of one goal, one try, three penalties and two dropped goals to a goal, a try and two penalties. Even in this more open semi-final, there were five penalty goals and four tries, and there was still need to redress the balance in favour of tries. One must be careful, of course, in suggesting that rugby union football is a handling game, because originally, the scoring of a try allowed a side the opportunity of kicking a *goal*, and goals were the decisive scores! In 1978 we were not far removed from a century previously, inasmuch as goal kicks still remain decisive: Grand Slam champions Wales kicked eight penalty goals to equal their tally of eight tries; their opponents scored four tries and kicked seven penalties; this gives a ratio in four matches of twelve tries to fifteen penalty goals.

WRU Cup Semi-finals
In the semi-final rounds of the WRU Cup (which is supported by the sponsorship of Schweppes), Newport defeated Aberavon at

Cardiff Arms Park (in torrential rain), 10-6. Newport took their two chances to score tries; Aberavon scored two penalty goals, although this latter side had far more of the play.

At Aberavon, Swansea defeated Cardiff 18-13 in an exciting match. Although Swansea deserved their victory, they were almost pipped at the post by Cardiff, who made a late and determined rally. Swansea scored three tries and two penalties to Cardiff's two tries and one penalty. For Swansea and Newport (the 1977 holders) it was a happy result: they had not only the honour of appearing in the final, but also the financial reward.

Reception for the Welsh Touring Party

On Monday 3 April, the Welsh team and squad members, selectors and WRU officers were the guests of the Prime Minister at No. 10, thus following in the footsteps of the 1971 British Lions. (For some of the senior Welsh players, it was their second visit.) Mr Callaghan was in good form as a friendly host, and the Welsh members of the Government enjoyed it all – especially the singing of Sir Geraint Evans. Mr Callaghan showed his guests the Cabinet Room. The MP for Newport, keen sports-fan Roy Hughes, was the happiest member: he had made the pilgrimmage to Dublin to watch the vital Triple Crown decider. He and I had sat in a bar in a Dublin side-street afterwards, drinking – naturally – Guinness, and I realized how pleasant it was to talk to an MP without mentioning politics! Mr Callaghan spoke well of the Welsh team and its achievements, and the WRU President, T. Rowley Jones, replied.

Police Rugby

The British Police do not play many matches a year. This is sad, since I believe that a four-team championship with the three Services and the Police would lead to more enthusiasm in Service rugby. I believe that Arthur Rees, former Welsh international flanker, and ex-Chief-Constable of Stafford, should now lead a campaign to this end, as a former RAF officer.

On 7 April, the British Police entertained the Combined Services at the Waterton Cross Ground at Bridgend, the home of the South Wales Police Club. A pleasant match ended in a win for the Police, 18-10. The occasion was intended as a dress rehearsal for the Combined Services match later in the year, against the All Blacks at Aldershot; it was felt that the incentive of the touring game would inspire Service rugby to rise to the occasion, and thus maintain a tradition that was particularly strong between the Wars. The continued reduction of the Forces has not helped to improve the sporting standards.

At this time, it was announced by the Rugby Football Union that in future they would participate in 'B' internationals rather than Under-23 matches and I am sure this was a wise decision and appreciated more by contending players. In France and Wales, the 'B' matches have been dress rehearsals for and stepping stones to senior honours, and now that Scotland and Ireland are happy with the principle of such fixtures, it was good to see the RFU fall into line.

The John Player Cup
On 15 April, Gloucester won the John Player Cup at Twickenham, defeating, in a rather one-sided match, Leicester, by a goal to a penalty goal. The 'cherry whites' had three-quarters of the play in possession and territory but revealed little imagination; Leicester could have won had the normally reliable international full-back, W. H. 'Dusty' Hare, not failed with several reasonable penalty goal attempts. Hare dealt admirably with the variety of kicks sent up field in his general direction, but although Referee Quittenton was stern in his decisions against Gloucester, Hare could kick only one goal.

The powerful Gloucester forwards – Burton, Fidler and Watkins all in form – controlled the play. Their backs, however, were not too clever, and Leicester revealed a most determined defence, despite their reluctance to run some of their penalty awards. Had Leicester read the play more wisely, they might still have carried off the Cup against considerable odds. A crowd of twenty-five thousand watched the match, the largest so far in the Competition, and there were lively scenes when the Gloucester captain, Peter Butler, received the Cup. Wing R. R. Mogg scored the try for Gloucester, following a good forward drive; Butler converted with an excellent kick. Hare kicked one penalty goal in six attempts for Leicester.

88

The Welsh Championship

On 22 April, Pontypridd became the Welsh Club champions, achieving a notable away victory over a much-improved Maesteg team, 14-8. The Taff Valley Club, led by Lion Tom David, thus gained their second Championship success in three years. It was a triumph of consistency through a long, hard season which included a notable 'double' over Cardiff. (Cardiff, without a championship success since 1958 – Cliff Morgan's last season – had to be content with second place, and Maesteg in third.)

Pontypridd are essentially a team rather than a collection of star players; their approach is both attractive and effective, and one cannot fail to be impressed by their team spirit. Cardiff also had a splendid season, but failed in moments of tension in both the Championship and the WRU Cup. One felt that their selectors did not always judge correctly those moments when they just had to play the best available fifteen players. The Club may think that prizes do not matter all that much, but it is time they won a *Western Mail* plaque to go with their many other trophies.

The 'Pony' Award

An interesting development in recent years is the Pony Award, given to the best performers in the Championship of Five Nations. The French sports-equipment firm runs a competition judged by a panel of leading rugby journalists from each of the countries. The six judges award points after each International to the players of each side. A maximum of three points is awarded to each player but, naturally, a player has to be outstanding to receive three marks. The winner for 1978 was the new French scrum-half, Jerome Gallion, with a total of 67 points out of a maximum of 72. It was a very close competition, as Gareth Edwards (Wales) and Jean-Pierre Rives (France) were equal second, only one point behind, and Tony Ward (Ireland) third with 65. When the result of the competition was announced, not one three-quarter from any of the five countries made the top fifteen places. There were five backs, Gallion, Edwards, Ward, Bennett (Wales) and Aguirre (France) and the remaining ten were forwards. Wales had six players in the top fifteen: Edwards, Bennett, Price, Quinnell, Cobner and Martin (in that order).

France had five players there, Ireland three and England one (Bill Beaumont). The highest position for a Scottish player was 26th (Jim Renwick). A presentation ceremony was held in Paris in May, at which Gallion received his award. Later in June, Gareth Edwards was the *Rugby World* magazine's 'Player of the Year' in a poll of readers' votes.

Rugby Union football was recognized in the appointment of former Lions scrum-half and England captain, R. E. G. Jeeps from Northampton, as the new Chairman of the Sports Council. Mr Jeeps, aged 45 at this appointment, made three Lions tours in 1955/59/62, and appeared in 13 Test matches with distinction. He also played twenty-four times for England in a colourful playing career, before becoming an administrator, and achieving the important office of President of the RFU. At the end of April 1978, he resigned as an RFU representative on the International Board and the four Home Unions. His place was taken by another former England player, Albert Agar, who for many years had been secretary of the Home Unions Tours Committee.

Mr Jeeps gave his reason for leaving the Tours Committee as 'pressure of work'; this appeared fair and reasonable, although it was suggested in some quarters that it may have been in order to avoid any clash of opinion over the maintenance of relationships in rugby football with South Africa. As the Sports Council appointment was a Government one, and they were totally against relationships with South Africa, Mr Jeeps, aged 45, may have adopted the wisest course. Since he is an outspoken administrator, the rugby brotherhood will follow his progress closely. He was a hard-working aggressive player who first achieved fame when touring with the 1955 Lions in South Africa; a previously uncapped player, he appeared in all four Tests as partner to Cliff Morgan.

The WRU/Schweppes Cup

On 29 April, Swansea won the WRU/Schweppes Cup, defeating Newport in the final at the Cardiff Arms Park, 13-9. After establishing command in the match, Swansea almost allowed it to slip from their grasp. Better fortune with his place kicking on the part of Newport's young full-back, Chris Webber, could have seen his club retain the Cup they won in 1977. There was only one try scored in the match, that by Swansea; there were four penalty goals, emphasizing the greater importance of the penalty goal relative to the try in even a clean and sporting match such as this final.

Swansea scored a try through hooker Jeff Herdman, and the Newport forwards, try as they did, could not master a powerful Swansea scrum which included four internationals and a 'B'-match player. David Richards and Gareth Jenkins dropped goals; Roger Blyth kicked a penalty for Swansea; Chris Webber kicked three penalties for Newport. A crowd of nearly forty thousand was present, representing the biggest gate since the competition was revived in 1972.

The competition was first launched in the last century, but discontinued because of rough play and disputes between the clubs involved. Revived again before and up to World War I, but not re-started after the break, and finally found favour again only in 1972, sponsored by Schweppes, who, offered, for a three-year period starting with the 1977-78 season, £85,000. Its third running has seen the Cup produce, in the main, good and exciting football; together with the John Player Cup, it can do much good for rugby football, providing opportunities for the smaller clubs to have a crack at the larger ones.

The season ended with seven-a-side tournaments in all four home countries; the Border Sevens as popular as ever in Scotland; the Middlesex Sevens at Twickenham; the Snelling and National tournaments in Wales; and competitions in the four provinces of Ireland. The top Clubs were Pontypridd (Wales); Hawick (Scotland); Ballymena, and Garryowen (Ireland); London Welsh, Gloucester, and Wakefield (England). Loughborough Colleges retained the UAU Championship, defeating Bristol 17–0 in the final at Twickenham.

In reporting all this, there should be a special word for Hawick, who became the top Scottish Club for the fifth successive year, ever since the new league in divisions was formed. All credit to their coach, Derrick Grant, a 1966 Lion and a whole-hearted flank forward with fourteen Scottish caps. The 'Greens' of Hawick are a well-balanced side and during the season supplied six players to their national XV.

In Ireland, British Lions captain and lock, Willie John McBride, the world's most-capped rugby player with his 63 appearances for Ireland and 17 for Lions Tests, was still playing with enthusiasm for the top club in Northern Ireland, Ballymena, in his 37th year. His friend of many years and tours, big Syd Millar (37 internationals and nine Tests), was also playing for one of the Ballymena sides. What tremendous enthusiasts! Will they carry on until they are sixty, as has done former Cardiff prop, war-time international and club committee man Stanley Bowes, making appearances in charity matches?

Matters to Discuss

During the close season, many subjects were discussed by the various unions and clubs at their annual general meetings. But uppermost in the minds of the executives of governing bodies was the problem of rough play, brought dramatically into perspective during the Welsh tour in Australia, when a player's jaw was smashed by an unseen punch, and by the court case arising out of a player punching a referee in a minor game in Gwent.

In a game of physical contact, one must accept that accidental injuries are inevitable. One should not accept injuries that one player inflicts upon another by dirty play or through opting out of the Laws. Referees should perhaps shoulder some of the blame, if they allow dangerous situations to develop. However, quite seventy-five per cent of illegal injury occurs when the referee is unsighted; hence the demand for touch judges to assist the referee in his task of spotting dirty play and ensuring that the 'clever' or 'crafty' player cannot continue without detection.

Many a touch judge would have had a player sent from the field in 1978 and saved a match by spotting the early trouble off the ball. The lesson of it all is that referees must be strict and unions must support referees to the full; club committees and unions must suspend players by not selecting them, no matter how useful they may be. There is no room on the field for 'rogue' players, no matter where or in what grade of play they appear. The Presidents of the RFU and the WRU warned their clubs' delegates that action would be taken. The future promised greater discipline, but the later New Zealand tour highlighted traditional laxity.

Steve Fenwick the Welsh centre crashes over for a try (*above*) against Ireland at Lansdowne Road, Dublin, in the match which decided the Triple Crown, giving it to Wales for the third successive time.

J-P. Rives, the brilliant French flanker, is just too late (*below*) to prevent the Welsh captain, world-record point-scorer Phil Bennett, from clearing to touch in the Grand Slam decider at Cardiff, between Wales and France.

France (v. Wales) (above). Standing (l. to r.): A. W. Welsby (referee), R. Paco, A. Paparemborde, J-P. Rives, J-C. Skrela, G. Cholley, F. Haget, M. Palmie. Sitting (l. to r.): D. Bustaffa, R. Bertranne, B. Vivies, J. M. Aguirre, J-P. Bastiat (capt.), J. Gallion, C. Belascain, G. Noves.

Wales (v. Scotland) (below). Standing (l. to r.): M. Watkins (reserve), J. R. West (referee), G. Price, J. Squire, D. L. Quinnell, A. J. Martin, G. A. D. Wheel, A. F. Faulkner, T. J. Cobner, J. Richardson (reserve), D. B. Williams (reserve), A. W. Bevan (touch judge). Sitting (l. to r.): G. Evans (reserve), R. W. R. Gravell, T. G. R. Davies, J. P. R. Williams, P. Bennett (capt.), G. O. Edwards, R. W. Windsor, J. J. Williams, S. P. Fenwick.

Scotland (v. Wales) (above). Standing (l. to r.): D. M. Rea (touch judge), J. R. West (referee), C. B. Hegarty, W. B. Gammell, M. A. Biggar, A. F. McHarg, A. J. Tomes, D. S. M. Macdonald, N. E. K. Pender, A. E. Bevan (touch judge). Sitting (l. to r.): C. T. Deans, A. G. Cranston, J. McLauchlan, D. W. Morgan (capt.), I. R. McGeechan, J. M. Renwick, B. H. Hay, D. Shedden.

Scotland *v.* England: (*below*) the nearest Scotland got to scoring! MacDonald and Gammell are stopped on the line.

J. P. R. Williams (*above left*) in a new role, playing as a flanker during the first half of the second Test at Sydney. Here he is seen at a lineout, marked by Australians Mark Loane and Greg Cornelson.

The price of Violence! (*above right*) Graham Price, the Pontypool prop, holds his broken jaw as he leaves the field early in the second Test between Wales and Australia at the Sydney Cricket Ground. Australia won 19-17.

(*Above far right*) Brendan Moon, the Queensland left wing, flies through the air as he is tackled by J. P. R. Williams, to score a try for his State against Wales at Brisbane.

Player of the Year: Gareth Edwards (*opposite*), the most capped scrum-half, scoring his last points in his last match for his country. He is dropping his goal against France at Cardiff in the Triple Crown decider.

The Barbarians Easter Tour (*below*). The Barbarians with their President, Herbert Waddell (centre), pictured at Cardiff Arms Park during their tour of South Wales.

A great wing steps down: Gerald Davies (*left*), the prince of modern wings, in action against Scotland. He retired after making a record 46th appearance for Wales and leading his country in the second Test against Australia at Sydney.

Terry Holmes (*below*), the player most likely to succeed Gareth Edwards as the Welsh scrum-half, in action against Queensland at Brisbane on the Welsh tour.

The Big Lift. Australian lock, David Hillhouse (*above*), is well and truly lifted by his captain, flanker Anthony Shaw (*6*) while Welsh lock Alan Martin has no chance of winning the ball at a lineout in the second Test at Sydney.

Paul McLean (*below*), the brilliant Australian place kicker, was responsible for his country's success in Test series against Wales. Here, he is in action in the first Test at Brisbane, challenged by J. J. Williams.

arry Nelmes (*above left*), the first Englishman to aptain Cardiff since Gwyn Nicholls in 1903-04, lays for England at prop.

listair Hignell (*above right*), the fine all-rounder ad double Cambridge blue, was plagued by ajuries during the early part of the year.

eter Butler (*opposite*), the Gloucester full-back nd record point-scorer, won the John Player RFU Cup with a conversion.

A. B. 'Sandy' Carmichael (*below*), an outstanding Scottish prop and rugby personality, became the most capped prop, with 50 appearances.

5

The Bitterness of the Australian Desert

The nine-match tour of Wales to Australia during May and June was launched in friendship, and ended in controversy, violence and ill-feeling. It damaged Australian–Welsh relationships, revealing the desperate desire for victory at all costs which exists in Australia following several years' little success. At times Wales did not play as well as was expected of reigning European champions, but there developed during the tour an increasing frustration on the part of the tourists, who saw the tour slipping away from their control.

Enjoyable to a degree off the field, it became something less attractive on it, as the odds against clean, open rugby increased with each match, resulting from the over-physical approach of Australian opponents, and the inefficiency – one would not like to think of it as bias – of the referees. The number of penalty goals against increased to more than that of tries scored for; the Welsh party left disappointed and disillusioned by what they had experienced.

Australia's desire for victory overshadowed all else; the Welsh party was led gently into a well-prepared trap, and when ensnared they found the trappers ready with platitudinous apologies which did not ring true. Sad, maybe, but an ever-increasing feature of modern touring.

The record of the tour suggests that Wales had paraded falsely as European champions, but there is much more to it than the apparent failure of the Welsh to produce their expected standard of play. The Welsh visit followed that of England in 1975 almost as an urgent remedy for Australian Rugby Union's empty coffers.

(Following the financial failure of three short tours by Japan, Tonga and Fiji, the ARU funds were low.) The last tour had ended in disaster, Fiji leaving the field during the second Test when one of their players was ordered off. Having seen the conduct in the second Tests which both England and Wales played, one might suspect that the 'unsophisticated' Fijians were equally disturbed by the standard of Australian refereeing!

Wales agreed to play nine matches, including two Tests, starting at Perth on 21 May, ending at Sydney on 17 June. It was a formidable task following a long, hard eight-month season at home and, for the majority of the players, a long, hard winter in New Zealand in 1977. When Wales left Australia on 18 June, they had won only five of the nine matches, and had suffered defeat in two Tests. But they had left behind a handsome profit for the uncompromising Australian Union, almost one hundred thousand dollars. It was all too evident that Australia wanted Test victories and cash, and to hell with the consequences. They achieved their ambition, but tarnished their reputation as administrators and as players on the field. This was particularly sad as there had been previously a close and happy relationship between the two countries; if Australia had hoped to come back into the international rugby scene out of the cold, they may have further delayed the process by the intensity of their ruthless endeavour.

It was inevitable that Manager Clive Rowlands could do little else but submit a report to the Welsh Union that was not particularly complimentary to the Australian Union or the game in Australia, although the rugby world may be prompted to believe that Wales and the Welsh party complained in a mood of 'sour grapes' arising from the intense disappointment at the loss of a proud record. Almost every Welsh tour abroad had been accompanied by criticism of poor or biased refereeing; the most severe critics have suggested rather bluntly that the Welsh are poor tourists. Could it be a combination of these three factors, or is it true to say that few tours nowadays, in any country, are happy?

The growing popularity of rugby has produced a new form of sporting nationalism; there has developed a fanatical desire, on the part of various countries, not to lose at home. The Welsh are as dedicated to this cult as any other nation; rugby is their national game, providing an outlet for national expression as opposed to

94

political nationalism. However, their followers have a genuine love of the game that encourages dedication on and off the field, and all the efforts of the Welsh in Europe are governed and controlled by neutral referees. These two points are important; the latter particularly should be kept in mind when comparing the game at the highest level in the Northern and Southern Hemispheres; it is the key to the complete disillusion experienced by Wales during their Australian tour of 1978.

The initial week's stay in the lovely City of Perth, full of warm hospitality, suggested that the whole of the tour would be a pleasant undertaking with none of the 'double talk' often present in modern international sport. Two reasonably easy victories over Western Australia and Victoria did nothing to dash such idyllic hopes (although the matches did suggest that the true strength of Welsh talent at international level might not have been as great as had been expected). An unbeaten tour was not expected, since there were nine matches to be played in four weeks. But there were genuine hopes of a record better than that eventually achieved.

While at Perth, influential members of the ARU eased Welsh fears of possible difficulty with referees and the interpretation of the Laws. President Bill McLaughlin, an old friend of the Welsh and an experienced administrator, agreed that there would be 'consultation', as the Tour Agreement allowed, between the ARU and the Welsh management, over the appointment of the Test referees. It was what followed in later weeks that produced the controversy; the Australian interpretation of the Laws seemed as far removed from the International Board's intention as is London from Sydney; further, there was no consulation upon the appointment of the Test referees. The volte-face on the part of the ARU, and the poor standard of refereeing plus the underlying violence (which at times erupted, highlighting the Australian determination to win at all costs) served to see the tour end in bitterness. Genuine compromise on and off the field would have saved the spirit of the tour, irrespective of which country won the series.

Analysing in retrospect the reasons for the Welsh failure, I suggest the following:

(1) The Australian approach on the field of play was over-physical and far harder than anticipated.

(2) Some Welsh players did not play as well on tour as they had in the previous season.

(3) The reserves of strength of Welsh rugby, as revealed on tour, were no more than reasonable. It is never easy to replace outstanding players immediately. However, the spirit and effort produced in the second Test was encouraging for the future. The absence of a second able full-back and experienced utility player (like Roger Blyth of Swansea) was a major selectorial error.

(4) There was an occasional lack of tactical direction behind the scrum, and too much emphasis upon 'crash ball' in midfield rather than the swift spinning of the ball to the wings.

(5) A party of twenty-five players is insufficient for any tour longer than five matches; Wales should have taken thirty, especially since the injury rate was exceedingly high, with players transferring from the soft grounds of the British Isles to the harder grounds of Australia.

(6) An alarming poor standard of refereeing was experienced; there is an overwhelming need of neutral officials in the Southern Hemisphere, and of greater uniformity of interpretation.

(7) Australia was obsessed with success at all costs, and the ARU should have conformed with the tour agreement and compromised over the appointment of Test referees.

(8) On occasions, Wales did not play as well as they should have done, especially at Canberra, where their frustration at the strange interpretation of the Laws bubbled to the surface. Refereeing greatly influenced the course of each match. The Referee of the first Test at Brisbane, revealed much when, on one occasion at a scrum, he said to Welsh scrum-half, Brynmor Williams, 'It is not your ball Williams, it is *ours*!' No side, even one playing supremely well, could overcome such extraordinary refereeing.

However, it should be recorded that, generally, the Welsh party enjoyed travelling through Australia and meeting Australians off the field, and appreciated to the full the genuine hospitality, and the support of their exiled country-folk. The accommodation and food provided was excellent. Liaison officers, especially Angus Campbell of the ARU, and those at Cobar and Canberra, were first-class.

The revenue for the tour reveals what a splendid return was

achieved for the investment in the Welsh visit. Yet the tour itself raised a number of vital points for the future, ones that cannot be ignored by the four Home Unions or by the International Board. By far the most important point is the essential need of neutral referees for all Test matches, wherever they may be played. Every tour, long, medium or short, should have an agreement which allows the visiting side to select a Test referee from an approval panel of at least three officials; this is vital for the visit of Ireland to Australia in May 1979. No tours should be undertaken in the Southern Hemisphere without written guarantees, protecting management, that neutral referees will be appointed to Test matches; that all violence will be curbed, and that the over-vigourous play which is now a feature of such tours will be eradicated. In addition, there should be firm reference to the exploitation of visiting sides for commercial purposes. Without such guarantees there is little or no hope of regaining the true spirit, ideals and well-being of such tours. This is much more than my personal view: players and officials from all four home countries have expressed a desire for such an 'overseas tour charter'.

Australia should not be invited to the British Isles until a 'cooling-off' period has elapsed. An apology from the ARU should be forthcoming to the four Home Unions for its volte-face over the appointment of referees during the Welsh tour. Finally, the International Board should have its eight member-countries agree that they will exercise greater power in ensuring the smooth running and improved on-field discipline in future tours.

Sadly, it is true that players on both sides often took the law into their own hands; this is no way to conduct a rugby tour, and one must look for the basic reasons. On returning from Australia, I discussed the tour with the England prop, an experienced and sensible player, Barry Nelmes; he played in the controversial second Test when Mike Burton was sent off at Brisbane by Referee Bob Burnett. Nelmes said, 'The standard of refereeing is so poor in Australia that Wales suffered in 1978, as did England in 1975.'

The Departure to Australia

The Welsh party spent a night at a London Airport Hotel, and then made the long flight to Perth by a Qantas 747B, arriving there on Sunday morning, 14 May, where they were greeted by a large gathering of Welsh exiles. It was a happy welcome, and ARU officials were glad to point out that the tour would enable their Union to achieve a complete financial recovery. Local officials were most helpful, and before the party retired early to bed, in order to overcome the 'jet lag', time was allowed to toast, in champagne, the health of Manager Clive Rowlands, to celebrate his fortieth birthday. Unfortunately, as events were to prove, he was not a lucky manager, however hard he tried.

The week's stay at Perth was enjoyed; and the team trained in rain and sunshine at Perry Lakes, the site of the Commonwealth Games arena. Even in training, the players suffered a series of nagging injuries (which were to these escalate to impossible proportions by the final Test). For five weeks, no one in the party worked harder than team masseur Gerry Lewis, without whose efforts the tour might well have broken down. One player received over twenty treatments for muscle injuries in six days. There was a never-ending queue of players outside Lewis's room for sixteen hours of most of the days in the tour.

Another feature of the tour which first showed at Perth was that only once in nine matches did the chosen team ever take the field because of niggling injuries that forced withdrawals on the morning of matches. Often players due for a well-deserved rest were forced to curtail lunch and prepare themselves for playing. This highlighted the need for at least thirty players on a tour of more than five matches. J. P. R. Williams played seven matches in succession between 27 May and 17 June; Ray Gravell played six; Geoffrey Wheel, the big lock, appeared in seven matches out of nine in twenty-seven days – one every four days, at representative level!

Tourists and hosts were amateur players, allegedly playing for the fun of the game rather than, as John Dawes suggested, taking part in a sporting war!

While at Perth the party visited an Australian Rules match, peculiar to Australia; those who remained to watch the last of the four quarters began to understand it. They were able to appreciate that the game (though hybrid in the sense that it is a pot-pourri of several games taken to Australia by emigrants from the four home countries) requires exceptional fitness, good eyes and hands, and varied skills, and it requires keen perception and fitness on the part of its umpires. I would put these officials in a class above those of Australian rugby referees and cricket umpires!

Match 1: v. Western Australia

The first match of the tour was played on Sunday 21 May. Early-morning rain freshened the pitch, but it was followed by a strong wind that did not help improve the standard of play. Indeed, the Welshmen found the going hard, against a much-improved Western Australia side that played with tremendous spirit. Although winning 33–3, the Welsh failed to amass the total of points anticipated; the final score was unchanged from the interval. Playing with the wind in the first half they scored two penalties through Steve Fenwick, and then a runaway try from sixty yards, following an interception by centre Pat Daniels, which was converted by Fenwick. Then Tim Davis, the WA full-back (now at Oxford University as a Rhodes scholar) landed a penalty goal, although he failed with two other attempts. Wales then scored four more tries before the interval: J. P. R. Williams, prominent in most movements, collected two of the tries, and Gerald Davies and Terry Holmes scored the others, Fenwick converting two.

In the second half, playing with the wind, the WA side gave a splendid account of itself, even if it rarely threatened to score tries. It revealed how to cope with the Welshmen. Their method consisted of maximum effort in front combined with hard tackling and swift covering behind. The fullness of the WA effort surprised the Welshmen. A basic fault was that the Welsh midfield trio failed to get the best out of two fast-moving wings, Gerald Davies and J. J. Williams; but then and for the rest of the tour, one noticed in particular that the marking of the Welsh three-quarters was intense (even if some defenders came up remarkably quickly and may in fact have been off side occasionally). In some matches, particularly the first Test, it was to prove decisive.

There was an over-emphasis upon 'crash-ball', although Dawes, in training sessions, encouraged the full flow of the three-quarter movement. As in the days of McRae for New Zealand, when a move proves successful at first, it continues to be employed even when it appears to have become less effective and should be used only occasionally.

Match 2: v. Victoria

This second match was played on an extremely heavy soccer pitch and, although the weather was dry, there was a considerable amount of water at one end. Wales did improve upon their showing at Perth: their handling was better, as was the cohesion of their forwards, which enabled them to enjoy better control. Having played many times together in club football, the two halves appeared to move more easily. Wales scored eight tries; five by backs and three by forwards. Every three-quarter scored a try, and Steve Fenwick and Gareth Davies collected fourteen points apiece. The Welsh try scorers were Fenwick (2), Evans, Gerald Davies, Lane, Gravell, Davis and Brynmor Williams. Gareth Davies converted four tries and kicked two penalties, and Fenwick kicked two penalties. Full-back Thornton kicked a penalty for Victoria.

Towards the end of the match, lock Allan Martin suffered a knee injury that was, on initial examination, believed to be extremely serious; as Wheel had left the field after 24 minutes with a dislocated thumb, there were thoughts of replacements. However, Martin recovered quickly, as did Wheel. One still feels that the injuries reduced their efficiency, if not their effort, until the second Test. They prevented them playing in the third match of the tour, which proved far more important than was expected.

Match 3: v. Sydney

Wales were beaten by Sydney in an exciting finish to a hard-fought match, one that set the pattern for the rest of the tour by indicating how desperately Australian sides desired to win. Sydney won 18–16, after a last-minute dropped goal, a splendid effort by full-back Laurie Monaghan, who was back in his favourite position after a long stay on the wing for both country and state. Sydney deserved their victory; they played more efficiently than the Welsh did. It was a hot day for rugby in the British sense, with the temperature in the 70s. The match was won and lost in the first quarter, before Wales could settle down.

Sydney collected two quick tries and then never looked back, even though they were overtaken at one point before the end, for Wales to lead 16–15. In injury time a Welsh clearing kick failed to find touch, and Monaghan, fielding near the touch-line, ran on to drop a superb goal from forty yards and snatch victory.

There was much to be observed by the discerning spectator. First, the comparatively poor standard of refereeing (Mr Byers missed so much); secondly, the physical approach of the Australian players; thirdly, the shortcomings of several of the Welsh, who needed to be quicker to the breakdown and the ball, and stronger in the tackle as well as in covering defence. It was a match in which Wales really allowed themselves to be beaten by a side that played above itself and took the game to Wales; Sydney risked everything in search of victory, before a crowd that gave them maximum support. There was a feeling in the Welsh party that some players had not given 'their all' in the match. The management warned that a greater effort was necessary from all players for the rest of the tour.

Points for Sydney were scored by centre M. Knight (try), wing P. Crowe (2 tries), full-back M. Ellem (penalty goal), and the final dropped goal by Monaghan. Wales replied with four penalties goals by Fenwick and a try by Gerald Davies. The score at the interval was 15–6 to Sydney. From then, Wales fought back bravely. They played with more purpose, and could have gone on to win, considering the pressure they exerted, and the good punting of Brynmor Williams. However, they did not take every chance, and few could begrudge Sydney their victory.

This first defeat of Wales for several matches (they were last defeated by France in Paris in 1977) had a salutary effect. Although the next three matches were won well, one still believed, deep down, that the Welsh, unless they played exceptionally well, were unlikely to win the two Tests. Australian officials were not particularly forthcoming over the referee question; the Welsh may have been lured into a state of false optimism, rather than facing reality.

Match 4: v. New South Wales Country Districts

The next stop was at the small copper-mining town of Cobar in the New South Wales outback. Here the atmosphere and friendliness were more like that of home for the tourists. The ladies' committee prepared the food, and local officials drove everyone everywhere and genuinely made the party welcome. This was pleasant and refreshing and of considerable therapeutic value.

The Welsh responded to this encouragement, and defeated the New South Wales Country Districts side 33–0. They revealed a greater sense of urgency, what was required of them in the different conditions prevailing in Australia. They were more at ease with the referee on this occasion – sadly that was to be an isolated case. The heavy rain which fell during the match, although extremely disappointing to the hard-working local officials, supporting spectators and the Press, was welcomed by the Welsh players after the burning heat and hard ground of Sydney.

Gareth Davies and Terry Holmes had a good day at half-back but the major improvement was at forward, where much good possession was won: this enabled Holmes to reveal his potential. After Ray Gravell had suffered a knock on the knee, he was replaced by Pat Daniels, and young Alun Donovan gave a sound performance in the centre. However, after this match, four of the uncapped players, Donovan, Daniels, Clegg and Davis, had to stand down from the next three matches as more experienced players had to be selected; a short tour is not necessarily the right occasion for 'blooding' young players although it was to become inevitable, as injuries took their toll, before the staging of the second Test and final match at Sydney.

The thirty-three points scored for Wales against NSWCD came from tries by J. J. Williams (2), Holmes (2), Terry Cobner and Jeff Squire; three conversions by Gareth Davies; and a dropped goal by Holmes. Apart from the forward effort, it was Holmes who impressed the critics of both countries.

Match 5: v. New South Wales

On the party's return to Sydney for the New South Wales match, one sensed a new spirit of determination pervading the atmosphere of the team's hotel, and that the fact that a defeat had to be revenged was uppermost in the minds of the players. A strong side was chosen, in the knowledge that New South Wales were eager to repeat the triumph of Sydney, who supplied twelve members of the NSW side. Conditions were reasonable, following heavy rain the previous day, and a large crowd gathered at the Sports Ground to witness the contest. A win for NSW would have seen Wales in eclipse before reaching Brisbane (a city that held painful memories for English followers). One recalled wondering, in 1975, what was happening to England; and half way through this Welsh tour, one sensed an air of similar inevitability, that Wales would be struggling to avoid misfortunes.

Wales played hard and well against NSW and, deserved their 18-0 victory (two goals and two penalties). Yet again, the match was not well refereed! Too much over-vigorous play was allowed by Mr Byers in the first half. One must state, however, that he did appear unbiased, at least from the Press box, although his performance evidently did not please one important member of the Australian Rugby Union, who rushed to the Press box and told me in no uncertain fashion that Mr Byers 'had favoured Wales, and we will not have him in a Test match.' I was completely taken aback as was my Press colleague, Ron Griffiths of the *Swansea Evening Post* who also heard the outburst. We sensed immediately that there was refereeing trouble on the way; there was.

Wales had won the larger share of the ball against NSW and refused to be intimidated. They won the physical contest, and went on to win the rugby contest in the second half, through controlled forward power and through discipline. Yet they should have scored more tries. The midfield play was still not right, as evidenced by only one try being achieved by a wing. The NSW defence was brave, especially in midfield and in covering. There were particularly good displays by Derek Quinnell, in his first outing as captain of Wales, and by Stuart Lane, whose play suggested he would be challenging for a Test place.

NSW were disappointed, but I believe now as I did then that this victory was the turning point in the methods employed on and off the field by Australia in order to win the Test series. Poor refereeing and an over-vigorous approach was to give Australia their hollow Test-series win.

Match 6: v. Queensland

Two days after this victory, Wales were in Brisbane to face Queensland, who were lording it as the new leaders of Australian rugby, after a long period of its dominance by NSW. Wales were put on guard when a local rugby writer revealed at a Press conference that Bob Burnett of Brisbane would be the referee, and that he would be wearing Queensland stockings! One had to suggest that they should be changed to a neutral colour on the grounds that even if the referee was not neutral, his clothing should be. A request by Wales Manager Rowlands to the Queensland RFU President, Joe Gibson, was acted upon (although Rowlands pointed out it was agreed to because the referee's legs could be confused with those of Queensland players rather than because neutrality should be evident).

Strange as it may seem (and in spite of Referee Burnett) this was in my opinion the best match and best victory of the tour. Wales won 31–24. Queensland were the strongest side Wales had until then met, and were not easily overcome. Although they trailed 25–12 at the interval, and appeared to be heading for a heavy defeat, they recovered splendidly, and were back to 25–24 before Wales kicked two penalties to ensure victory.

Again, the details of the points raised several important matters; Wales scored four tries against one in a final score of three goals, three penalties and a try against a goal, a dropped goal and five penalties. Australian Paul McLean, a beautiful kicker of the ball in every way, collected twenty of his side's points. Here was the potential match-winner. Poor refereeing, combined with a notable variation in Law interpretation, could be turned into match-winning scores by the accurate kicking of McLean. (He is in no way to blame for anything that was to follow, except that a bad refereeing decision in the second Test allowed him a decisive dropped goal which in fact sailed well outside the upright!) The morning after the match, the Australian Rugby Union, *without* consultation with the Welsh management, announced in the local Press that Mr Burnett, hero of the England Test, would have charge of the first Test against Wales on the Saturday. Welsh hearts plummetted. The odds against them were then stacked extremely high. This was the one thing Wales wished to avoid;

it was the decision that soured the tour, and the ARU must be held responsible, since, after comment in the previous weeks, it was a complete volte-face.

The Welsh scorers against Queensland were David Richards, Terry Cobner, Stuart Lane and Gareth Evans with tries, Steve Fenwick with three conversions and two penalties, and Allan Martin with one penalty. The Queensland try, and it was a good one, was scored by a promising left wing, Brendan Moon.

The standard of play in this match was the highest of the tour from either Wales or their opponents. It came as no surprise after the match when the three Australian selectors nominated ten Queensland players in their first Test team.

The next two days were unpleasant, to say the least, at Welsh headquarters. The Australian Rugby Union failed to change the referee, despite the fact that at one stage Manager Rowlands threatened to return home with his party. Two members of the ARU dashed from Sydney by air at short notice, to join Joe Gibson in a meeting with Rowlands and Dawes. Gibson stood firm about his stable-mate Burnett, and whilst Peter Falk and John Howard were sympathetic, there was to be no change of heart by the ARU. Little did they realize at the time that it could well have been the last occasion for some time for them to be so dictatorial about the appointment of a referee. They believed they had won a notable tactical, off-the-field victory (as it was to prove in the Test); what they failed to realize was that the eyes of the rugby world were upon them, and the days of the 'home' referee in Tests were numbered. I must admit that, even allowing for the Sydney outburst of the ARU official, I did expect the Union to reveal a change of heart. With Byers at Brisbane and Burnett at Sydney, why not Kevin Crowe? He was probably the best of the three, although even he was not of top Test standard.

I lost considerable faith in the ARU at this time. I had known many of their members for years, and their action was unbecoming to generous and polite hosts entertaining guests who were there to save them from bankruptcy. It was an unforgivable act of bad manners. It should be contrasted with the dignity of the Rugby Football Union, who were informed by France in 1977 that they did not wish to have the (neutral) referee Norman

Sanson of Scotland in charge of their match with England at Twickenham. The RFU, in keeping with the spirit of the game and with the accepted principle of neutrality at top level, immediately asked Mr Sanson to stand down and requested Jeff Kelleher of Wales to take charge of the match. The unreasonable determination on the part of the ARU to 'have it their way', with their own referee, lost the ARU many friends; it was to set ablaze the controversial demand for universally neutral refereeing at Test level. It was the first Test which produced the remark from Referee Burnett mentioned earlier. It explained much; and is one that both he and the ARU will regret. Burnett said to scrum-half Brynmor Williams at a scrummage, 'It is not your ball, Williams, it is *ours*!' This will remain an after-dinner joke in the British Isles for many a season. It did more for the cause of neutral referees than did the tragic 18-17 defeat of the 1959 Lions at Dunedin. I was not at first prepared to believe such a preposterous story, but when other players confirmed it, my disbelief turned to laughter. Indeed, the entire Welsh Press party laughed and laughed; it revealed everything.

From then on, one realized that success for Wales was unlikely. Knowing this, one merely set out quietly to enjoy the fine land of Australia and the company of its pleasant and generous people. One began to pity rather than criticize the Australian Rugby Union, trying so hard and so desperately to regain status as a world rugby power. The ARU believed evidently that this would be achieved by defeating, (by hook or by crook), the visiting Welsh. What a pity they did not set out to defeat the Welsh in the manner of the 1927-28 Waratahs or the 1966 Wallabies! Even President Bill McLaughlin must have appreciated this; the two best luncheons I enjoyed in Australia was that as the guest of the Waratahs, and that of my Press colleagues, Australian and Welsh, to mark the official end of my touring days. I confirmed on these occasions there was nothing wrong or unfriendly about Australia, and came to the conclusion that the ARU had been misdirected and had tried too hard to win. (They had, indeed, bitten the hand that had come to save them financially.)

Welshmen may not have enjoyed the two Test defeats, but their disappointment soon passed; Australia may not so easily dismiss from their conscience the story of the 'home referees'. The four

Home Unions may be more than wise to allow them to rest awhile, as time is a great healer, even in rugby football. There have been major administrative changes in Australian rugby in recent years, and younger, more ambitious men have taken over the reins. They are impatient and want to succeed in a hurry. At what cost?

Match 7: The First Test

The first Test was won 18-8 by Australia; it was the first Test defeat suffered by Wales in eight matches and the largest margin of defeat in nine years. Several factors contributed to the Welsh defeat. One of them was the improved showing by the Australian forwards, another was the disappointing play of the Welsh centres, who were drawn into the 'physical contest' rather than disciplining themselves to stand off and run the ball along to the two match-winning wings; a third reason was the expected poor refereeing of Mr Burnett discussed above; a fourth was the kicking of Paul McLean, a match-winner in his own special way.

The Welsh forwards were often confused by the referee's rulings, and especially by his interpretation of the offside law, which was as far removed from the British habit as Twickenham is from Brisbane. The Australians argued that theirs was the right interpretation, and Mr Burnett gave this theory a touch of arrogance that was not appreciated by the Welshmen. Wales scored two tries against one; but it was still the penalty goal that mattered and McLean, as an all-round kicker, was better than any of his opponents. McLean scored fourteen of his side's points.

Had Wales been steadier at centre and not allowed themselves to be disturbed by Mr Burnett's antics (however hard that might have proved) they would have scored more tries and won. McLean's points came from a conversion and four penalties, and throughout I had the impression that at any time a penalty award would provide him with the opportunity of keeping Australia in the lead. The Australian forwards revealed tenacity, and none worked harder than those in their back row.

Lifting at the lineout, as many a Press picture and television film revealed, was blatantly allowed for Australia, as was the angled put-in at the set scrum. One felt that it was really not worth bothering against such odds, and that it would have been a much better game for both sides, win or lose, with a neutral referee.

Gerald Davies appeared in his 45th match for Wales as a three-quarter, creating a new Welsh record. He scored a try too, placing him just one behind his great rival and friend, Gareth Edwards. Gareth Davies and Brynmor Williams, as new caps, gave a promising display, despite having to follow in the place of Europe's most devastating match-winners of the era, Edwards and Bennett.

McLean played splendidly, easily the best of the Australian backs. His cleverly placed attacking kicks, whether just over the top or deeper to the corners, disturbed J. P. R. Williams and the Welsh centres; all three perhaps missed the superb, intelligent covering of the absent Bennett. Brynmor Williams did a great deal of able covering in emergency.

The turning point in the match was the first fifteen minutes of the second half. Wales, trailing 9-4, fought back to 9-8, and exerted intense pressure. However, indifferent centre play and an over-emphasis upon crash-ball play against a brave defence, prevented their continuing to success; Australia, with a little help, were able to weather the storm and return to the attack. They clinched the match amidst the adulation of a happy and partisan crowd (such as can be found, on occasions, in Wales!).

In the first half, McLean kicked two penalty goals, giving Australia the lead; they had been awarded five of the first six penalties. (This was to be expected of Mr Burnett acting within the Australian interpretation of the Laws.) Wales struck back with a try by Gerald Davies on the right wing: Fenwick switched the attack through Windsor; Gareth Davies punted deftly and diagonally; the bounce beat Crowe, and allowed Gerald Davies to gather and dash over in the corner. McLean then followed with a third penalty from a harsh award after Martin followed a ball through the ruck. It was thus 9-4 in Australia's favour, at the interval.

In the second half, Wales pressed with determination, but the centre play still was not of sufficient orthodoxy and efficiency to work Davies and Williams clear on the wings. Australia's centres and backs defended doggedly. However, after fifteen minutes of pressure Wales scored a second try. Once again, Fenwick switched

108

from left to right; he was supported by Gravell, who galloped away and passed inside to Brynmor Williams. Williams then gathered the ball off the ground and dived over. Unfortunately, Gareth Davies' conversion attempt sailed just wide of the upright; a successful kick would have given Wales the lead and might have altered the course of the match.

A harsh penalty was then awarded against Wheel, caught in the web of indecision through confusion over the Australian interpretation of the offside law. (It allows for 'loiterers' inside the ten-yard limit ahead of one's own kicker, and because Wheel moved he was trapped.) McLean kicked deep into Welsh territory and the Welsh pressure was eased.

Next, Australian centre Martin Knight kicked down to J. P. R. Williams who was held. Australia won the ruck, and then moved the ball quickly to Phil Crowe on the left wing. He slipped a diving tackle, and moved inwards to cross at the posts; McLean converted easily to make it 15-8. Wales were too far behind now and tiring, and yet another penalty by McLean, following an alledged offside, made it 18-8.

Australia had beaten Wales, to achieve what was for them a notable victory. The crowd went mad with delight. ARU President Bill McLaughlin commented, 'It is the grandest of Grand Slams as far as we are concerned. I'm so proud I cannot tell you!'

John Dawes commented, 'We did not turn pressure into points. At 9-8 down, we should have made the game safe. Australia kicked very well, but they were also allowed to enjoy the privilege of a number of collapsed scrums without penalties and were lifting continually at the lineout. Yet we did not take our chances.'

The great Australian 'plan' had worked. Their ambition had been achieved. It was not the defeat that disappointed Wales, but the manner of it. The truth was slowly revealed. The Welsh players spoke of the arrogance of Mr Burnett. He will be remembered always for 'Our ball!', and for the accusation made to Cobner on the field that Wheel had punched him, Burnett. 'I'll send him off next time,' Burnett told Cobner. Cobner replied, 'If you send him off, I'll take the Welsh team off!' It was that sort of match; the atmosphere was far removed from that of a European Test; worse was to follow in the first half of the second Test. There was simply no way that Wales were going to win a

Test match, even if they played like supermen. It is true that they were not really at their best in the first Test, but the odds were never even from the start.

Sections of the Australian Press made great play of the allegations and counter-allegations; the tour was soured completely. The journey had made money for Australia, but by this stage the Welsh players, although not unhappy solely because of losing, were frustrated and despaired of having to play in an atmosphere loaded against them. As one said, 'We have enjoyed our tour off the field and have been well treated with hospitality by friendly people, but it is great to think that we are returning home to play the rest of our football in Europe. We may lose matches there in the future, and our run of success may have come temporarily to an end, but on the field in Europe we will have fair play!' This was to me the saddest commentary of the whole tour. I recalled that I had heard it said before, by an English player returning home from Australia in 1975. When I returned home this time and met the powerful and pleasant England prop, Barry Nelmes, he commented, 'I could have written the story of the Welsh tour even before they left; it has proved exactly the same on the field as ours! You just cannot win!'

On the Sunday, the Welsh party moved off to Canberra. No Australian official was there to see them leave the airport at Brisbane. The evening paper stories reached us as we boarded the Canberra plane. The Welsh team was really under fire, but Manager Rowlands wisely refrained from engaging in a slanging match. It was Geoffrey Wheel who denied the allegations made by Mr Burnett.

Summary: First Test

Sunday 11 June   Ballymore Park, Brisbane

Australia 18 points (1 try, 4 penalties, 1 conversion)
Wales 8 points (2 tries)

Crowd: 14,000   Weather: Sunny and warm
Ground: Hard

Australia: L. Monaghan (NSW); P. Crowe (NSW), M. Knight (NSW), A. Slack (Qu'nd), P. Batch (Qu'nd); P. McLean, R. Hauser (Qu'nd); S. P. Finnane (NSW), P. Horton (NSW), S. Pilecki (Qu'nd), D. Hillhouse (Qu'nd), G. Fay (NSW), G. Cornelson (Qu'nd), M. Loane (Qu'nd), A. A. Shaw (Qu'nd, capt.)

Wales: J. P. R. Williams; T. G. R. Davies, S. P. Fenwick, R. R. W. Gravell, J. J. Williams; W. G. Davies, D. B. Williams; A. G. Faulkner, R. W. Windsor, G. Price, A. J. Martin, G. A. D. Wheel, J. Squire (sub: S. Lane), D. L. Quinnell, T. J. Cobner (capt.)

REFEREE: R. Burnett (Queensland)

SCORERS
Australia: Crowe, 1 try; McLean 1 conversion, 4 penalties
Wales: T. G. R. Davies, D. B. Williams, tries

Match 8: v. ACT

The team were welcomed by friendly officials at Canberra, the capital city of Australia and the headquarters of the Australia Capital Territories Rugby Union. The temperature and weather were more in keeping with winter at home. One sensed that the Welsh party had been disturbed by the severe press criticism but Manager Rowlands steadfastly refused to be drawn into further argument at the Press conference of the afternoon of arrival at Canberra. When he announced the side for the following day's match, it included all players who had not appeared in the first Test. One local Press man asked if he felt it was strong enough to beat the ACT. The answer was, 'We hope so!'. Several key players were injured, and he needed to rest the remainder. Cobner and Squire were extremely doubtful starters at this stage for the second Test. Quinnell assumed the captaincy, Alun Donovan was out on the wing in order that Gerald Davies could rest; however, Wheel played in his fifth consecutive match and J. P. R. Williams in his sixth, suggesting the Welshmen were under pressure.

Both sides were presented to the Governor General of Australia, H E Sir Zelman Cowan before the kick off, and Wales started happily enough. The opening suggested that they would achieve a comfortable victory; in the event, they received a sad and ignominious defeat. They scored four tries in the first half, to lead 16-6 at the interval, only to lose the match at the very last kick, the fourth penalty goal for ACT in the sixth minute of injury time; the final whistle was blown at a score of 21-20.

Manager Rowlands was brutally honest when he opened the after-match Press conference by saying, 'At times today, I was ashamed to be a Welshman. It was the worst display by a Welsh team I have witnessed since 1963.' These were harsh words born out of disappointment. Rowlands continued; 'I just do not know why it happened. I thought the referee did well, apart from his last decision. I was most unhappy that the mark was not given to J. P. R. before the last ruck, at which Wales were penalized and the winning goal was kicked.'

John Dawes agreed that it was a thoroughly bad Welsh performance, and that the ACT side played with remarkable spirit in the second half after the Welshmen had appeared to relax. It was humiliating, but once the ACT got into the game, the Welshmen just could not regain the initiative. ACT came from 16-6 down to 18-20; Wales held on desperately before the final controversial incident. In Australia, referees appear to blow for 'marks' when it suits them: when, in the sixth minute of injury time, the ball was kicked high downfield to J. P. R. Williams, he called a mark before being bowled over. It was not given, and a ruck formed with the Welsh forwards, not surprisingly, going over the top in sheer frustration. A penalty was awarded to the ACT in a position that allowed full-back Dominic O'Connell to kick the goal and thus become the local hero. (It was his day, with six goals – four penalties, a dropped goal and the conversion of a try by flanker Peter O'Neill.) The Welshmen scored four tries (through Daniels, Richards, Evans and Holmes), and Donovan converted two. Once again it was the penalties that beat the Welsh, who, after all, scored four tries to one. Nevertheless, it is true that in the second half, ACT proved themselves the better side.

Match 9: The Second Test

After this defeat, spirits were low. But then it was suggested that as rock bottom had been reached, only the way back remained, up the slope. However, Quinnell joined the list of injured, and Wales would obviously be without their Lions back row of Cobner, Quinnell and Squire. In order to maintain morale, the final side was not announced until Saturday morning, although it was clear all along that Cobner would not make it. Emergency plans had been prepared, and the side had J. P. R. Williams as flanker instead of Cobner, and Alun Donovan at full-back, with Clive Davis at number eight and Stuart Lane on the other flank. Terry Holmes was at scrum-half, and Gerald Davies was asked to lead the side for the first time: this pleased him, in his 46th international match, but little did he realize on that Saturday morning that it was to be one of the most controversial matches for many years.

Australia fielded the same side as won the first Test. Dick Byers of Sydney was the referee, about whom many Australians complained after the NSW match, despite having previously praised him to the skies. Wales had no reason to complain about him, but many believed he was not strict enough. There was no bias, but this weakness meant a start every bit as unhappy as that suffered by England in the second Test at Brisbane in 1975. The shame of the first ten minutes of both matches was to lose Australian rugby many friends, and set the game there back instead of forward. Condemnation was universal; although Wales narrowly lost the match, they gained all the glory!

There was an atmosphere of inevitability when the Welsh Press party journeyed out to the famous Sydney Cricket Ground, the Oval of Australia; I doubt if even the 'bodyline' days of 1932-33 produced a crowd so tense in anticipation. It was *the* big match; it was going to be Australia's big day in rugby union football. It could have been so, had the Australians not been carried away, as they have been in many matches; as it was, this match began exactly like that at Brisbane in 1975.

An attempt to intimidate the below-strength Welsh side was launched at the kick off; although it may never be clear as to which player on which side struck the first blow, there was soon a true punch-up; players paired off in various sections of the field. Some carried on with the ball towards the right hand corner: Wales almost scored. But the Referee then returned to the left touch-line, where he found Graham Price, the Welsh prop, bleeding profusely from the mouth while lying on the ground. Gerry Lewis was called to attend to him, and after a quick inspection waved for a doctor. Price was helped to the side line where he was examined: his jaw was broken. He had been punched from behind. Colleague Ron Griffiths, sitting next to me in the Press box, saw No. 1 (Finnane) punch Price from behind; some Welsh players saw it. Rowlands named Finnane in a radio interview immediately after the match. Price went to hospital, and John Richardson took his place.

Many sports-loving Australians were shocked by what they had seen. Many said so, but two, prop Finnane and coach Daryl Haberlicht, appeared to think it was all justified. Rowlands called it 'thuggery' in his after-match reception speech, and President McLaughlin agreed with him (only to modify his opinion some weeks later). Rowlands warned Australia to mend their ways or lose friends.

It was a day that Wales will remember with pride. Their gallant players, especially the new men, did their best in adverse circumstances. Near the interval, Alun Donovan damaged a knee ligament in a ruck and Gareth Evans replaced him. Then Evans, in making his first tackle, gained a depressed fracture of the cheek bone. Then J. J. Williams twisted an ankle and started to hobble. Wales could have no more replacements, and the two backs, Evans and Williams, not really fit to continue, had to remain on the field. J. P. R. Williams had to be withdrawn from the pack but the seven forwards stood up bravely to the Australian eight in the last half hour.

Wales's ill-fortune continued: the Referee awarded a dropped goal to Paul McLean that passed two feet outside the upright; Wales made a couple of decisive errors, first when they left Mark Loane unmarked, for him to drop over for a try at a lineout outside the Welsh line, and then, when a penalty had been awarded to Wales, Welsh hooker Windsor made some comment which caused the Referee to reverse his decision: McLean kicked the penalty. Had either of these scores been prevented, Wales would have won.

Summary: Second Test

Saturday 17 June   Cricket Ground, Sydney

Australia 19 points (1 try, 3 penalties, 2 dropped goals)
Wales 17 points (2 tries, 2 penalties, 1 dropped goal)

Crowd: 41,632 (record)   Weather: Sunny and warm
Ground: Firm and grassy

TEAMS
Australia: L. Monaghan; P. Crowe, M. Knight, A. Slack,
P. Batch; P. McLean, R. Hauser; S. P. Finnane, P. Horton,
S. Pilecki, D. Hillhouse, G. Fay, G. Cornelson, M. Loane,
A. A. Shaw (capt.)
Wales: A. Donovan (sub: G. L. Evans); T. G. R. Davies (capt.),
R. W. Gravell, S. P. Fenwick, J. J. Williams; W. G. Davies,
T. D. Holmes; A. G. Faulkner, R. W. Windsor, G. Price (sub:
J. Richardson), A. J. Martin, G. A. D. Wheel, J. P. R. Williams,
C. Davies, S. Lane

REFEREE: R. Byers (NSW)

SCORERS
Australia: Loane, 1 try; Monaghan, 1 dropped goal: P. McLean
3 penalties, 1 dropped goal
Wales: T. D. Holmes and T. G. R. Davies, tries; W. G. Davies,
1 dropped goal, 2 penalties

The next day, Wales flew out of Sydney for home. The British
Press supported them fully, even though they had made mistakes
and had sometimes not played well. The Australian Press were
divided, with David Lord (a stranger to the Welsh party, and to
them an unknown columnist) the most extreme, critical and cruel;
Bill Casey was the kindest, in that he apologized for what had
happened, and asked the Welsh not to blame Australia and the
Australian people for what had happened. I don't think they will,
but the Welsh will blame the ARU and the referees, and certain
players. This second Test match, and the refereeing problem,
plus the refusal to compromise of Joe Gibson, cost the Australian
team a return trip to Wales in 1979.

The Welsh knew their disappointment would pass. What Australia did not realize in the euphoria of success was that they had really made no headway or impressed anyone by their attitude and approach. They were still miles away from their dream. It was their magnificent touring schoolboys side that won the admiration of the British!

6

The Wallabies in New Zealand, Argentina in Britain

The Wallabies in New Zealand

After defeating Wales in the two-match Test series in Australia, the Wallabies set off later on a thirteen-match tour of New Zealand. They finished in a blaze of glory, despite winning only eight of the matches and losing five. They won the last four, including the third and final Test, this handsomely, 30–16, mainly through the splendid work of scrum-half John Hipwell and the back-row forwards, plus the brilliance of Ken Wright, who played superbly at centre. This victory alone was enough to satisfy the most critical of the followers at home, and stirred New Zealand supporters into thinking that hard times might lie ahead of their team setting out for Britain in October.

The Wallabies selected those players who appeared against Wales – at least all those who were available – and the remaining best ten; the party thus comprised twenty-five players, with the same management as that against Wales. The mighty puncher, prop Steve Finnane, was selected: the team, indeed, said they would not travel without him. Diplomatically, he withdrew before the start of the tour, owing to pressure of business; this may have proved a blessing in disguise for this fiery player. In the words of the New Zealand sporting Press, he would have been given a 'warm welcome'!

The tour did not start well. Three of the first five matches were lost. Nelson Bays were defeated 16–9, but then defeats were suffered at Invercargill against Southland, and at Dunedin against Otago.

Hawkes Bay were beaten at Napier, where Ken Wright, taking over from an injured Paul McLean as first-choice place kicker, appeared. He scored in each of the next six matches. Against Manawatu, the Wallabies went down 20–10; at Napier, Wright kicked two penalties after kicking three goals (two penalties and one conversion) for eight points.

However, there was still something wrong with the Wallabies: they were not the power they had been at home against Wales. Then there was trouble at scrum-half, and an injury to Rod Hauser brought the discarded John Hipwell to New Zealand as a replacement. Hipwell should have been selected in the first place, but domestic opposition had prevented this; he helped transform the side into a confident and consistent machine.

The early troubles of the Wallabies were due to poor tight forward play at set scrum and ruck, and this weakness nullified much of the good work achieved at the lineout by Gary Fay and Peter McLean, and in the loose by the side's captain Tony Shaw, Greg Cornelson, and Gary Pearse. Peter McLean created history when he made the first Test side; his family became the first to provide three generations of international players, with Peter following grandfather George and father William; it is a remarkable record. (Father 'Bill', who had hoped for such an occasion when I met him in Brisbane in June, was highly delighted. He was the ill-fated captain of the 1947-48 Wallabies in the British Isles, who broke his leg in the seventh match of the tour, that against the Combined Services.)

John Hipwell played in five of the last eight matches and in all three Tests. His mere presence was a boost for the side. He directed the tactical approach with shrewdness, and Australia all but won the first Test, losing only 12–13 (in that, they were unlucky, in that Wright just failed with a penalty attempt at goal in the closing minute). Hipwell's influence upon the Australians was profound and he made good, together with Wright, the loss of ace place kicker, Paul McLean, whose injury was a severe blow.

Another replacement was called upon, Englishman Geoffrey Richards, as full-back, following McLean's injury; he did well. Having lived in Australia for two years, he was a Sydney Grade player. He was flown out on the eve of the second Test at Christ-church to stand by in case McLean, chosen to play, broke down. McLean was not able to play, and Richards did take the field as a replacement. He played well, developing into one of the successes of the tour.

Still one more replacement was called for, and 19-year-old centre Tony Melrose (who had captained the unbeaten Australian Schoolboys in the British Isles in the first half of the 1977-78 season) arrived to play an important part in the memorable third Test victory. He looked amazingly mature for his years (maintain-ing the tradition that Australian players develop more quickly than those of other countries). The second Test was the low point of the tour, as the Wallabies went down 22–6 at Christchurch, to lose the series, being two down with one to play. However, it was also the turning point in the tour, as the replacements settled in and Hipwell took command of the tactical approach.

The remaining four matches were won. Hipwell played regularly and Ken Wright moved into the centre to partner Bill McKid; while Tony Melrose (normally a centre) played at outside half. On the wings, Paddy Batch and Brendan Moon (both from Queensland) did well, and Richards behind them was sound in defence and attack, suggesting that he could well have played for England while a member of the Wasps. These backs were the best combination tried, working more effectively for having the out-standing back row of Shaw, Cornelson and Pearse. As a whole, the side developed, to prove itself far superior in broken play than the All Blacks.

Thus the tour re-created a respect for Wallaby rugby in New Zealand; as the countries are physically close together, and play each other regularly, this cannot be bad for the game in either. By their free and open play, far removed from the 'blood and thunder' favoured against Wales, the Wallabies did much to restore their tarnished image. The return to playing the game as much for enjoyment as for victory can be credited to Hipwell (the veteran), and to Wright (a brilliant young player who soon after the tour succumbed to the temptation of a big fee from the Rugby League code, and thus was lost to the Union game just as he was approach-ing his peak in a career that was developing the promise of brilliance shown when he was a schoolboy playing in Britain).

The third Test

The ninth of September will remain a memorable day in the history of Australian rugby. At Eden Park, Auckland, New Zealand, a record crowd of 50,000 was present, expecting a third successive New Zealand victory to produce a clean sweep by the favoured All Blacks in the Test series. As one New Zealand critic wrote, 'They were present to watch the *coup de grace* being administered to the beleagured Australian side'! The tourists had suffered five defeats, including two Tests, and sustained innumerable injuries, they had had four replacements flown out, and had left their coach Daryl Habericht behind at Wanganui, suffering from a heart attack. Whatever happened in the match, it could not be worse than that which had gone before. With commendable determination after facing these disasters, the Wallabies said, with typical Aussie optimism, 'We'll give it a go!' They arrived at Eden Park in happy mood and never lost faith, despite their problems.

In particular, the list of injuries in the 13-match tour was an unusually long one. Full-back Laurie Monaghan broke a collarbone before the second Test. The second full-back, Roger Gould, spent only 17 minutes on the field of play before suffering a hamstring injury. Mark Loane, the leading number eight, joined the tour after it was underway, played two matches, and then became another hamstring sufferer, and returned home. Paul McLean damaged a cartilage during the second Test. Three test players failed to make the tour at all: David Hillhouse, Phil Crowe, and the much-publicized lawyer and prop, Steve Finnane.

So the team took the field for the last Test in the old-fashioned manner of Australian sides. They did not care about errors; they determined to run the ball, and they did. Actually, they did much more, they ran the All Blacks off their feet! They played so well, and produced fine football of a style rarely seen in Test matches. They won over the large crowd, who had come prepared for a Roman holiday. The All Blacks looked poor opponents as their defence crumbled.

The hero of the day was the bearded Greg Cornelson. He scored four tries, becoming the tenth player in international rugby to do so in one match. The tall, powerful loose-forward scored one from the back of a loose maul, one from a rash long throw-in by New Zealand on their own goal line (which manoeuvre they also did to their cost against Cardiff later in the year), and two through close support inside the right wing Paddy Batch. The fifth try was also scored by a back-row forward, Gary Pearse, after centre Ken Wright had scattered the defence. This was only the second time ever that New Zealand had conceded five tries in a Test match. It was a triumph for running, attacking rugby. Even Terry McLean admitted that the All Blacks had been annihilated. Not since the 1937 Springboks visit had New Zealand conceded so many tries in a match. New Zealand were poor at the lineout; poor in defence, and dropped passes. The prospects for the British tour were not good. Would British teams heed the lesson of this Test, and run with the ball?

The Australian record

29 July, Nelson: Nelson Bays 9, Wallabies 16
2 August, Invercargill: Southland 10, Wallabies 7
5 August, Dunedin: Otago 10, Wallabies 8
9 August, Napier: Hawkes Bay 6, Wallabies 16
12 August, Palmerston North: Manawatu 20, Wallabies 10
15 August, Pukehohe: Counties 8, Wallabies 17
19 August, Wellington: 1st Test: New Zealand 13, Australia 12
22 August, Ashburton: Mid Canterbury 12, Wallabies 19
26 August, Christchurch: 2nd Test: New Zealand 22, Australia 6
30 August, Wanganui: Wanganui 3, Wallabies 8
2 September, Rotorua: Bay of Plenty 7, Wallabies 34
5 September, Whangarei: North Auckland 11, Wallabies 16
9 September, Auckland: 3rd Test: New Zealand 16, Australia 30

A personal note

Australian assistant manager and coach, Daryl Habericht, a tense personality (as revealed in the series against Wales), suffered a heart attack while at Wanganui and could not continue in his post in the three remaining matches. He recovered but did not seek re-election as national coach upon his return. His experience merely emphasizes the demands made upon management and players on tours. It is true that the pressures have increased; part of cause for Mr Habericht's illness could have been the worries of his side's constant misfortune and the disappointment at the loss of the series. To any tense and dedicated person in sport, disappointment is not easily acceptable.

The Argentinians in the British Isles

The second official team from the Argentine to visit the British Isles gave a much better account of itself than was anticipated, and developed into a popular and successful side. It left its native shores almost an unknown combination, but developed so rapidly, and with such spirit and enthusiasm, that it almost toppled England at Twickenham. It won the hearts of spectators, and left for home knowing that it had made safe the future of its country's rugby, and that further invitations for tours would follow in the years ahead.

Since the visit to Wales in the autumn of 1976, with a much stronger side, there had been a rugby 'revolution' with a considerable change in personnel. Dr Carlos Contepomi, a highly successful manager, had resigned; also, many players were upset as their captain Arturo Jurado had been discarded. Ten leading Argentinian players were suspended by their Union for five years as a disciplinary measure after they refused to play in the South American championship as a protest against the treatment of Jurado. Another player, the big centre Alejandro Travaglini, was suspended for three years after being away from the Argentine when he had been required to attend the hearing concerning his being sent off in a championship match. One would not have expected anything like this to have happened in any other rugby country, but the Argentine RU was determined to remain the authority in power.

So in September, a new manager, Eric Kember (a talkative one, who became something of a character on tour) arrived in London with a new side. He had three assistant managers (a coach, assistant coach and a doctor), but only two players who had been in Wales and England in 1976. (Fortunately, these two were brilliant players of world class, Hugo Porta at outside half, and Martin Sansot at full-back.)

The tour will be remembered for the lively play of a young pack, play which developed immensely during the tour, and for the outstanding all-round play of Hugo Porta. It was truly his tour!

122

He scored 88 points out of 151; his running was elusive; his passing was accurate and slick; his tactical kicking was superb. By the end of the tour he could justly be considered the World's Number One as an outside half, following the retirement of Phil Bennett from international rugby.

Match 1: v. Southern Counties

The tour began at Oxford, on the University Ground at Iffley Road. The Southern Counties were beaten comfortably, 39–9, and 'Mr Porta' claimed the headlines with his quality of play and style of action. He scored a try, three penalties, and three conversions. The Argentinians needed to give greater attention to their scrummaging, but their backing-up was excellent and their tackling strong. Their back row impressed with its covering work, and Petersen and Silva on the flanks were to achieve much praise during the tour for their tackling, foraging and support work (especially so in the international – albeit unofficial – match against England).

The Southern Counties, though game enough, were a scratch side, and not particularly strong; the French referee was quick to spot infringements by both sides whilst not disturbing the flow of the game. Full-back Sansot indulged in many attacking forays, delighting the crowd.

Match 2: v. London Counties

The tourists moved on to their second match at Twickenham against the London Counties, with enthusiasm. This match turned on the points made by the London Counties just before the interval, at which point they were trailing 9–3, having spent most of the half defending. Preston, the Counties outside half, ran across the defence and scored a try in the corner. Bushell did well to convert it; the score was 9–9. Then, with ten minutes left, it was 15–15; finally, an unconverted try and a penalty made it 22–15 for the Counties. A strong wind swirled round Twickenham and made kicking difficult even for Hugo Porta, although he did manage to collect three goals, one penalty, one conversion, and one dropped. In only one match did he fail to score, and that was in the third, against the Northern Division of Counties at Headingley.

Match 3: v. Northern Division of Counties

At this Northern Division match, the Pumas suffered their heaviest defeat, 20–6. The Northern pack included four powerful England forwards, and was a good one (especially the sadly neglected Tony Neary, whose omission from the England side previously selected remained a puzzle).

The Pumas always tackled hard, but, with little good possession, they found life difficult and, at that stage of the tour, it was not anticipated that they would prove to be as successful and attractive as they were by the end of it. The rucking and mauling of the Northern pack was better than that of the England pack in the international later; Martin Young at scrum-half and Tony Bond in the centre were in particularly good form. The Pumas left for Moseley to meet the North Midlands, anticipating little that was to happen at the Reddings on 7 October.

Match 4: v. North Midlands

The Pumas won this match 22–14; sadly, there were incidents and a growing violence that led to the sending-off of a player from each side. This unnecessary incident tarnished the tour, and was made worse when each offending player received only a week's suspension. Such a mild – almost friendly – attitude on the part of the disciplinary sub-committee did not meet with the approval of Stanley Couchman, President of the RFU. He commented, 'The incidents, which had all the ingredients of everything we have been fighting to eliminate, saddened me. All I can assure you of is that nothing will be swept under the carpet. Everyone connected with rugby must realize that the future of the game is being placed in jeopardy.' Strong words by an experienced administrator, not afraid to speak out, stand up, and be counted, both for his principles and for what the RFU was seeking. He added that the North Midlands, the Pumas' management, and the Referee would all be asked for detailed reports of what really happened.

The trouble appeared to start after the North Midlands had executed one of their wedge-like charges from a tapped penalty, which the Argentinians attempted to halt by charging in similar fashion! The result was physical confrontation, and from then on the violence was continual, spoiling an otherwise lively match. The younger Pumas may have been inexperienced and a little stupid but the senior North Midlands players set a poor example. It was a sad day for Midlands rugby after such a fine record over the years; for an excellent Irish referee, David Burnett, it was an embarrassing situation. Two players were sent off in the final free-for-all (it might reasonably have been five men from each side summarily dismissed). They were Derek Nutt, the North Midlands forward, and Alfredo Soares-Gache, the Pumas' scrum-half, who had already scored a try for his side. It was his first match of the tour, and his suspension prevented him from being considered for the international match against England then seven days ahead.

Match 5: v. England Students XV
The following Tuesday, the Argentinians moved to Kingsholm at Gloucester, in recent years a home of successful club and county rugby, and one which generates as much enthusiasm as at Welsh grounds. Any side that wins at Kingsholm does well; Welsh teams have told me that a win there is worth two victories at any other ground! The opposition in this match was provided by an England Students XV. (It was an excellent idea to give them a match, an encouragement for student rugby outside Oxbridge. No rugby follower wishes to take anything away from Oxbridge, but there are other universities which deserve encouragement and recognition. More rugby players now enter colleges of physical education, whereas in the pre-war years a good rugby man of average academic achievements might often win a place at Oxbridge. The drop in standards of Oxbridge rugby in recent years has revealed this all too clearly, and many believe that the two senior universities should encourage a high standard in all walks of life, including sport.)

The Students, to their credit, gave the Pumas a hard match; it required all the ingenuity and skill of Hugo Porta to see his team through to victory. They achieved a 15–9 win. He scored all fifteen points, with a try (converted) and three penalty goals. He is a unique player, gifted and confident and refreshing in approach.

Match 7: v. England
From Kingsholm it was back to Twickenham, to 'the big one' against England; the English selectors had paid the Pumas the

compliment of fielding a really strong side, almost the strongest available.

Most followers and critics, however, thought that the match would provide a comfortable England victory in the build up for the All Blacks match to follow. England captain Billy Beaumont, a likeable realist and never one to boast, admitted that every member of the side was playing for his place and that victory would not be achieved without hard work. The critics suggested a runaway England victory and one was so bold as to hint that the Englishmen would use the match to 'frighten the All Blacks', who would be in attendance, the day after their arrival in London. How wrong everyone was!

The match was drawn, 13–13; many an English face was red with embarrassment. The *Sunday Times* headline summed it up: 'Day the Pumas Pounced'.

The All Blacks, freshly out of their plane, refused to be conned by England's poor form. Coach Jack Gleeson, having his first sight of rugby in England, sniffed the air and said, 'We will not be conned by the England showing. They will be far better by the time of the full international against us. Perhaps they were short of a few key players and it was early in the season for them to be at their peak.' This was a touch of shrewd diplomacy, one thought; having watched the match closely I was tempted to believe that the new young Argentine side, guided by Porta, had found itself. Even allowing for the fact that it was the first outing by England, so early in the season, there was every reason to praise the tourists. Their achievement was as good as a victory; it was splendid to see the 20,000 crowd give them such a good reception at the end. Argentina has proved itself a country fit to play with the 'big boys', and they were indeed happy with their effort; manager Eric Kember afterwards talked continuously, and with evident delight.

The Argentine forwards worked hard and got about the field. They excelled themselves at the lineout, and were superior in the loose (especially in the back row, where Petersen and Silva had a wonderful day). They were here, there and everywhere. They showed up the England selectors' need to change their back row. The link between backs and forwards, control in the loose, and the cover in defence must all come from the back row; the modern game demands it and there is no alternative.

Hugo Porta was at his best, and worried the England back row. After a good start by the England halves their effectiveness faded, mainly because they neglected the basic principles. Squires and Slemen are good wings by any standard; sadly, they had little possession to reveal their talent. Gifford, having scored a good blind side try from near the Pumas' line, became obsessed with the blind side, and Horton at outside half, who can be a clever runner at his best, kept jinking back inside. When he did send Squires off for a try, it was because he had gone one way and then changed his mind, hoping to get clear, rather than by intent. England, generally, have good wings and all that is needed is accurate orthodox rugby to get the ball to them quickly.

England took the lead with a dropped goal by Horton, then the Pumas' right wing Campo scored in spectacular style, flying over full-back Bushell's head (in the manner of Carson Catcheside scoring against France in the 1920s). Gifford's try put England back in the lead before the interval, only for the Pumas to recapture it in the second half with a try from lock Passaglia, following a timely peel-off from the lineout. Porta converted before England got their second try, a good one by Squires which was converted by Bushell. Porta then made it 13–13, with a penalty goal, and this remained as the final score.

TEAMS

An England XV: K. M. Bushell (Harlequins); J. P. Squires (Harrogate), P. J. Warfield (Rosslyn Park), P. W. Dodge (Leicester), M. A. C. Slemen (Liverpool); J. P. Horton (Bath), C. J. Gifford (Moseley); J. P. Scott (Cardiff), P. J. Dixon (Gosport), M. J. Colclough (Angouleme), W. Beaumont (capt.) (Fylde), M. Rafter (Bristol), F. E. Cotton (Sale), P. J. Wheeler (Leicester), B. G. Nelmes (Cardiff)

Argentina: M. Sansot; M. Campo, N. Loffreda, R. Madero, A. Cappelletti; H. Porta (capt.), R. T. Landajo; G. Travaglini, H. Silva, I. Iachetti, R. Passaglia, T. Petersen, H. Nicoli, A. Cubelli, A. Cerioni

REFEREE: C. Norling (WRU)

SCORERS

England: Gifford, Squires, tries; Bushell, 1 conversion; Horton, 1 dropped goal

Argentina: Campo, Passaglia, tries; Porta, 1 conversion, 1 penalty

The rest of the tour

Only one visit was paid to Wales, and one to Ireland. Both were successful. A Welsh 'B' XV was beaten at Stradey Park, Llanelli, in an exciting match, and Leinster were defeated at Lansdowne Road, Dublin. Both matches provided good football and further valuable experience for the young tourists.

The Welsh match was played beneath the new floodlighting system at Stradey Park, before a large and generous crowd. (Amongst it was the Italian coach, Pierre Villepreux, whose observations were later to prove of immense value to his team.)

The lead changed hands regularly at Stradey Park. Porta started off with a penalty goal, and his opposite number David Barry equalized for Wales with a penalty. Prop David Lewis got a try for Wales before Porta set one up for wing Campo to score. It was 7–7 at the interval.

In the second half, Porta regained the lead with an excellent dropped goal; a strong young centre, Hutchings, got a try for Wales and the lead was then back again in Welsh hands at 11–10. Flanker Serrano then scored a try, and Sansot put over a superb penalty from forty-five yards. It was 17–11 to the Pumas.

This burst was decisive, even though Barry collected another penalty goal for Wales to make the final score 17–14. The match was won in the set scrums where the tourists proved far stronger than their opponents, continually driving back the Welsh. In the loose and at the lineout, the Welsh held their own, but it was a deserved victory for the tourists. They moved on to Dublin in a happy frame of mind, and there ended the British section of their tour with a good win, and another bumper personal performance from captain, Hugo Porta.

The Irish side included ten international players who were expected to be out to make a bold impression and help the national selectors, then searching for a side to overcome the All Blacks two weeks ahead. As Paul MacWeeney reported from Dublin for the *Guardian*: 'The Argentinians achieved a notable advance in playing standards and, just as important, a big step forward in temperamental stability.'

During the match Porta attempted six kicks at goal. He succeeded with all of them, recording a conversion, a dropped goal and four penalties, a total of 17 points, which brought his total for the tour to 88. Leinster collected 12 points through a try by centre Adreucetti and three penalties by outside half, Quinn. In addition for the Argentine, number eight Travaglini scored a try and Sansot kicked a fifth penalty goal.

Although the match provided eight penalties and only two tries, this did not give quite a fair story of the play as there were some excellent handling movements from both sides.

The Argentinians victory, 24–13, suggested they would have little trouble overcoming Italy four days later. As it was, the celebrations, the flight to Italy, and the resting of Porta after a heavy tour, saw the tourists go down by 19–6. It was rather a sad end to an otherwise splendid tour.

In the whole tour, thus, the final record was: Played 9. Won 5. Lost 3. Drawn 1. 156 points for, 135 against. As a tour it was invaluable for Argentine rugby, consolidating technical proficiency, temperament and approach, while many young players 'came of age' in rugby terms on the tour. It promises even better things for the future. British rugby liked them, enjoyed their company and grew to respect them. They proved that touring need not be a grim experience!

7

The All Blacks in
the British Isles

In the end, the eighth New Zealand All Blacks blew it! The last
week of their tour was a disaster of their own making. Much of the
good work off the field was ruined by that sense of arrogance
which is never far below the surface in their rugby. Maybe they
believed they could 'get away with it all'. They became over-
confident.

John Ashworth, a prop from Canterbury (NZ), stamped twice
upon the unprotected face of the British Lion, Wales and Bridgend
captain J. P. R. Williams, at the Brewery Field, Bridgend after
four minutes of the match there; he left this country refusing to
show any remorse for his action. This will remain an incredible
and callous approach to an act of violence on the rugby field, one
magnified by the stupidity of the New Zealand management in
their subsequent behaviour. My views are those of Dr Peter
Williams, father of J. P. R. I admire the father of the injured
player for speaking out against violence; the New Zealand management have tried to infer that they did not see it (Jack Gleeson
providing the most glib explanation of all). Gleeson is reported to
have said, 'I saw Mourie's shoulder make contact with Williams's
face'. If one believes that glib statement after seeing the television
film of the incident, then there is no point in continuing international relationships.

Twice in one year, in tour matches, I have seen vicious physical
damage being inflicted upon unsuspecting players, at Sydney and
Bridgend; after fifty years of watching and forty-five of writing
about the game, I am sickened by it all. I cannot forgive the conduct of the New Zealand management, who made John Ashworth

130

a replacement for the subsequent match, that three days later against the Barbarians, actually sending him onto the field at half time to play in the match. It was an affront to British rugby, adding a major insult to a major injury. I never thought that Messrs Gleeson and Thomas would have done this. In the action, I saw the arrogance that lies below the surface in New Zealand rugby. When my Editor Duncan Gardiner asked Russell Thomas about the choice of Ashworth as a replacement, Thomas replied, 'Would you let the crowd make your selection for you?' He refused to look at the incident on a television replay. He should have gone to see J. P. R. Williams the next morning, with J. Ashworth, and made a public apology. All the pleasantries quoted will never alter the fact that British sportsmen do not accept those who believe they are never wrong. The cause of rugby football, which the New Zealanders allege they guard so jealously, was seriously damaged. I emphasize again the need to consider seriously how conduct on the field which is not seen by the referee but is detrimental to the game, can be dealt with quickly and sternly by the authorities. Without action, the game will lose its way.

The traditional retort is that such dirty play is just the 'emnity' in rugby between New Zealand and Wales. If this is believed, then I think everyone is missing the point: this was a wanton act (not even one of retaliation). To condone it, as did the New Zealand management, is to destroy the pleasure of the whole tour.

Perhaps weariness got to some of the New Zealand players in the end. There were other minor incidents on the field. It was in striking contrast to the behaviour *off* the field. There, it was a happy tour, one of the best by a New Zealand side since 1953–54.

The activities of Andy Haden were brought to a head when he carried out his now-famous act in the fatal and decisive lineout against Wales at Cardiff (see page 159). I thought the film exposure of this would have been a lesson for the team, but the New Zealand management refused to discuss it. Then came Haden's k.o. punch of Alistair McHarg at Murrayfield, actually in front of Referee John West. But there was no comment; life was 'charmed' on the field; British referees leaned over backwards to please.

The vicious Bridgend incident brought matters to the eyes of the world. Even the Director of Public Prosecutions became interested but still the All Blacks brazened it out.

I doubt these All Blacks will be remembered as a great side; sadly, it is the last week of their tour that will be remembered. Let there be no continued criticism now of the 1977 Lions, called 'animals' by certain sections of the New Zealand Press: they did not engage in 'malicious wounding'. Most of the 1978 All Blacks were decent fellows on and off the field. Most were real sportsmen. Some members did not measure up to this standard. In the end, they were protected by the management.

The NZ Press party was the happiest to visit us for some time, and most of their copy – at least that airmailed back to me – was fair. I want to record what their senior photographer, Peter Bush, a real rugby man, told me before he left London, 'They should have sent on anyone as a replacement at Cardiff at half-time in the Barbarians match, except Ashworth!' It is sad, too, to have to record a report that NZ Manager Russell Thomas was 'man-handled' by a couple of hooligan spectators after the match. One can have only genuine disgust for that, whatever one may feel about the incidents.

Now I will analyse the tour technically. New Zealand achieved a very successful playing record, seventeen victories in eighteen matches (even if several of them were hair-raising cliff-hangers which could have gone either way). They were a lucky, rather than a great side, and the tour was influenced considerably by British referees being lenient to the tourists. Some of their decisions were appalling. One much-travelled official commented, 'If this is how neutral referees perform, let each country supply its own!' Several referees had poor matches, including Messrs Sanson, West, Quittenton and Norling. However, many observers missed the gentle 'pressure' applied to British referees by New Zealand captain, Graham Mourie, who queried most penalty awards against the All Blacks in kickable positions. It was interesting to check this observation while watching BBC tele-recordings. Andy Haden enjoyed a 'charmed life' on the field. He should have won his Oscar for his performance at Cardiff against Wales.

The laxity of refereeing may have helped the New Zealand playing record, but it did not help rugby football, and certainly not British rugby. Equally it must be recorded that several British teams did not play well against the tourists. In all, I often found the whole course of this tour bizarre, and often embarrassing. It was not the defeats that really worried me, but the latitude allowed to a touring side that really did not need such treatment. They enjoyed latitude in offside play at the lineout, as well as the ruck and maul, where they were as often on the 'wrong side' as their opponents. They engaged in unobtrusive but clever obstruction, and they chatted up referees! One cannot blame them totally: they played right up to what each referee allowed or did not allow. That was in keeping with modern 'gamesmanship'.

Maybe all these criticisms of themselves, their opponents and the referees will be refuted by the All Blacks. But it happened; if most British officials and critics were too polite to say so, then just think of what the 1977 Lions had to suffer.

There were players in the party who impressed me for their approach, attitude and effectiveness. I liked Brian McKechnie, because he was a sound full-back and a good match-winning kicker. He had nothing to do with the awarding of the last-minute penalty against Wales, but he kicked a good goal. Stuart Wilson was a darting wing who made the most of poor tackling and defensive lapses by opponents. Bruce Robertson has always been a favourite of mine; a fast upstanding centre who handles well and runs hard, he is always eager to make use of the slightest chance and opposition error. Douglas Bruce, the old man of the side, was an old-fashioned, traditional All Blacks first five-eighth who kicked accurately for position and kicked well.

Dave Loveridge proved to be as sharp as a needle, a quick passer and runner, and quite an astute kicker of the ball. He is a better player than many realized (he shared in three victories at Cardiff Arms Park). Graham Mourie was as shrewd a captain as they come on the field, and a pleasant fellow off it. His unobtrusiveness disarmed any critics, and hid his native shrewdness in the game. Quick and opportunist, he made it his business to pounce on opposition errors. His side respected him. I hope he was not concerned with the Cardiff 'con trick' against Wales.

Leicester Rutledge, also on the flank, became the most improved player in the side, a first-class, hard-working loose forward. He was tenacious and persistent. Andy Dalton, from a famous All-Black family, was a splendid quick-striking mobile hooker; he did extremely well to appear in all the Tests. He is a compact player, and a competitor much in the mould of Ron Hemi.

Manager Russell Thomas talked a lot and talked well. He said the right things and side-stepped the difficult issues, dismissing the Bridgend business too easily. When he left for home with the team, the issue had not been clarified. But he worked hard for the team. Coach Jack Gleeson was deep and observant, but played it all very close to his chest. He made occasional outbursts about the predictability of British rugby, and he was upset at the Munster defeat 'because the opposition tackled too hard and wouldn't allow his team to play rugby'. He worked hard as a coach, with a good training system. He is a disciple of the ruck, the most controversial phase of play in the modern game.

The player deserving most sympathy was Ash McGregor, a flanker who played only three times on tour. He is a nice guy, but was his journey really necessary?

Technically, the eighth All Blacks did not leave behind many lessons of which British rugby was not already aware, but there were a few points that British rugby needs to re-think. Firstly, there is the vital matter of close support, at which the New Zealanders were far better than their opponents, especially at forward. They recovered more quickly in defence, so as to plug all the gaps (though British sides did not run at them often enough), and everyone tackled and brought his opponent to ground or prevented him playing the ball easily. The forwards accomplished far more close-tackling than opponents, and they did ruck better (although there was an element of danger, sometimes violence, in their approach, with little thought for the man trapped on the ground).

They did not run all that much, preferring to kick for position rather than create running openings. Gleeson said he adjusted his tactics after Munster because of the stern tackling. The truth is that as a running side they were not happy against a quick-marking, strong-tackling side. The kicking in attack was good, especially to the wings (occasionally Osborne kicked for Wilson to score in the right corner), but the All Blacks kicked too frequently with the overlap.

Their lineout play improved; they frequently employed the combined move across the line but were rarely penalized. If

134

Haden was properly marked, the All Blacks did not win a lot of ball in the middle of the line, but he was better 'protected' as the tour developed. At the end of the line, Seear did some good work, but was a clumsy forward on occasions. Their best front row was Johnstone, Dalton and Knight. When Knight recovered from his herpes illness, he made a marked difference to the rigid strength of the set scrum. Their scrum taps and lineout call-signs could be 'read', but they excelled best at the drive forward, and the rolling smuggle proved most effective.

The scrum-halves were nippy and quick-serving: although Donaldson had the longer pass, Loveridge was the better all-round player. Bruce was the sounder outside half, and a good general; Dunn was unsure under pressure, although with play flowing and in receipt of plenty of ball, he was more imaginative than Bruce.

Bryan Williams looked a little past his best, often unhappy in defence or in wet conditions on the wing. Ford was unlucky with injuries. Taylor looked a more than useful player. Osborne was a hard tackler but wasted too many chances in attack. Kururangi never really made it. Currie was improving, before his injury against Wales. McKechnie, however, as the more accurate place kicker, was always a better bet for the full-back position.

The side is young enough to enjoy a good series against France in 1979 and they should feel quite at home with neutral referees from the British Isles. When Russell Thomas commented, 'I think your referees are wonderful!', he was being a shrewd administrator.

Next winter, England and Scotland have the All Blacks back, and they visit Wales in 1980. I hope there will be no more incidents like that at Bridgend.

The Start of the Tour
The Eighth All Blacks arrived at London Airport on Thursday 12 October, full of humour and a willingness to meet the people. Manager Russell Thomas shook hands with all the Press representatives, and even remembered most of their names and their papers. It was a good start, and he continued to smile and chat his way easily through the crowded first days in London when everyone had to be met. (It is always a punishing time, the start of any tour, and the All Blacks did the job well.)

At the special welcoming reception given by the New Zealand High Commissioner Sir Douglas Carter, and his wife, there must have been five hundred guests to meet the tourists – quite the largest gathering ever at New Zealand House for such an occasion. There was considerable interest in this new-look All Blacks party, and the next day the tourists visited Twickenham to watch England struggle against the Argentine. (It was a difficult match for England – slightly embarrassing, even – but the All Blacks, especially coach Jack Gleeson, said they were not conned by England's rather lethargic performance.)

On Sunday the All Blacks were officially welcomed by the Four Home Unions Tours Committee, and on Monday by the British Sportsman's Club which had Edward Heath in good form as the chairman of one of the famous club's largest gatherings, and Russell Thomas in equally good form when responding to the toast to his team. He called for a good, hard, enjoyable and clean tour. 'We are proud to come to these Islands, as Britain has a style of life that is unequalled. Everyone is worried about sport today. It faces greater challenges than ever before, with the advent of television, commercialism and violence. Every step should be taken to ensure that sport is protected, and I feel that the privilege of coming to Britain should ensure an exchange of friendships; winning and losing should be treated equally.'

Mark these words, honestly delivered: they were put to the test during the tour on several occasions, as much by the All Blacks themselves as their hosts.

On Monday afternoon, the party were on their way to Cambridge. It is a busy city, traffic-blocked, but friendly; one sensed that the team were happy with their lot, even though anxious to get underway. They enjoyed the quiet but comfortable hospitality of the University Arms and the green splendour of the adjacent Parker's Piece.

Match 1: v. Cambridge University

The opening match of the tour was blessed with truly magnificent weather that can prevail only in autumn in certain parts of the Northern Hemisphere; the sun shone as brightly as ever it did in high summer of 1978. Grange Road was full to capacity.

136

The All Blacks fielded a good side; the University had some of their leading young performers supported by bandage and injection, especially a particularly brave captain, Irish international scrum-half, John Robbie. The Cambridge coach, humorist, BBC reporter, horse owner and former Cambridge and Scotland outside half, Ian Robertson, did not believe his side had a chance; he uttered the encouraging words, 'If our tackling improves one thousand per cent, and our handling five hundred per cent, all we need to win is a miracle.' In the event, the All Blacks proved utterly human, and the University side, blessed with courage, ensured that the final score was highly respectable.

The undergraduates provided no Roman holiday for the visitors. The heading to the *Guardian* preview, 'Blacks Set to Make Blues Look Green' could be taken in light-hearted fashion, as Cambridge scored 12 points against the 32 of the All Blacks. Terry McLean, having his first taste of yet another tour, cabled home to his *Herald*: 'While they scored an encouraging victory, the All Blacks did not manage to achieve dominance, and could face many hard tests ahead.' This was an honest and fairly accurate prophecy.

It was the first match of the tour, but there were certainly areas of vulnerability in the side. Two assets were to carry it through the tour with few defeats; the traditional New Zealand tenacity, and a generous amount of good fortune (this normally attends their rugby efforts at home, in the British Isles, and in Australia – but never in South Africa!).

In the first half, the All Blacks were comparatively untroubled. A nervous University side struggled, and their errors were punished by the accuracy of full-back Brian McKechnie as a place kicker. (His in-and-out form was to trouble the tour selectors, yet helped them to achieve their most desired triumph later at Cardiff.) He kicked three penalties, and converted tries by Donaldson and Wilson, giving a 21–0 lead at the interval. Robbie must have convinced his Cambridge side that the Men in Black were not super-human during his interval team talk. He inspired his pack, and Butler, Heath and Ford set nobly about winning the ball. The score changed to 24–12, as cries of 'Come on, Varsity' echoed across the Grange Road ground from nearly 9,000 spectators. In the last ten minutes the less experienced side tired a little and the All Blacks, after further tries by Donaldson and Ford, left the field with a 32–12 victory, one flattering in many ways, but one that could point them in the right direction. Wing Tyler scored the Cambridge try; Robbie converted it, as well as landing two fine penalties.

Summary: Match 1

Wednesday 18 October   Grange Road, Cambridge
Cambridge 12 points (1 try, 2 penalties, 1 conversion)
All Blacks 32 points (4 tries, 4 penalties, 2 conversions)

TEAMS
Cambridge University: I. Metcalfe; P. Frackleton (sub: M. Parr), M. Fosh, A. Laycock, R. Tyler; J. Thornton, J. C. Robbie (capt.); R. J. Brooman, J. Grant, S. Killick, N. R. M. Heath, J. N. Ford, C. O'Callaghan, S. J. Glanvill, E. T. Butler
All Blacks: B. J. McKechnie; R. R. Kururangi, B. J. Robertson, N. M. Taylor, B. R. Ford; O. D. Bruce, M. W. Donaldson; J. C. Ashworth, J. E. Black, W. K. Bush, J. K. Loveday, J. K. Fleming, B. G. Ashworth, G. N. K. Mourie (capt.), A. A. McGregor

REFEREE: K. Rowlands (Wales)

SCORERS
Cambridge: R. Tyler, 1 try; J. C. Robbie, 2 penalties, 1 conversion
All Blacks: M. W. Donaldson, 2 tries: G. N. K. Mourie, 1 try; N. M. Taylor, 1 try; B. J. McKechnie, 4 penalties, 2 conversions

Match 2: v. Cardiff

The New Zealand party moved on the next day to Wales, via Oxford where they trained. They enjoyed their long coach ride, and arrived in Cardiff during the early evening with less apprehension than many a previous side, and certainly without the mafia-like snarls and strange headgear of some members of the 1972 side. The friendly confidence of the latest tourists did not pass unnoticed, and the Royal Hotel at Cardiff, once the stately headquarters of the Welsh Rugby Union on such occasions, was alive

138

again. Nowadays, it is a rugger man's haven only at Easter time when the Barbarians, less demonstrative than in the former Esplanade Days at Penarth, enjoy the privacy of their own team room.

There was talk of a hard match against Cardiff, although the Club, by constant selectorial experiment following a high scoring start to the season, did not really arrive at its best XV, even for the most important match of the season. Nevertheless, tickets for the encounter sold well, and the eventual gate receipts produced £87,000 for the Welsh Rugby Union, the largest figure for any club match in the British Isles, and £4,000 from programme profits for the Club in addition to considerable takings at the bar!

The team trained on the Friday at Sophia Gardens, next to the Glamorgan County cricket pitch. The training impressed a hero of former years, Wilfred Wooller, who had helped topple the 1935 All Blacks. Jack Gleeson was methodical and efficient, if not inspired, as a coach. He knew what he wanted, and he never expected too much. He rarely ranted and raved. He was a sensible man who did his homework, and who spent as much time as he could upon two maxims: 'Take your chances' and 'Cut down on errors.' The evening of Friday was spent in Cardiff Castle with Stan Bowes and his Jubilee Reunion Dinner for the members of the 1953 Cardiff side. At £25 per head he found plenty of takers for tickets. (At one stage the enjoyable affair was misconstrued as Cardiff's official welcome to the tourists!) Russell Thomas spoke well and even brought a recorded message from the 1953 All Blacks captain, Bob Stuart – a clever touch, and excellent p.r. work. Again, conditions were good on the day. The All Blacks survived their first stiff hurdle because they made fewer errors than Cardiff, and took their chances more readily; this is almost the entire story of British teams in opposition to New Zealand. Some loose passing and tackling nullified good work by the Cardiff forwards, and brought about the downfall of the Club side hoping to achieve a Jubilee victory. It was 3–3 after 30 minutes (Gareth Davies had countered a Currie penalty for New Zealand with a dropped goal from a tapped penalty). Cardiff were doing well and were actually on the attack, when one centre got ahead of the other and the long pass was intercepted by Stuart Wilson. He galloped away for nearly seventy yards to the posts. Although it was before the interval, the match was effectively almost over. It was the decisive score, because it hit the Cardiff forwards extremely hard. Arriving at the interval at 9–3 down after their tireless work was not a happy moment for them: the young Cardiff back division had failed – probably through a lack of experience of close-marking – to rise to the occasion.

After the interval the All Blacks put themselves well clear with a good try. Outside half Dunn, moving left, booted ahead with his left foot. Although the kick was not a particularly good one, it hung long enough for centre Jaffray to get to it, draw the full-back, and send Osborne on a long fifty-yard dash for the line. Currie kicked wide, but a lead of ten points (13–3) made a Cardiff comeback unlikely. Nevertheless, the gallant pack never gave up trying. It was bad handling errors that led Cardiff to fail to take their chances.

The All Blacks, after surviving a long period of pressure, then came back again to execute one of their favourite scoring ploys, achieving their best try of the match. Good possession was won from a lineout (something not often achieved), and B. G. Williams moved in from the left wing to make the extra man. The ball moved right, quickly, to Wilson, who got between the full-back and the touch-line (when he should have been tackled), and dived over in the right corner. Currie again failed with the kick.

At 17–3, it was only consolation when Carl Smith, the Cardiff flanker, scored at the posts. Cardiff kicked deep, and at the lineout the All Blacks threw a long one. Centre Jaffray, who gathered, was trapped immediately in a maul, and Smith ripped it away to gallop to the open side and crash over between the posts. Incredibly, such a good place kicker as Gareth Davies only hit the post. It was 17–7 at the end.

The All Blacks deserved their victory; they were more efficient, defended strongly, and took their chances. Cardiff won enough ball to have scored many more points; they did especially well at the lineout. Their backs were poor; chances were missed in attack, and points conceded in defence, revealing a lack of cohesion and urgency that could well have resulted from continual changing of the side during the weeks of preparation.

Some of the younger All Blacks proved their worth in this match. There were good displays by Wilson, Dunn and Loveridge

140

(although Dunn was to experience harder times in later matches). Terry McLean was critical of the failure of his country at the lineout, which emphasized the weakness observed at Cambridge; it was to be revealed yet again in various matches on the tour.

This was the 100th match played by B. G. Williams in an All Blacks jersey. He was presented with a souvenir to commemorate the occasion by the Cardiff Club, and was honoured by leading the team on to the field. At the after-match function, attended by the N Z High Commissioner and other dignitaries, he was presented with another souvenir from his colleagues. It was made a day to remember for one who has served his country well. Joy is often followed by disappointment, however, and a short while later Williams was dropped for the first time in his career as a Test player, finding Brian Ford preferred to himself for the match against Ireland! Fame may be a spur, but once achieved it is a tantalizing mistress!

Summary: Match 2

Saturday 21 October   Cardiff Arms Park
Cardiff 7 points (1 try, 1 dropped goal)
All Blacks 17 points (3 tries, 1 penalty, 1 conversion)

TEAMS
Cardiff: P. Rees; D. Thomas, P. Daniels, M. Murphy, C. Camilleri; W. G. Davies, T. D. Holmes; B. G. Nelmes (capt.), M. Watkins, F. M. D. Knill, H. de Goede, R. Norster, R. Dudley-Jones, C. Smith, J. P. Scott
All Blacks: C. J. Currie; S. S. Wilson, W. M. Osborne, J. L. Jaffray, B. G. Williams; E. Dunn, D. S. Loveridge; B. R. Johnstone, A. G. Dalton, G. A. Knight, A. M. Haden, F. J. Oliver, L. W. Rutledge, G. N. K. Mourie (capt.), G. A. Seear

REFEREE: R. Quittenton (England)

SCORERS
Cardiff: Smith, 1 try; Davies, 1 dropped goal
All Blacks: S. S. Wilson, 2 tries; W. M. Osborne, 1 try; C. J. Currie, 1 penalty, 1 conversion

Match 3: v. West Wales

The success against Cardiff, before 40,000 spectators, cheered the tourists for their next match, one against a side which appeared, on paper, a powerful West Wales combination (including eleven Welsh international players and one Lion – of the internationals six were Lions) led by Derek Quinnell, a most experienced number eight from Llanelli. All the players had been drawn from the four big clubs in the West, Aberavon, Llanelli, Neath and Swansea. The tourists were not unwise to regard it as almost a sixth Test match!

Swansea provided a warm welcome for the tourists, who responded readily, accepting as many invitations as possible from local government chairmen, and small rugby clubs. This may be one of the chores of a long tour but the All Blacks made light work of it at this stage, in a happy and unassuming manner so vastly different from the 'sourpuss' attitude of 1972. No folk more than the Welsh (for all their apparent partisanship) are better able to appreciate this happy socializing. The way was led by the effervescent Russell Thomas and the more retiring Jack Gleeson.

At this early stage of the tour, the All Blacks were troubled by two things; injuries to their lock forwards, and an outbreak of herpes, a nasty skin rash. Several of the prop forwards were affected but the best of them, Gary Knight, was the worst case, eventually forced to enter hospital whilst the party was in Dublin. At the time it was believed it may have been caught at Cambridge. The worry was that it would spread through the team. The WRU honorary surgeon, Gordon Rowley, dealt with it first, and later his colleague in Ireland, Bob O'Connell. It is unpleasant and irritating – in former times it was called 'scrum pox', as suffered by front-row men.

For the match itself, conditions were perfect. A mid-week crowd of 40,000 recalled the golden days of Swansea rugby when international matches were held at St Helen's (although had it rained it would have been a different story; unpleasant for the majority of spectators!). The ground looked splendid, and Groundsman George Clement, complete with pipe but minus his daily glass of Guinness, had worked hard with his staff to make the occasion a great one, helping to justify to the full the award once again of a big match to St Helen's.

The first twenty-five minutes of play were hard, as the All Blacks, employing forwards and backs in unison, probed deeply into the defences of the West. Violence erupted after ten minutes: there was a punch-up that had to be quelled by referee Alan Welsby. Play then remained hard for the rest of the match, but without anything over-vigorous. Referee Welsby was particularly hard on the West pack, especially in his interpretation of the pile-up law; the crowd as a whole were unhappy about the New Zealand method of rucking, however legal. They saw it as I do, as something that the game can do without. However unintentionally, players on the ground can be hurt, often badly. It is little use suggesting that players have no right to be on the ground!

New Zealand took the lead after twenty-five minutes, when Donaldson shot away smartly to the blind side, and fed Wilson on the right wing, who left a couple of defenders easily before reaching the line, feeding Seear as he was tackled. Seear was grounded, but New Zealand won the ruck speedily, and prop Gary Knight gathered and dived over the West line for an unconverted try.

West Wales rallied and hammered away at the All Blacks line but fortune did not favour the brave: Quinnell actually lost his grip on the ball as he was diving to score!

Then there followed several hard tackles at the other end of the field. J. J. Williams was left prostrate with a deep gash in his left thigh, and was carried from the field by stretcher, with someone staunching a wound that required a large number of stitches. Mr Gordon Rowley, honorary surgeon to the WRU commented, 'Such a deep wound could not have been caused by a normal stud.' Later, he prepared a report for the four Home Unions.

David Nicholas replaced Williams. He started well, but soon suffered a broken nose to add to the West's tale of woe. Even so, he did not leave the field.

In first-half injury time, Bryan Williams landed a splendid 58-yard penalty. The All Blacks led 7–0 at the interval.

When Trevor Evans, the West flanker, was forced to leave the field with a knee injury, he was replaced by Richard Moriarty. He in turn suffered a similar fate to Williams; he too was prostrate on the ground, knocked out in boxing-ring fashion. There were

143

no more replacements available. Mr Rowley examined Moriarty. Moriarty recovered amazingly quickly, and took the field again. Mr Rowley reported: 'I asked him his address and telephone number, and he replied correctly, so back on he went. Obviously, had he been a boxer he would have lost the fight!'

The West got an early second-half try to raise the hopes of their followers. Outside half Richards kicked deftly to the left corner to turn the All Blacks defence; that always creates a little panic among them. McKechnie got to it, but mis-kicked, and Roy Bergiers was able to charge down, gather and dive over for a try. Blyth failed to convert, so it was 7–4. The West had something to build on, but the All Blacks rapidly came back, gaining a penalty goal with a good kick from 25 yards by McKechnie, which atoned for his previous error.

Nevertheless, the West kept at it, and Blyth landed a 35-yard penalty to make it 10–7. This was really the last time the West were in contention, however; they then allowed the match to slip from them. Richards dropped out poorly, and Donaldson gathered to send Seear galloping away to the right. He handed on to Wilson and the West appeared to check, expecting the whistle to blow, and so Wilson began a 'charmed' run that should have been stopped to the line for a try. He got to the posts and McKechnie easily converted. This was the decisive score; the match was virtually over. McKechnie kicked another penalty goal and Bryan Williams came inside from the blind side wing to help create the overlap for Wilson to achieve his second try. The final score of 23–7 left no doubt as to which was the better side.

The interpretation of the new pile-up law, enforced with some severity by Referee Alan Welsby, indicated quite clearly that it had caused a minor revolution in British forward play, one not for the better. It merely played into the hands of the hard-rucking New Zealand forwards.

Summary: Match 3

Wednesday 25 October   St Helen's, Swansea

West Wales 7 points (1 try, 1 penalty)
All Blacks 23 points (3 tries, 3 penalties, 1 conversion)

West Wales: R. Blyth (Swansea); E. Rees (Neath), R. T. E.
Bergiers, R. W. R. Gravell, J. J. Williams (Llanelli), (sub:
D. Nicholas (Llanelli)), D. Richards (Swansea), C. Shell; J.
Richardson (Aberavon), J. Herdman, P. Llewellyn, G. A. D.
Wheel (Swansea), A. J. Martin (Aberavon), T. P. Evans (sub: R.
Moriarty (Swansea)), G. Roberts (Swansea), D. O. Quinnell
(Llanelli) (capt.)

All Blacks: B. J. McKechnie; S. S. Wilson, N. M. Taylor,
W. M. Osborne, B. G. Williams; O. D. Bruce, M. W.
Donaldson; B. R. Johnstone, J. E. Black, G. A. Knight, J. K.
Fleming, A. M. Haden, G. N. K. Mourie (capt.), W. G.
Graham, G. A. Seear (sub: L. Rutledge)

REFEREE: A. Welsby (England)

SCORERS
West Wales: Bergiers, 1 try; Blyth, 1 penalty
All Blacks: Wilson, 2 tries; Knight, 1 try; Williams, 1 penalty;
McKechnie, 2 penalties, 1 conversion

The pile-up interpretation problem was to be highlighted in
match after match; one can only say that most British referees
appeared to take unusual pleasure in enforcing the law harshly.
(The words of Des O'Brien came to mind, 'The referees are
watching one side more than the other.' The side or sides in
question were the opponents of the All Blacks, a fact even more in
evidence in the next match when a Welsh referee, Clive Norling,
had charge of the London Counties game at Twickenham. He
did not please some commentators or players and, if unintentionally, appeared to be all too lax in dealing with All Blacks infringements.)

Having won two important matches in Wales, the tourists returned to London in good heart. They were happy with their
successful start. Although during the tour they rarely made any
comment beyond the normal platitudes (even after the strange
happenings in the Welsh test) they did say after their Twickenham
victory, 'We've had no problems with the refereeing.' True. It
was the opposition who had the problems!

145

Match 4: v. London Counties

There was, of course, little chance of London Counties winning. They were a scratch side in every sense of the word, never having played together and having engaged in only a few training sessions. The critics forecast a thirty-point victory for the tourists; in fact the tourists achieved more than thirty points in total, and a winning margin of twenty-five: 37–12. This was satisfactory for them, but an unhappy day for English rugby, giving fresh power to the argument that divisional sides in England were easy to overcome by any established touring team. *The Observer* headed its report, 'The Retreat from London'; *The Sunday Times* suggested, 'The Tourists don't need Gifts'; the *Western Mail* said, 'Counties no Test for All Blacks.'

It is fair to say that the match proved to be an additional 'easy one' for the tourists. Such an event is in striking contrast to the experiences of British Lions sides in the Southern Hemisphere.

This victory brought the All Blacks' record to four wins in four matches, with 109 points including sixteen tries. In this match they scored six tries, with Currie making five conversions and kicking a penalty goal. The try scorers were Kururangi (2), Robertson, Dunn, Oliver (captain for the day), and Ford. The Counties replied with four penalty goals, three kicked by full-back Billy Bushell, who then suffered a badly cut head, and one from Williamson who replaced him. Bushell had to have fourteen stitches in a gashed ear. It was a case of the pounding hooves again!

Officials simply said after the match, 'Thank you, All Blacks, for reminding us of quick ball and pressure.' So it will go on, tour after tour; it is always a case of being kind to the visitors. The All Blacks were in for a surprise, however – a very big one, in a few days time in Ireland.

Summary: Match 4

Saturday 28 October   Twickenham
London Counties 12 points (4 penalties)
All Blacks 37 points (6 tries, 1 penalty, 5 conversions)

TEAMS
London Counties: K. M. Bushell (Harlequins) (sub: I. D.

Williamson (Blackheath)); R. O. Demming (Bedford), K. Hughes (London Welsh), P. J. Warfield (Rosslyn Park), D. M. Wyatt (Bath); R. Wilson, A. J. M. Lawson (London Scottish); T. C. Claxton (Harlequins), P. d'A. Keith-Roach (Rosslyn Park) (capt.), A. J. Cutter (Harlequins), M. J. Colclough (Angouleme), C. W. Ralston (Richmond), S. R. G. Pratt (London Scottish), R. J. Mordell (Rosslyn Park), A. C. Alexander (Harlequins)
All Blacks: C. J. Currie; R. R. Kururangi, B. J. Robertson, N. M. Taylor, B. R. Ford; E. Dunn, D. R. Loveridge; J. C. Ashworth, A. G. Dalton, W. K. Bush, A. M. Haden, F. J. Oliver (capt.), L. M. Rutledge, B. G. Ashworth, J. K. Fleming

REFEREE: C. Norling (Wales)

SCORERS
London Counties: Bushell, 3 penalties; Williamson, 1 penalty
All Blacks: Kururangi, 2 tries; Robertson, 1 try; Dunn, 1 try; Oliver, 1 try; Ford, 1 try; Currie, 1 penalty, 5 conversions

Irish selection
The Irish Selectors announced their team to meet the tourists soon after the All Blacks had reached Limerick on the Sunday. There was one major surprise in the choice of new cap, Colin Petterson of Instonians, at scrum-half, in preference to the captain of the previous season, John Moloney. One Irish critic believed the Selectors' choice to be 'illogical and unjust'. Otherwise, the side was much as anticipated, with Mike Gibson, at 36 years of age, in the centre (a choice which the same critic believed to be 'a mistake that could prove costly'). Some Irishmen believed that Gibson, once an outstanding player, was being chosen on reputation as a centre, when he would have been more comfortable on the wing. Heroes go on for ever in Irish rugby: to most Irishmen, Gibson is a hero like McBride, Kiernan and others. In fact this was to be his last (66th) match for Ireland. The new captain, Shay Deering of St Mary's College, said he was astounded when he heard that he had been given the leadership:

'It is a great honour, and the nicest thing that has happened to me in my career.' (His father, Seamus, played for Ireland against Jack Manchester's Men in 1935, and Shay Became the third successive Irish captain from St Mary's College.)

Match 5: v. Munster

Before the first international at Lansdowne Road, Dublin on the Saturday, there was to be played one of *the* matches of the tour, that against Munster at Limerick. It was not expected that here – at a place traditionally respected for the warm welcome afforded to touring teams both on and off the field – Munster would provide a major upset. If there be fire in the heart of Irish rugby, it is in Limerick; mighty are the men who have played there in the scarlet jerseys. But well as they have done against touring teams, not even the proudest boasted too freely that Munster would win. They would suggest that it would be a very hard match; Donal Canniffe, a big strong scrum-half, and his men would give the tourists a match to remember. These words were to prove right in an unexpected sense at a crowded Thomond Park on 31 October.

Munster won 12–0, recording the first defeat ever suffered by New Zealand on Irish soil in all the 24 matches in the history of the two sides' meeting. Of the previous 23, in 73 years of challenge, 19 had been won by the All Blacks, and four drawn. (In 1972 Tom Kiernan's Munster men had shared a draw at 3–3 at Limerick; a few days later, Ireland shared a draw at Dublin under Kiernan's leadership). It was indeed, a glorious achievement and a great day. It was Ireland's 1905.

Even the serious and dedicated Edmund Van Esbeck in *The Irish Times* allowed himself a little looser vein, writing, 'All those privileged to have seen it will talk with pride of this victory to the end of their days.' How true! Irishmen will claim 'We were there', as did Welshmen after the Welsh victory over New Zealand of 1905 at Cardiff. (The 40,000 present at the Arms Park then became ten times that number with the passing of time. Such is the happy folklore of rugby football!)

There were 12,000 spectators at Thomond Park.

Coach Tom Kiernan joined the exuberant celebration, but made the following coherent and accurate observation amidst the wildness of the moment: 'Our discipline and control combined

148

wonderfully with our traditional aggression. Against this, New Zealand's play deteriorated to frustration. This game will really matter in Irish rugby history.'

New Zealand Manager Russell Thomas answered: 'It was a marvellous effort by Munster – a great thing for Irish rugby. We made too many mistakes, as we have done even in our first four victories. This time we paid for them, but we will learn much from today.' The Captain, Graham Mourie, explained, 'Munster played the type of game we tried to play – pressure and cutting down on mistakes – but they played it better.'

It was both a joyous and desperately sad moment for the successful captain, Donal Canniffe; shortly after the match he was informed that his father had died listening to the radio commentary. Naturally, he had to leave the ground hurriedly to join his family in Cork, having to leave the scene of both celebration, and one of his own great triumphs as a player.

I enjoyed the *Guardian* headline, the crisp 'Munster pot the Blacks'; it was outside half Tony Ward who did the 'potting'. He collected eight points with three kicks, with the accuracy of snooker's Ray Reardon.

The initial lead was achieved after eleven minutes by the only try. Ward, kicking from well inside his own half, and to his left, found his kick gathered by Jimmy Bowen in full stride. This was clever enough, but then this left wing got past Wilson and McKechnie and, after a fifty-yard gallop that brought the crowd to its feet, he sent inside to the supporting flanker, Christy Cantillon. Cantillon pounded the last fifteen yards to the line. The try was at the posts and Ward kicked the conversion.

Some seven minutes later, Munster went further ahead. McKechnie, who had missed Bowen (a lapse that was to cost him his Test place against Ireland) failed to gather a penalty attempt from Ward that fell short. The knock-on brought a scrum, immediately in front of the posts. The powerful Munster forwards returned the ball to big Donal Canniffe, who quickly fed Ward, who in turn dropped a goal. The move proved the value of a quick heel in such a position, over the holding of the ball in the back row.

The All Blacks, trailing 9–0 at the interval, were expected to make a special effort in the second half. They did for a while, putting Munster under the severest of pressure. But the Irishmen did not waver in their defence, as both coverers and tacklers. When the All Blacks conceded another score it was all over: Wilson knocked-on a kick behind his own goal line (probably through nerves), and a five-yard scrum followed. Ward sent his second kick sailing between the posts, to make it 12–0.

Ward was the individual hero for Munster, but all the side earned glory. Referee Corris Thomas ensured that the match was sporting and clean. He stood no nonsense and made known what he required, early on. A couple of Munster forwards nodded to each other, as if to say, 'He knows all the tricks; there'll be no trouble today. We can get on with the winning!'

Terry McLean was sincere in his cable to New Zealand; 'Although the resounding defeat was due to three inexcusable blunders, the All Blacks never really looked like scoring. They displayed so much tactical ineptitude that the probability of further defeats must be faced. The errors were all in the back line.' Yet he ended his cable by looking ahead and stating, 'Hard days await, but the 1978 All Blacks, who have set the fine standards in the first third of the tour, still have the chance by winning the big five matches to return to the strains of "see the conquering heroes come".'

The next day, surprisingly, Jack Gleeson complained about the kamikaze tackling of the Munster players, saying his men could not play fifteen-man rugby against such defenders. Come on Jack! What did you really expect? It was high time for someone to tackle sternly following the poor defence of opponents in previous matches. Either Mr Gleeson was naive, or he believed that British rugby men were.

In New Zealand, they never let it remain easy for opponents to score. It was up to Gleeson to counter such methods of aggressive tackling. Tom Kiernan suggested that the All Blacks should have used the ball better, by making an attempt to stretch the defence, rather than set itself up for tackles. (I can recall many matches in New Zealand, against various touring teams, where the same tactics – all of them legal – were applied against visiting sides early in the tour, reducing confidence.) This first defeat, coming on the eve of the Ireland game, could have proved either a help or a hindrance; it was even suggested that the tourists had their backs to the wall.

Summary: Match 5

Tuesday 31 October   Thomond Park, Limerick
Munster 12 points (1 try, 2 dropped goals, 1 conversion)
All Blacks 0 points

TEAMS
Munster: L. Moloney (Garryowen); M. Finn (UCC), S.
Dennison (Garryowen), G. Barrett, J. Bowen (Cork Const.);
A. J. P. Ward (St Mary's Coll.), D. Canniffe (Lansdowne)
(capt.); G. McLoughlin (Shannon), P. Whelan (Garryowen),
L. White (London Irish), M. Keane (Lansdowne), B. Foley
(Shannon), C. Cantillon (Cork Const.), C. Tucker (Shannon),
D. Spring (Dublin University)
All Blacks: B. J. McKechnie; S. W. Wilson, B. J. Robertson
(sub: W. M. Osborne), J. L. Jaffray, B. G. Williams; E. Dunn,
M. W. Donaldson; B. R. Johnstone, J. E. Black, G. A. Knight,
A. M. Haden, F. J. Oliver, G. N. K. Mourie (capt.), W. G.
Graham, A. A. McGregor

REFEREE: Corris Thomas (Wales)

SCORERS
Munster: Cantillon, 1 try; Ward, 2 dropped goals, 1 conversion

Match 6: v. Ireland Test

The tourists desperately wanted to include prop Gary Knight in
their team, but he was ill on arrival in Dublin, and had to be
admitted to hospital with herpes. (The official number of persons
on the tour who suffered from it was never revealed.) When the
team for the Test was announced, Currie replaced McKechnie
at full-back; Robertson could not play because of a gash in his
leg that required stitching; Bryan Williams was dropped for the
first time in his career, being replaced by Brian Ford. (This
decision shocked many, in the British Isles as well as New Zealand,
although Williams was in fact to take the field as a replacement,
when Ford was injured and put out for a long time with knee
trouble.) Billy Bush got Knight's place as the tight-head prop.

    There was special interest in the match for two cousins, famous
Irish players and coaches Tom Kiernan and Noel Murphy.
Kiernan had achieved his ambition with Munster, and the stage

was set for Murphy with Ireland. The Irish naturally wanted victory more than anything, but wondered if lightning could possibly strike twice on a rugby pitch in Eire. On Saturday 4 November Dublin was alive with rugby football.

Dublin is a fine city. It is a splendid one for the visitor, and it is easy to understand why so many New Zealanders enjoy their visits to Ireland: they live in fine hotels, enjoy superb hospitality, and never find the Irish, outwardly at least, as fanatically dedicated as their Celtic cousins in Wales.

Never having lost to Ireland, the All Blacks were eager to maintain their record. The plan was to run the Irish about the field, attempting to keep the ball away from Ward and thus keep him under control. Much depended upon the All Blacks' loose forwards in attack and defence, plus the kicking of Donaldson and Bruce. The match would be decided by which side won more of the ball and used it most wisely.

As it turned out, New Zealand won most of the ball, but did not use it too wisely. They managed to win the match only in injury time. Ireland did not play as fiercely as Munster and could not win enough ball (especially at the lineout). Although holding on for a draw, they made one slip just before the final whistle, to lose by a try and two dropped goals to two penalties. It was hard and exciting, but never a great match. The All Blacks were too intent upon not making errors, and Ireland had to live off the crumbs from the rich man's table as far as possession was concerned. The All Blacks may have been a shade fortunate to win – although certainly not to the same extent as they were against Wales seven days later!

The All Blacks had more of the play territorially. Also, for once (although he kicked two penalties) Ward was not really himself, missing one decisive penalty kick that would have put his side ahead in the second half, something that could have encouraged eventual victory. Much of the match turned on the play of 'Oscar' Haden, as successful at the lineout then, against Spring and Duggan, as he was unsuccessful a week later against Martin of Wales. Ireland were shut out of the lineout, and Ward never had the possession needed to control play.

This was a bonus for the All Blacks, and a crucial advantage. Full-back Currie, in his first Test, played with admirable skill and courage, standing up well to the periods of bombardment by high punts from Ward. Douglas Bruce, at outside half for the All Blacks, kicked well, dropping two fine goals, although he once grub-kicked to touch with players outside him and a try on. Yet if he was rather slow, it was his steadiness (compared with the uncertainty of Dunn at Limerick) that helped the All Blacks to victory. The forwards, too, were better together, and the Irish were never able to take charge, hard though they tried.

The match appeared to be heading for an inevitable draw at 6–6 (two dropped goals to two penalties) when injury time was entered. Both sides seemed prepared to settle for a share of the spoils. But there was a lineout near the Irish '25' on the left. The ball was won by the tourists, and gathered by Donaldson as he shot off toward the blindside at the front of the lineout. The first Irish forward was checked from getting at Donaldson who dashed up the touch-line, his forwards galloping with him. Scrum-half Patterson and right wing Kennedy could not stop them. The ball went inside to hooker Andy Dalton, and he got over in the corner, at the bottom of a heap of players. It was a try! Ireland were beaten. The All Blacks cliff-hanging approach had saved them yet again.

McLean suggested that the All Blacks, in the final analysis, were a little lucky to get home; the Irishmen were deeply disappointed. They had believed they had a chance and, until injury time, were deserving of a draw. British critics were quick to emphasize the fact that in their successful bid for victory, the All Blacks discarded their fluid style of earlier matches. They were nervous, less confident and unsure of themselves. In turn, Ireland were not solid enough in the set pieces in front, although lively in the loose, if never quite matching the fire and brimstone of the Munster men. Three of the Irish forwards and four of the All Blacks forwards had been in action in Limerick. That special occasion may have dampened their fire a little for the more important match to follow.

Throughout the match, the Irishmen kept after the All Blacks as best they could, sometimes achieving slight hope of victory. They also moved the ball, allowing the backs a run on occasions. The All Blacks covered well, with every man helping his colleagues, and there was always Haden at the lineout to win the ball and send it back for Donaldson or Bruce to clear. There was not a great deal of positive rugby, and much of the play was in the mould of the Triple Crown days of the late 1940s, when the idea was to play it tight and kick accurately in support of the forwards.

Each side hoped that the other would make mistakes. The Welsh team watched the BBC's video-tape of the Dublin match the next day. The All Blacks were not as menacing as some of the teams of the past, and so there was a chance for Wales, starting as rank outsiders, to succeed, even though New Zealand were bound to start as favourites.

Summary: Match 6

Saturday 4 November   Lansdowne Road, Dublin
Ireland 6 points (2 penalties)
All Blacks 10 points (1 try, 2 dropped goals)

TEAMS
Ireland: L. A. Moloney (Garryowen); T. J. Kennedy (St Mary's Coll.), A. R. McKibbin (London Irish), C. M. H. Gibson (N.I.F.C.), A. C. McLennan (Wanderers); A. J. P. Ward (St Mary's Coll.), C. S. Patterson (Instonians); P. A. Orr (Old Wesley), P. C. Whelan (Garryowen), E. M. J. Byrne (Blackrock Coll.), M. I. Keane (Lansdowne), D. I. Spring (Dublin Univ.), J. F. Slattery (Blackrock Coll.), S. M. Deering (St Mary's Coll.) (capt.), W. P. Duggan (Blackrock Coll.)
All Blacks: C. J. Currie; S. S. Wilson, N. M. Taylor, W. M. Osborne, B. R. Ford (sub: B. G. Williams); O. D. Bruce, M. W. Donaldson; B. R. Johnstone, A. G. Dalton, W. K. Bush, A. M. Haden, F. J. Oliver, L. M. Rutledge, G. N. K. Mourie (capt.), G. A. Seear

REFEREE: G. Norling (Wales)

SCORERS
Ireland: Ward, 2 penalties
All Blacks: Dalton, 1 try; Bruce, 2 dropped goals

Match 7: v. Ulster

Following the Dublin triumph, and a happy after-match party with traditionally lavish Irish hospitality, the All Blacks moved

154

north to Belfast. Some members of the party were a little worried at visiting the troubled city but, as George Morgan travelling with the team told me, 'It was amazingly quiet, and no one was disturbed. In fact, the players really enjoyed their stay in Ulster.' Rugby football is one of the few things which appears to unite the north and the south in Ireland. Players combine together for Ireland, and on tour with the British Lions, in perfect harmony: this is a tremendous confirmation that the game knows no boundaries in class, race or religion. Not even politicians can disturb its brotherly comradeship!

The match against Ulster in Belfast was played at a once-famous rugby ground, Ravenhill Park, in windswept conditions. It was the first really unpleasant weather of the tour. The 'dirt trackers' (the players not selected for the day) were called in for duty so as to make sure in the minds of the selectors that they were not being neglected. Ulster were in no way as strong as yesteryear, understandably in view of the decade of trouble in the City. Yet the spirit was willing, and the side contained several internationals. It did not have the fire and purpose of the Munster side, however.

The All Blacks forwards were never really successful at the lineout, but in every other phase they did well, and their driving was particularly effective. It enabled them to pin down Ulster for long periods and provide their backs with good possession. Unfortunately, the backs were poor and made little use of this possession. It was not a happy day for back play. Eddie Dunn fell away still further, failing to live up to the early good impression created in the more favourable conditions against Cardiff. He and Jaffray believed that kicking was better than running; the All Blacks machine consequently never really appeared to move into top gear.

This was symptomatic of the tour. One section of the side always played well, but the team rarely played well as a whole. Even if they were just good enough, generally, to beat most sides, it was often without full satisfaction to themselves, to their own management, or to critics, or to those who paid good money to watch them. It is equally true that sides opposing them often played badly. There were several matches during the tour that were dull and boring. The lack of true enterprise in the side hung like a cloud over the tour. It was difficult to pinpoint it when a side

155

continued to win its matches, but it was as if the approach was simply 'we have to win each match, even though we may not enjoy it to the full'. Winning is vital on tour – let no one argue otherwise – but the fulfilment of the game is to play at one's best and give full expression to one's ability. Harping back to the past is often cruel, but better New Zealand sides have produced marginally poorer records but entertained more. In the rest of the tour, British sides were often to play poorly against them. Even referees, sometimes, appeared to be merely going through the motions.

Ulster started well enough, but faded, even failing with reasonable place kicks. Bryan Williams, eager to prove himself after being dropped against Ireland, landed a 50-yard penalty to launch the scoring for New Zealand, and then completed a good break by acting captain Robertson to score a try, giving an interval lead of 7–0. As they had achieved this against the wind, there was really no hope for Ulster in the second half. The All Blacks went on to add another 16 points to their total, while Ulster could achieve no more than a penalty goal. John Black and Kururangi got further tries, one of which Brian McKechnie converted. McKechnie also kicked two penalties, the second in injury time. Outside half Adrian Goodrich kicked Ulster's penalty.

The final score, then, was 23–3. It was not as convincing a win as the All Blacks needed to return to Wales with confidence for the international match at Cardiff Arms Park. No player in the Ulster match had really excelled, although it was obvious that Williams could not be ignored a second time. (As Brian Ford had suffered a leg injury, Williams was certain to be chosen.) Several players ruled themselves out of Test match consideration, and increased the decisive gap between the Wednesday and Saturday players. However, as Mark Donaldson had entered Belfast on crutches with an injured ankle, the chance for Dave Loveridge to win a cap was more real than the management led us to believe. Loveridge did play against Wales and he did exceedingly well, but it was Donaldson who was named in the team when it was first announced.

The England team (*above*) line up before the start of the match against Argentina at Twickenham. From r. to l.: W. B. Beaumont (capt.), M. J. Colclough, J. P. Scott, P. J. Wheeler, C. J. Gifford, P. J. Dixon, P. J. Warfield, P. J. Squires, M. Rafter, M. A. Slemen, B. G. Nelmes, F. E. Cotton, J. P. Horton, P. W. Dodge, K. M. Bushell.

The England–Argentine match (*below*): the two tall Argentinian locks, R. Passaglia and I. Iachetti out-jump England at a lineout. The match was drawn 13–13.

Wales 'B' v. Argentina (*left*), Stradey Park, Llanelli: the Wales 'B' scrum-half, Gerald Williams, sends out a long pass from a lineout in this floodlit match. Argentina won, 17–14.

The All Black wing Stuart Wilson (*below left*) races for the line against Cardiff, having intercepted a pass before making a 65-yard gallop to the vital try. The All Blacks won 17–7.

In this All Black–Cardiff match (*right*), All Black Wing Bryan Williams made his one-hundredth appearance for his country. Here, he leads the team out, followed by the team's captain Graham Mourie.

As always before tour matches, the All Blacks (*below*) danced the traditional Maori *Haka* at the Arms Park before the match. This leap completes it.

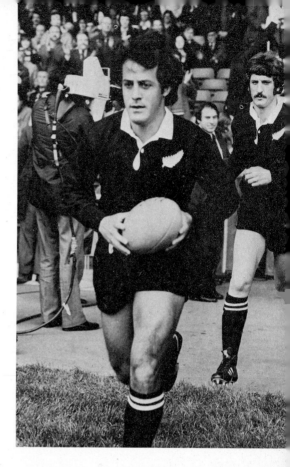

Referee Roger Quittenton of England, the man who had to make the decision about the incident shown in the following sequence: the lineout in the Wales—New Zealand match.

The ball has just been thrown in by Wales and Haden (centre of line) is already leaving it. Oliver in front is turning towards own goal line.

The ball has still not arrived or been touched by a player. Haden (centre) is now well out of the line; Oliver is facing his own goal line, with arms outstretched ready to leave.

Haden has started to fall clear and Oliver is on his way from the lineout.

Haden is now down, and Oliver on his way towards his goal line.

Referee Quittenton awards the controversial penalty. Haden is out of sight, Oliver on the ground (*centre*). The Welsh forwards, Quinnell and Squire, point to the out-of-sight Haden.

The victorious Munster team before the game at Limerick (*above*). From l. to r., standing: Sean Gavin (President, Munster Branch, IRFU), touch-judge Johnny Cole, Ginger McLoughlin, Les White, Moss Keane, Donal Spring, Colm Tucker, Pat Whelan, Brendan Foley, referee Corris Thomas, touch-judge Martin Walsh. Sitting: Tony Ward, Christy Cantillon, Mossie Finn, Seamus Dennison, Donal Canniffe, Greg Barrett, Jimmy Bowen, Larry Maloney.

John Robbie, Cambridge captain and Irish international, kicks away in the Varsity Match.

Further proof that violence is all too common in modern rugby (*above*). J. P. R. Williams, Bridgend captain, leaves the field after being violently stamped on. The blood is streaming from his face. After fifteen minutes and eight stiches, he returned to play.

C. M. H. 'Mike' Gibson (*right*) played his last international for Ireland against the All Blacks at Dublin in November.

David Leslie (Scotland) (*above*) gets the ball away before Mark Donaldson (NZ) or Leicester Rutledge (rear) can intervene

NZ *v.* Barbarians (*below*). Phil Bennett makes a break.

Summary: Match 7

Tuesday 7 November   Ravenhill Park. Belfast
Ulster 3 points (1 penalty)
All Blacks 23 points (3 tries, 3 penalties, 1 conversion)

TEAMS
Ulster: R. Elliott (Bangor); J. Myles (Malone), C. M. H.
Gibson (NIFC), A. Irwin (Queens), C. Gardiner (Queens);
A. Goodrich (Ballymena), C. Patterson (Instonians) (sub:
R. Stewart (Malone)); A. Henry (Malone), G. G. Berenger
(London Irish), B. O'Kane (Ballymena), W. Anderson
(Dungannon), D. Dalton (Malone), S. A. McKinney (Dungan-
non) (capt.), H. Steele (Ballymena), A. McLean (Ballymena)
All Blacks: B. J. McKechnie; R. Kururangi, B. J. Robertson
(capt.), J. L. Jaffray, B. G. Williams; E. Dunn, D. S. Loveridge;
J. C. Ashworth, J. E. Black, W. K. Bush, J. K. Loveday, J. K.
Fleming, W. G. Graham, B. G. Ashworth, L. W. Rutledge

REFEREE: P. E. Hughes (England)

SCORERS
Ulster: Goodrich, 1 penalty
All Blacks: Williams, 1 try, 1 penalty; McKechnie, 2 penalties,
  1 conversion; Black, 1 try; Kururangi, 1 try

When the Irish team left Ireland for Porthcawl, it was announced
that prop Gary Knight would be released from a Dublin hospital
to join at Porthcawl. The management were now fully aware of
the disturbing effect of herpes within the side, but were reluctant to
discuss it. There were more players affected at this stage of the
tour than they cared to admit. In accordance with Home Union
policy, the Irish Union's medical officer sent a full report to the
Welsh Union's officer, this being necessary in view of the chances
of it being communicated to opponents. Knight was told that he
would have to miss the Welsh match, much as he wanted to play
and the management to play him.

A reception was held after the final work-out of the Welsh XV
arranged by the Welsh Rugby Writers' Association with the help
of the South Wales Police Club at Bridgend. For the first time in
many a year the Welsh XV did not include such brilliant players

F

as Gareth Edwards, Phil Bennett, Gerald Davies and Terry Cobner. Filling the vacancies were three young men already capped, and a new player, the 27-year-old flanker Paul Ringer from Ebbw Vale, who had won his spurs a few weeks previously in a 'B' international against the Argentine, at Llanelli. Senior cap and battling full-back, J. P. R. Williams, who had played many times against New Zealand and toured there in 1971 with the Lions, took over the captaincy from Bennett. Edwards was by this time a BBC commentator and Sunday-paper columnist. Gerald Davies had joined him with occasional articles in the *Guardian*. Terry Cobner joined John Dawes as assistant coach with special responsibility for the forwards.

Match 8: Test v. Wales

Wales took the field with a new-look side including the Cardiff halves Terry Holmes and Gareth Davies. The tourists were slight favourites. But the Welsh team spirit was as good as ever and they began as if they would win comfortably; the forwards made the best start for many a season, carrying the play strongly to the opposition. They put the All Blacks under pressure. Referee Quittenton of England had to admonish a couple of All Blacks for being 'carried away'. One forward, Frank Oliver, struck Ringer a blow on the chin while the Welshman was on the ground; he was fortunate indeed not to be sent off!

The capacity crowd of 45,000 were in great voice. After the first twenty minutes of play Wales actually led by nine points to nil, something totally unexpected. They had four kicks at penalty goal during the period; Gareth Davies landed two and Steve Fenwick one. However, New Zealand hit back with the only try of the match, when Osborne kicked one to the right corner after the ball had been won on the left, inside the Welsh '25'. The Welsh defence had been falsely committed, and Stuart Wilson was able to chase ahead of the covering Gareth Davies, winning the race to the line. Brian McKechnie could not convert, however.

Clive Currie, who started the match at full-back, was injured in a tackle after ten minutes of play, and forced to retire with a jaw injury that was to keep him out for the remainder of the tour. Currie was replaced by McKechnie, a much more reliable place

158

kicker. His taking the field, as a replacement, was eventually to decide the match in favour of New Zealand.

Gareth Davies then kicked his third penalty, the fourth for Wales, making it 12–4. In first-half injury time, McKechnie kicked the first of his three decisive penalties to make the interval score 12–7 in favour of Wales. This was not as good a lead as the early minutes had suggested was possible. It was not enough to win them the match. But at this stage, hopes were high. Thirteen minutes into the second half, Wales had a kick at penalty goal. It was from 40 yards, and one would have thought it more suitable for Fenwick than Davies, but the latter took the kick, and sent the ball just wide. Had Fenwick tried and kicked successfully it would have settled the match.

Three minutes later, McKechnie landed a 38-yard goal for New Zealand, to make it 12–10 and give his side a fine chance of retrieving the match. Immediately afterwards, Wales missed a rare chance of scoring a try when Terry Holmes made a splendid break of fifty yards downfield and sent a long pass to his right. J. J. Williams tried to gather but had to wait for a bounce and, in that time, the All Blacks' cover defence was able to get back to stop him. Wales still tried hard but New Zealand were encouraged to hold on. Then, in the fortieth minute, the controversial incident occurred that was to highlight the New Zealand approach and leave an unhappy taste in the mouth.

There was a lineout near the Welsh '25' on the South side. Referee Quittenton asked for it to be reformed. A bit of a kerfuffle took place, and Quittenton awarded a penalty to New Zealand. Although one could not see clearly what happened, it was obviously the death-knell for Wales. One member of the Press box, Clem Thomas, felt that someone had 'taken a dive' on the All Blacks side. He discussed it with Barry John sitting near him, and mentioned it in his Sunday copy for *The Observer*, after checking with the BBC commentary staff, who also believed that all was not right.

Brian McKechnie calmly kicked a goal. It was 13–12 to New Zealand. Yet again, they had escaped from defeat, but few realized at that moment what had really happened. The *Sunday Express* carried the following comment: 'Bitter Welsh players said that Andy Haden had "taken a dive" when he went spilling out of the lineout. Referee Roger Quittenton said, "There is no secret about it. A Welsh player climbed up on the inside shoulder. That is why I gave a penalty." Quittenton refused to identify the forward who gave it away. Welsh lock Allan Martin said angrily, "Haden went for a penalty and got it. No one touched him. You don't find a 17-stone man catapulting out of the lineout like that." Geoff Wheel backed up Martin by saying, "Haden took a dive." Haden's team mates refused to allow him to answer.'

At the official after-match dinner, three Welsh forwards approached me and suggested I watched the tele-recording of the match, and especially the fatal lineout. They said, 'We do not wish to put words into your mouth, and would rather you judge for yourself, but we feel the All Blacks took a dive.'

New Zealanders, from Manager Russell Thomas down, admitted they were fortunate. They had wanted to win this match more than any other of the tour. Although they would only say, 'We accept the referee's decision', I felt they were rather more subdued than one might have expected had it been a clear-cut win.

Sunday's Press gave the match a good working-over. Gareth Edwards had been in the South stand, and wrote in the *News of the World*: 'The match-winning penalty goal by McKechnie seemed to me a dubious decision. . . . It looked as if the All Blacks had said to themselves that the only way they were going to snatch victory was to get a penalty by some means or other. They succeeded; more's the pity, for this was an international Wales deserved to win.'

When asked about the rough play, Manager Thomas commented: 'Some of the incidents were a bit disappointing. It appeared the tension in front of a vast crowd affected some players. I think some of the play was indiscriminate and it does not do the game any good.' Captain Graham Mourie commented, 'The Welsh got a lot of ball, but could not use it as constructively as they wanted. We felt we could win at any stage; we were playing well enough behind the scrum.' But New Zealand were not winning until that vital lineout.

The BBC, on the Sunday afternoon, were able to reveal that Haden had taken a dive. Four critics sat in the BBC studios at Cardiff and watched the replay of the lineout half a dozen times and then commented on it. Clem Thomas, one of the four, had no hesitation in calling the action a dive. He accused the All Blacks of 'cheating'. He was in no doubt.

When I watched the replay, I came to the conclusion that not only did Haden take a dive with no one near him, but Frank Oliver ran out of the lineout with arms outstretched: he had leaned into Wheel at the front of the line, and had made no attempt to jump for the ball. Haden fell out of the line, the ball never travelling far enough down the line to reach him. If they wanted to win, why did both these lineout experts not try to jump for possession?

Once the BBC programme ended, every pressman was after the story. The main New Zealand Press party had reached Bristol by this time, however, and only NZ television commentator Kevin Quinn was left behind to share in the BBC programme, together with that splendid former All Black prop 'Snowy' White. Naturally, they denied any suggestion of 'cheating', but the die was cast. John Humphries, the eager deputy editor of the *Western Mail*, obtained permission to use a selection of sequence pictures from the BBC tele-recording, which appear in this book (between pages 156 and 157), and he arranged interviews with Clem Thomas, Geoff Wheel and the All Blacks manager, for a page one splash. When interviewed, Mr Thomas said Haden was not available for interview as he was ill in bed. He then stood beside the reporter Gail Foley while she telephoned her piece back to Cardiff, saying that he did not wish to become involved in a slanging match. The referee made the decisions on the field; he had also made decisions, which they accepted as justified, against New Zealand. 'I am certain that the Welsh people will accept the decisions given on the field. We were satisfied with the referee.'

Mr Thomas could hardly say otherwise.

Under no circumstances can any blame be attached to himself, or to Coach Jack Gleeson for the incident: it would appear to be a ruse employed after three forwards, Haden, Oliver and Billy Bush, had got together on approaching the lineout.

Monday's Press was really controversial. Barry John's report of the match in the *Daily Express* was headed, 'Yes, I call it a dive', and Gren, in the *South Wales Echo* on the eve of the Miss World 1978 competition, drew Miss New Zealand falling out of line.

The controversy produced the largest number of readers letters to the *Western Mail* on any one sporting topic in my long association with the paper. They came from all over the British Isles.

Despite having lost through the unsatisfactory ending, the Welsh selectors were disappointed. Although delighted with their side rising to the occasion they knew that the match could have been won, easily, had Wales taken all their chances.

The Welsh forwards were in splendid form; it is no criticism of the two young halves, both playing for the first time before the knowledgeable but emotional Cardiff crowd, to suggest that had Edwards and Bennett been at half-back instead of in the stand, New Zealand would never have caught up with Wales, even with the employment of distasteful lineout ruses. The Welsh three-quarters did not play as well as they could have done as a unit, although Steve Fenwick had a splendid match, and there were times when J. P. R. Williams found life a shade difficult.

The All Blacks were shaken and mightily relieved to escape. Their forwards were held. However, the backs defended extremely well, and the major stroke of fortune (although no consolation for poor Clive Currie) was the emergence of Brian McKechnie: New Zealand would not have won without his place kicking. He has followed in the line of recent New Zealand full-backs, Don Clarke, Mick Williment, Fergie McCormick and Joe Karam, who have all helped to beat Wales with their accurate place kicking.

Perhaps, as a last comment on the match, I should emphasize my concern that the penalty goal, despite the law changes, continues to grow in importance. Never was a year more demonstrative of the importance of penalties than 1978. In this match Wales kicked four penalty goals, and New Zealand three. Who believes now that the try remains more important? An accurate kicker is more useful than a try-scoring wing, because the kicker will now receive so many more chances. This reflects as much on the Laws as upon the contemporary approach to attacking rugby.

Summary: Match 8. Test v. Wales

Saturday 11 November   Cardiff Arms Park
Wales 12 points (4 penalties)
New Zealand 13 points (1 try, 3 penalties)

Crowd: 45,000

Wales: J. P. R. Williams (Bridgend) (capt.); J. J. Williams (Llanelli), R. W. R. Gravell (Llanelli), S. P. Fenwick (Bridgend), C. F. W. Rees (London Welsh); W. G. Davies (Cardiff), T. D. Holmes (Cardiff); A. G. Faulkner (Pontypool), R. W. Windsor (Pontypool), G. Price (Pontypool), G. A. D. Wheel (Swansea), A. J. Martin (Aberavon), P. Ringer (Ebbw Vale), D. L. Quinnell (Llanelli), J. Squire (Pontypool)
New Zealand: C. J. Currie (sub: B. J. McKechnie); S. S. Wilson, B. J. Robertson, W. M. Osborne, B. G. Williams; O. D. Bruce, D. S. Loveridge; G. A. Seear, G. N. K. Mourie (capt.), F. J. Oliver, A. M. Haden, L. M. Rutledge, W. K. Bush, A. G. Dalton, B. R. Johnstone

REFEREE: R. C. Quittenton (RFU)

SCORERS
Wales: G. Davies, 3 penalties; Fenwick, 1 penalty
New Zealand: Wilson, 1 try; McKechnie, 3 penalties

Match 9: v. South Western Counties

Rugby in England has given, and will continue to give, great pleasure to many people on and off the field. England is the last of the major countries in the game to play it for fun. Everywhere else, it is highly competitive in nature, and nowhere more so than in New Zealand. If English rugby were to become totally competitive, then England would rule the rugby world once again, as it did from the inception of the game up to World War II.

After World War II, England reluctantly refused to join in the revolution that was taking place; it preferred to play with the traditional approach. Rugby was a game to be enjoyed. Who can say Englishmen are wrong to treat it thus. The problems arise when they fail, far too often, to do themselves justice at top level. In other chapters I have referred to the rival merits of the club and county systems in the development of players for international competition. The tour's next match, that against the South Western Counties at Bristol, indicated the basic weakness in the existing system.

Combined-county sides have no real chance of attaining the standards of outstanding club sides, even though in the subsequent match the Midland Group did well, and later the Northern Group went near to triumph. The South West selected from Cornwall, Devon, Somerset and Gloucestershire; they were a scratch side in every sense, not because the players as individuals were unworthy of selection, but because of the precious few opportunities of training together and blending into a unit. They lacked cohesion. This weakness, and the bad weather, plus obvious refereeing errors, saw them defeated by 20–0. (This final score flatters the All Blacks, however.)

Referee Norman Sanson, an official of considerable experience, awarded two extremely doubtful tries to the All Blacks, including a penalty try which according to Law 12 was not really justified. The other was awarded to the All Blacks' outside half Eddie Dunn: Counties defender John Palmer believes it was not touched by a tourist before it carried over the dead-ball line.

I do not suggest that the Counties could have won; they lacked pace behind, and the forward effort faded a little in the closing stages. But they deserved a much more respectable scoreline.

The South West did not yield until 37 minutes of play had passed. A couple of penalty chances had been missed by SW fullback Peter Butler and one certain try lost; Bryan Williams then scored a good try for the All Blacks, giving a four-point interval lead. It was to be a day to remember for Williams who scored 12 of his side's points, really out of 16 rather than 20, as four were awarded by the Referee. He kicked two penalties and converted the try by Dunn in addition to scoring his own try.

The penalty try was given when the South West were seen to collapse the scrum on their own line as the ball was emerging cleanly on the All Blacks side. It was gathered and Seear, the number eight, was sent charging for the Counties line. Quite rightly, Mr Sanson had played the advantage law, but Seear was tackled and held up on the line in the normal way. Sanson ran across to the posts and awarded a penalty try. Law 12 says that a referee can award a penalty try when he believes an infringement has prevented a score. If Mr Sanson believed that to be true in this case, he was leaning too heavily towards the tourists. There was no certainty they would have scored. The decision did not affect the result, but it produced a scoreline that was not in keeping with the play.

Summary: Match 9

Wednesday 15 November   Memorial Ground Bristol

South West Counties 0 points
New Zealand 20 points (3 tries, 2 penalties, 1 conversion)

TEAMS
South West Counties: P. J. Butler (Gloucester); A. J. Morley (Bristol), S. Donovan (Torquay Ath.), R. Pellow (Falmouth), R. Mogg (Gloucester); J. Palmer (Bath), P. J. Kingston (Gloucester); B. G. Nelmes (Cardiff), S. Mills (Gloucester), J. Doubleday (Bristol), B. G. Corin (St. Ives), P. Ackford (Rosslyn Park), J. A. Watkins (Gloucester), J. P. Scott (Cardiff), M. J. Rafter (Bristol) (capt.)
New Zealand: N. M. Taylor; B. G. Williams, B. J. Robertson, L. Jaffray, R. R. Kururangi (sub: S. S. Wilson); E. J. Dunn, D. S. Loveridge; J. C. Ashworth, J. E. Black, G. I. Knight, J. K. Loveday, J. K. Fleming, G. N. K. Mourie (capt.), G. E. Seear, W. G. Graham

REFEREE: N. R. Sanson (Scotland)

SCORERS
New Zealand: Dunn, 1 try; Williams, 1 try, 2 penalties, 1 conversion

Match 10: v. Midland Counties

From Bristol, the All Blacks moved on to the Midland city of Leicester to face a strong Midland Counties side, one that included several players bidding for places in the national XV due to be selected the next day. The Midlands front row, internationals Cowling and Wheeler and a 'Mighty Mouse' type of prop, tight head Willie Dickenson, promised to give 'battle' to the tourists' Test trio of Johnstone, Dalton and Knight. The All Blacks fielded a side of Test quality. In charge was a second Scottish referee bidding for an international match, Alan Hosie.

Several members of the Midlands side had played for England and lock Nigel Horton was bidding for a place in the England side after fifteen appearances since 1969. A lineout expert, he was expected to strengthen the England pack in this skill. Full-back Dusty Hare had every chance of playing at Twickenham, with both Hignell and Caplan out of the running through injury.

As expected, it proved a hard match. Once again, the All Blacks finished strongly, winning 20–15. Horton failed against Haden at the lineout, but the front row did well, and Hare kicked himself into the England side by scoring all of his side's fifteen points. At one stage the Midlands led 12–4, but they faded in the second half, when the tourists' opportunism plus the goal kicking of replacement full-back Ron Wilson enabled them to move ahead to 20–12; there was then no chance of the Midlands ever regaining the lead, although Hare kicked his fifth goal, to make it 20–15, before the end.

The match turned on a long and quick throw-in from touch by Peter Wheeler for the Midlands. It was smartly intercepted by Mark Taylor running from the centre. The doubt was whether a lineout *had* been formed; if so, was he offside, or was a lineout forming before the throw took place? Had he been declared offside, the Midlands were likely to have kicked the goal and gone back into the lead with about ten minutes of play remaining. If he was not offside, then good luck to him, but it was marginal, and fortune always seemed to be one-sided when the All Blacks played a match.

As the tour progressed, one became aware of the tourists' growing determination in defence, and their determination to prevent any team scoring a try against them. They were expert in cover defence; if their attack had equalled the skill of their defence, they could have become one of the great sides. It is true that for those who followed, match after match, there was a predictable sameness about them, but they developed into the most efficient defensive side to pounce upon opposing errors since Bill McLean's Wallabies of 1947–48.

In this match against the Midlands, the All-Black front row was in trouble, especially the tall prop Brad Johnstone against the smaller Willie Dickenson; four tight heads were won by the Midlands trio. Dickenson was not selected for England, but he won a place in the Barbarians side, staking a claim for an England place in the New Year. At full-back for the All Blacks, Ron Wilson was playing his first match a few days after his arrival as a replacement for Currie; jet-lag could well have disturbed his early kicks at goal, but he recovered to drop a goal, and kick a penalty and conversion.

Jack Gleeson, a perfectionist in some ways, was not too happy with his side. He spoke out strongly: 'The team failed to give me a fifteen-man performance I was hoping for in this match; we are still not putting our game together. The early scratchiness of the halves and the failure to release the ball quickly after winning the lineout was noticeable. I told them to stand closer together, but they turned a deaf ear and many passes were dropped.'

Mourie was as alert as ever on the flank, and John Fleming at number eight turned in a good performance. Referee Hosie had a reasonable match but the choice for the England match, as expected, was Norman Sanson.

The scorers were Dusty Hare for the Midlands with four penalties and a dropped goal, and Bryan Williams, Graham Mourie and Mark Taylor, who collected tries for the All Blacks, plus Wilson's three goals.

Something disturbed the even tenor of the Rugby Football Union's administration as John Reason leaked the England side to meet the All Blacks in *The Daily Telegraph* on the Monday morning, before the official announcement was made at 10.30; consequently the Twickenham headquarters were besieged with phone calls from the rest of the rugby writers. Furthermore, Reason was correct in his pronouncements, Barry Nelmes was moved to tight-head, for Robin Cowling to come back as loose head, and John Scott was moved up to the second row from number eight, and Roger Uttley returned. A new cap was brought into the centre, Tony Bond of Sale, a promising young player who had been challenging for some time. Dusty Hare was the full-back and Billy Beaumont retained the captaincy.

Summary: Match 10

Saturday 18 November   Leicester

Midland Counties 15 points (4 penalties, 1 dropped goal)
New Zealand 20 points (2 tries, 2 penalties, 1 conversion)

TEAMS

Midland Counties: W. H. Hare; M. J. Duggan, P. W. Dodge, B. P. Hall (Leicester), P. F. Knee (Coventry); M. J. Cooper, C. J. Gifford (Moseley); G. J. Adey (Leicester), I. R. Smith (Leicester), N. E. Horton (Toulouse), B. F. Innes, J. Shipsides (Coventry), W. Dickinson (Richmond), P. J. Wheeler (Leicester) (capt.), R. J. Cowling (Leicester)

New Zealand: B. Wilson; B. G. Williams, W. M. Osborne, N. M. Taylor, S. S. Wilson; O. D. Bruce, M. W. Donaldson; J. K. Fleming, G. N. K. Mourie (capt.), F. J. Oliver, A. M. Haden, A. A. McGregor, G. A. Knight, A. G. Dalton, B. R. Johnstone

REFEREE: A. M. Hosie (SRU)

SCORERS

Midland Counties: Hare, 4 penalties; Horton, 1 dropped goal
New Zealand: Williams, Mourie, Taylor, tries; Wilson 1 penalty, 1 dropped goal, 1 conversion

Match 11: v. Combined Services

The All Blacks left Leicester for London and their Park Lane Hotel headquarters ready to face a pleasant match at Aldershot on the Tuesday against the Combined Services.

The Combined Services did remarkably well for a scratch side in the first half. The All Blacks, possibly surprised by the enthusiasm of the opposition, failed to make an impression. They led by no more than a point at the interval, 7–6, and the Services won good possession from lineout and ruck without being able to press home their advantage. Green at outside half did not move the ball, preferring to kick. Although some of his kicks caused trouble, greater variation might have proved more beneficial. The All Blacks had become used to the fact that no one would run at them.

Fabian, a Royal Navy centre, kicked a penalty, and Green, (RAF) dropped a goal for the Services. So it was six points, against a try by Brian Ford and a penalty by Brian McKechnie,

168

before the teams changed ends. In the second half, McKechnie led a points rush: he kicked another penalty and converted four tries splendidly with wide-angled kicks, as well as scoring a try. Seear got a push-over try; then a try followed from Jaffray, and a good one from Robertson (acting captain for the day), and finally McKechnie's.

The final score was thus 34–6, a little hard on the Services, who faded only in the closing stages. Whilst scrum-half Ken Pugh was on the field, they had played well. His injury after 25 minutes was unfortunate.

The All Blacks came together in the final quarter and ran freely. It suggested that they would remain cautious in attack until it was obvious that the opposition had been fully contained and could not win. Services flanker, Williams, had an outstanding match in attack and defence. It is he and McKechnie who will be remembered from this match.

NZ Coach Jack Gleeson could not have been pleased with the indifferent play of his halves. On the wing Kururangi had another match in which his hands let him down. After this match, the All Blacks appeared to have some 24 players in contention for Test places, and 6 who were unlikely to make the grade. Eventually, the Test side almost selected itself; scrum-half Mark Donaldson and prop Gary Knight were fit, and replaced Bush and Loveridge from the Welsh match. McKechnie remained at full-back. The NZ team to meet England was announced on the next day.

Summary: Match 11

Tuesday 2 November   Aldershot
Combined Services 6 points (1 penalty, 1 dropped goal)
New Zealand 34 points (5 tries, 2 penalties, 4 conversions)

TEAMS

Combined Services: Lt P. Lea; Lt C. English (Navy), Cpl S. Jackson (Army), Lt G. Fabian (Navy), Jun-Tech. S. Rogers; Cpl A. Green, Jun-Tech. K. Pugh (RAF) (sub: Cpl G. Davies (Army)); Cpl N. Gray, Cpl R. Matthews (Army), Lt J. Ackerman (Navy), SAC J. Orwin, FO N. Gillingham (RAF); Cpl G. Williams (Army), SAC G. Still (RAF), Lt S. Hughes (RM).
All Blacks: B. J. McKechnie; R. R. Kururangi, J. L. Jaffray,

B. J. Robertson, B. R. Ford; E. Dunn, M. W. Donaldson; J. C. Ashworth, J. E. Black, W. F. Bush, J. Fleming, J. K. Loveday; B. G. Ashworth, L. M. Rutledge, G. A. Seear.

REFEREE: K. Parfitt (WRU)

SCORERS
Combined Services: Fabian, 1 penalty; Green, 1 dropped goal
All Blacks: Ford, Seear, Jaffray, Robertson, tries; McKechnie, 1 try, 2 penalties, 4 conversions

Match 12: Test v. England

As the critics of both countries forecast good and ill in turn, two players, Andy Haden the controversial lock and England hooker Peter Wheeler, fought hard to get fit for Twickenham. Both succeeded but the comments before and after the match by critics were strangely contrasted in some instances. *The Times, Daily Express* and *Daily Mail* believed England would do well, but after the match had some scathing things to say about the selectors. One selector commented: 'If England win, it is the team that does it; if England lose, of course, it is the selectors' fault. We may make mistakes on times but, we cannot play the matches for the players!' England did lose, rather miserably, 16–6. They conceded two tries for eight points, far too easily, and there was none of the fighting spirit of previous years. It was this, more than anything, that saddened the loyalists.

The ground was full, with over 70,000. Conditions were ideal. England took the lead after five minutes with a dropped goal by Hare following an indirect penalty award, and then Osborne messed up a back movement and McKechnie missed a simple penalty from in front of the posts. However, England were put under pressure, and after 17 minutes' play a lineout was staged 10 yards from the England goal line. Wheeler threw in, but England lost control of the ball and it went loose towards the England line. Oliver gathered and dived over for a try. McKechnie failed with the conversion attempt and a penalty kick shortly afterwards. England scored next, to regain the lead. After 25 minutes, Rutledge fell offside, and Hare kicked the penalty for 6–4. It was near the interval before New Zealand regained the

170

lead. Again, it was as a result of England's poor play at a lineout almost on their own goal line. Wheeler threw to the middle of the line (apparently the call was wrong, as a long throw would have been more favourable). Prop Brad Johnstone snatched the ball and crashed over for a try. This time McKechnie put over a lovely conversion from the touchline, and the interval score was 10–6.

England's play had not been particularly clever. The forwards were having a harder time than anticipated, and when they had possession, John Horton at outside half appeared intent on kicking it away. Vivian Jenkins, a shrewd but fair critic, commented to me: 'England look as though they could have played forty years each way and still not scored a try!'

The second half produced poor stuff on the part of both sides. England had chances, winning good attacking positions and then forfeiting them. New Zealand appeared content to take no risks. Hare, Young and Slemen were the best of the England backs, and Rafter the hardest-working forward. Haden won a great deal of ball for New Zealand and Johnstone, Oliver and Rutledge were foragers. The backs did comparatively little in attack although defending as well as ever.

New Zealand exerted the greater pressure. After 13 minutes McKechnie popped over a penalty off the near upright for 13–6; it was now a match out of England's reach. After 32 minutes, McKechnie kicked a good goal from 40 yards after a scrum offence. The crowd remained silent until the end and, when it came, a regular follower behind the Press box stood up and remarked to his wife, 'Was all that worth £7.50 apiece?' No, it was not.

John Read's sub-editor in the *Sunday Express* rather overdid it in calling New Zealand 'Mourie's marvels'. There were no marvels in this match. The heading over Clem Thomas's piece in *The Observer* read, 'England are easy meat'. I liked the *Sunday Times* heading (in many ways it was the story of the tour): 'Never mind the quality, the All Blacks get the result'. Monday's papers brought forth abundant criticism of the selectors; the *Daily Mirror* proclaimed: 'Loose in the head'. The *Sun* quoted England captain Billy Beaumont as saying, 'We're just not fit enough. We cannot blame our backs this time. They never really had a chance because we were absolutely outgunned up front.'

David Frost in the *Guardian* thought that the victory over England, which put the All Blacks 3–0 up with one to play, would make things hard for Scotland.

The trouble for England started in the set scrum and developed through the lineout. Young was a brave soul at scrum-half, but Horton had an indifferent match with the three-quarters left flat-footed. Slemen did noble work in defence and Hare improved after a shaky start. Overall, though, it was extremely disappointing. England were left to ponder. Little *constructive* criticism followed. It was not that the All Blacks were in any way outstanding. The All Blacks won a lot of ball, but they did not use it well. They were efficient in defence, but lacked flair and creative ability in attack. (Admittedly, this has always been their approach to Test rugby in recent years, to make no mistakes and pounce upon opposing errors. It is a method that often succeeds in winning, but is rather boring to watch.)

John Reason in *The Daily Telegraph* argued, 'The entire predictable poverty of the England pack enabled New Zealand to win despite making so many mistakes in attack. Condemned by selectors to play without a scrummage and a lineout – surely a resignation issue – England found their opponents apparently doing their best to play down to their level.' These harsh words did not please the selectors, especially after the *Telegraph*'s leak of the team!

In the *Western Mail*, I asked, 'Where has all the midfield flair gone? The match, comfortably won by New Zealand, lacked flair, imagination, creative ability and many of the joys of rugby.' I went on to suggest, 'It is now time to forget the big money involved and the mass media treatment, the intense organization and the concentration upon technique and ploys, and attempt to rediscover flair and the true charm of the game we enjoy. In criticizing this match we must criticize rugby as a whole.'

The 1978 All Blacks went on to win the Grand Slam with only one try scored against them in the four matches. Their defensive efficiency was first class; opportunism substituted for creative ability. They played, in all respects, the modern game; they concentrated on confined areas with extreme dedication: no risks, no flair; just the winning of matches.

Summary: Match 12. Test v. England

Saturday 25 November   Twickenham, London
England 6 points (1 penalty, 1 dropped goal)
New Zealand 16 points (2 tries, 2 penalties, 1 conversion)

TEAMS
England: W. H. Hare (Leicester); P. J. Squires (Harrogate), A. M. Bond (Sale), P. W. Dodge (Leicester), M. A. C. Slemen (Liverpool); J. P. Norton (Bath), M. Young (Gosforth); R. M. Uttley (Gosforth), M. Raster (Bristol), J. P. Scott (Cardiff), W. B. Beaumont (Fylde) (capt.), P. J. Dixon (Gosforth); B. G. Nelmes (Cardiff), P. J. Wheeler (Leicester), R. J. Cowling (Leicester)

New Zealand: B. J. McKechnie; S. S. Wilson, B. J. Robertson, W. M. Osborne, B. G. Williams; O. D. Bruce, M. W. Donaldson; G. A. Seear, G. N. K. Mourie (capt.), F. J. Oliver, A. M. Haden, L. M. Rutledge; G. A. Knight, A. G. Dalton, B. R. Johnstone

REFEREE: N. Sanson (Scotland)

SCORERS
England: Hare, 2 penalties
New Zealand: Oliver, Johnstone, tries; McKechnie, 1 penalty, 1 conversion

Match 13: v. Newport

After celebrating their victory, the tourists returned to Wales to start a difficult week that included two important matches, forcing them to divide their forces in the selection room. Monmouthshire had to be met at Newport on the Wednesday (29 November) and the Northern Division of the English Counties at Birkenhead on the Saturday (2 December).

They chose to field only five of the Test XV against Monmouthshire. This was a brave decision, but in the end they need not have worried, as Monmouthshire proved extremely disappointing, especially at forward, with six members of the Pontypool side, including four British Lions from the 1977 tour.

The Monmouth match attracted considerable interest, however, and over 20,000 spectators packed into the historic Rodney Parade Ground at Newport.

On the morning of the match, coach Jack Gleeson, interviewed for the *Western Mail*, was quoted as saying that he found British rugby predictable and that far too much of it was premeditated. 'Sides are obsessed with the high kick towards our line. Good possession is being kicked away instead of being used among the backs.' He admitted that in the Test, Wales had played a lot better than he expected, but he felt that the possession had not been used imaginatively. Actually, what he was saying of British rugby was almost true of his own side. It is a condemnation of modern world rugby. The only difference between the All Blacks as winners and British sides as losers was the greater number of errors made by British opposition, and perhaps the tendency on the part of British referees to be over-kind to the tourists.

Just before the Monmouthshire match it was revealed that the Barbarians had invited the French pair of flankers, Rives and Skrela, to play for them against the tourists, and invited Phil Bennett as well. Such a decision did not please members and officials of the WRU. They felt the tour was confined to the British Isles and the Frenchmen should not have been invited. The Welsh selectors felt it was something of an affront to invite Bennett: he had retired from representative rugby. The Barbarian reply was that all three players were active members of the Club, having played for them during the previous two seasons. It was not a representative match in the full sense of the word, but another club match on the fixture list. The WRU were acting as hosts, but it was a Barbarian Club match.

The Monmouthshire side included six internationals in the pack and two behind the scrum. However, any hopes they had of achieving a victory, avenging the Welsh defeat, were sunk in the first twenty minutes of play. By that time the All Blacks were 13–3 in the lead. The tourists were putting their game together. The new full-back, Ron Wilson, was kicking goals like a man shelling peas. At this stage some felt it was all over, but the brave young full-back, Peter Lewis kicked his second and third penalties to make it 13–9, and there was still just a chance! However, the All Blacks made it 22–9 in the ten minutes before the interval.

Monmouthshire, for all their preparation, were disappointing. Their forwards failed, completely dominated at the lineout by Andy Haden; behind there was not enough pace or penetration to disturb the efficient All Blacks' defence. Scrum-half Brynmor Williams worked hard, with little support, and did enough to win his Barbarians place. Full-back Peter Lewis and wing Tony Browning tried extremely hard. The rest could not match the tourists. It is true that in the second half Monmouthshire were stubborn, but they never appeared capable of scoring points, although the tourists could do no more than collect one more try, finishing at 29–6.

The All Blacks thus thoroughly deserved their victory. Manager Russell Thomas was pleased with the victory. It proved that his party was not divided into two sides, one for Wednesday and one for Saturday. 'We know now we have thirty equal players in the party. They put their game together and scored tries.' Wilson at full-back had an excellent match and Graham Mourie enjoyed himself: 'It was hard but I always felt we were going well enough to win. It was a good victory over a strong side.' He played well himself. At forward, Black, Fleming, Loveday and Haden gave him excellent support.

This was the 13th match, but still no side had scored a try against them since Limerick. Obviously, the desire to maintain such a defensive record became stronger with each match. Monmouthshire had failed to revenge the Welsh defeat; it became the turn of the Northern Division to attempt it on behalf of England.

Summary: Match 13

Wednesday 29 November   Rodney Parade, Newport
Monmouthshire 9 points (3 penalties)
New Zealand 26 points (3 tries, 4 penalties, 1 conversion)

TEAMS
Monmouthshire: P. Lewis (Pontypool); A. Browning (Newbridge), D. H. Burcher (Newport), I. Goslin (Ebbw Vale), G. Davies (Pontypool); D. Barry, D. B. Williams (Newport); A. G. Faulkner (capt.), R. W. Windsor, G. Price, S. Sutton,

J. Perkins (Pontypool), R. C. Burgess, P. Ringer (Ebbw Vale),
J. Squire (Pontypool)
New Zealand: R. G. Wilson; R. R. Kururangi, B. J. Robertson,
N. M. Taylor, S. S. Wilson; E. Dunn, D. S. Loveridge;
B. R. Johnstone, J. E. Black, W. K. Bush (sub: J. C. Ashworth),
A. M. Haden, J. K. Loveday, W. Graham, G. N. K. Mourie
(capt.), J. K. Fleming

REFEREE: J. R. West (Ireland)

SCORERS
Monmouthshire: Lewis, 3 penalties
New Zealand: Loveridge, Dunn, Robertson, tries; Wilson,
4 penalties, 1 conversion

Match 14: v. North of England

The weather took a turn for the worst, especially in the North.
There was doubt for several days as to whether the snow-covered
ground at the Birkenhead Park Club would be fit. Hot air was
blown beneath the sheeting covering part of the pitch. Eventually,
it proved to be playable, following a great deal of work by the
club (most of it voluntary). In 1972 the North had beaten the All
Blacks in the League town of Workington; everyone believed that
they could repeat the performance, even though Fran Cotton,
still plagued by injury, had to withdraw from the pack. Enthusiastic coach Desmond Seabrook forecast that his side was determined to prove that England players were better than had been
suggested at Twickenham. He commented: 'We must play the
All Blacks at their own game with the same amount of aggression
and commitment.' Unfortunately, the weather had proved to be
a handicap in his preparation of the side, but they did really try.
    The Northern side included five of the England backs of the
previous Saturday and three of the forwards, plus Tony Neary
who should have played for England. Many believed the Northern
XV was stronger than England. Events were to prove that it was,
and it went very near to overcoming the tourists. The *Observer*
headline read, 'Cocks o' the North scare the All Blacks'.
    Billy Beaumont was the captain of the North. His forwards
gave him everything, with Uttley and Dixon much more promin-
176

ent. The match gained the ranking of fourth in the tour, behind Munster, Wales and Ireland; it was only the All Blacks' fitness and tenacity that enabled them to survive, plus the kicking of McKechnie (an invaluable member of the side). They achieved a narrow 9–6 victory. (A last chance for the North sailed just wide in the closing minutes.) Perhaps a critical difference between the sides was the superiority of Bruce at outside-half for the All Blacks over his England rival John Horton. Horton did not look quite a big-match player.

Half Doug Bruce had an excellent match and was the All Blacks hero, but the victory was achieved by the short recovery time in defence. The All Blacks plugged the gaps readily, even though there was never any great danger from the Northern opposition once the ball had been handed on by Young at scrum-half. With Horton refusing to carry the ball to the opposition and providing an indifferent service for his centres, and Bond almost committed to the crash-ball technique (now an over-used ploy in British rugby), the All Blacks' alert defence was able to contain the North behind the scrum.

The three players who worried them most were the back row, the experienced Neary, Uttley and Dixon. This trio, but for injury and indifferent selection, could have represented England throughout 1978: the discarding of Neary can hardly be fathomed by those critics close to the England side. The three of them gave a superb exhibition of combined loose forward play.

The North took the lead after four minutes with a penalty goal by Young following lifting at a lineout. He kicked a second when the All Blacks punched the ball deliberately forward at a later lineout. Immediately, the All Blacks came back to level the scores, driving through to ruck the ball, and moving it across to Wilson. When challenged, Wilson sent it inside to the supporting McKechnie, who scored and then converted the try. The North thus had to face the wind after the interval with the scores level. It was a stern tussle, and neither side could make any great impression upon the other. McKechnie made sure of a victory for his side with a penalty goal after obstruction midway through the second half. Young had a chance to level the scores. As Beaumont remarked, 'A draw would have been a fairer result.'

John Reason's comment on the tourists after this match, was:

'Although they are sadly short of class attacking players, they are probably the fittest and the best-organized team of spoilers and poachers ever to visit these islands.' I agree with this, although I suspect that either their speed to the break-down and tackle suggested a shade of offside play, or else British rugby is considerably slower. Television often revealed technical infringements that were unsighted by British referees!

Summary: Match 14

Saturday 2 December   Birkenhead Park
North of England 6 points (2 penalties)
New Zealand 9 points (1 try, 1 penalty, 1 conversion)

TEAMS
North of England: D. R. Boyd (West Hartlepool); P. J. Squires (Harrogate), R. Cardus (Roundhay), A. M. Bond (Sale), M. A. C. Slemen (Liverpool); J. P. Horton (Bath), M. Young (Gosforth); F. Blackhurst (Waterloo), R. Tabern (Fylde), J. A. H. Bell (Gosforth), W. B. Beaumont (Fylde) (capt.), J. Butler, P. J. Dixon (Gosforth), A. J. Neary (Broughton Park), R. M. Uttley (Gosforth)
New Zealand: B. J. McKechnie; S. S. Wilson, L. J. Jaffray, W. M. Osborne, B. G. Williams; O. D. Bruce, M. W. Donaldson; J. C. Ashworth, A. G. Dalton, G. A. Knight, A. M. Haden, F. J. Oliver, L. M. Rutledge, G. N. K. Mourie (capt.), G. A. Seear

REFEREE: D. I. Burnett (Ireland)

SCORERS
North of England: Young, 2 penalties
New Zealand: McKechnie, 1 try, 1 penalty, 1 conversion

Match 15: v. North of Scotland

The All Blacks moved from Chester, where they had stayed for the Northern match, to Aberdeen for their only visit to Scotland. Whilst there, the tourists heard the announcement of the Barbarians side to oppose them at Cardiff on 16 December. It must have contained a few surprises for them. The Barbarians gambled on all-out attack; they refused to nominate a British Isles team, and included three non-capped players. Phil Bennett had been recalled and the two Frenchmen had been invited to provide back-row mobility and handling skill. The team was composed of six Welshmen, four Englishmen, two Scots, two Frenchmen, and one Irishman.

The North of Scotland XV, chosen from second-division clubs, may well have appreciated that trying to overcome the All Blacks was an Everest-like task but their veteran scrum-half, international Ian McCrae of the Gordonians, was as optimistic as ever. 'I will be playing against a fourth successive All Blacks side. As this will be my last season in representative rugby, it would be nice to win!' At 37, McCrae was revealing more-than-average courage and enthusiasm.

The North started well, snatching the lead with a dropped goal by outside half Colin High, which they held until just before the interval, when the All Blacks took charge.

The North had the cold wind behind their backs in the first half. McCrae was an inspiration to his team, energetic and tireless, but once Bryan Williams had made a try for full-back Ron Wilson, giving a 4–3 lead to NZ with the wind to come, one realized there would be no 'Munster surprise' at Aberdeen. The All Blacks pounded away. Although the North's cover defence was brave, tries were scored by Rutledge, Robertson, Ashworth (2), and Kururangi. Wilson converted two and Dunn dropped a goal. Bryan Williams was the outstanding All Black player.

Ian McCrae, the pint-sized terrier-like worker, commented on the match, 'I really enjoyed the first half. It was marvellous being in the big time again (he played six times for Scotland). Having played against two successive All Black sides, I am convinced that this team has the more skilful backs, and they are prepared to use their ability at every opportunity.' This was an interesting comment. The six tries scored by the All Blacks equalled the total achieved against the London Counties; had Wilson been in better form as a kicker, the All Blacks could have achieved their highest score of the tour. In the second half, as the opposition weakened, the All Blacks played fifteen-man rugby, something all too rare on the tour overall.

Summary: Match 15

Tuesday 5 December   Aberdeen
North of Scotland 3 points (1 dropped goal)
New Zealand 31 points (6 tries, 1 dropped goal, 2 conversions)

TEAMS
North of Scotland: A. Croll (Gordonians); S. Mackenzie (Kirkcaldy), J. Adams (Glenrothes), S. Irvine, P. Robertson (Gordonians); C. High (Highlands), I. MacCrae (Gordonians); G. Mackenzie (Highland), A. Hardie (Gordonians); G. Brown (Dunfermline), A. Dunlop (Highland), C. Snape, C. Watt (Gordonians), I. Paxton (Glenrothes), A. Angle-Finch (Highland)
New Zealand: R. G. Wilson; R. R. Kururangi, B. J. Robertson, N. M. Taylor, B. G. Williams; E. Dunn, S. Loveridge; B. R. Johnstone, J. E. Black, G. A. Knight, J. K. Loveday, F. J. Oliver, B. G. Ashworth, L. M. Rutledge, J. K. Fleming

REFEREE: J. R. West (Ireland)

SCORERS
North of Scotland: High, 1 dropped goal
New Zealand: Rutledge, Robertson, Kururangi, tries; Ashworth, 2 tries; Dunn, 1 dropped goal; R. G. Wilson, 1 try, 1 conversion

Match 16: Test v. Scotland

New Zealand selected the same team for the final international match against Scotland as defeated England. They were going for the Grand Slam. Those near to the selector-in-chief Jack Gleeson said there was a long discussion about the side, especially concerning the number eight and second five-eighths (inside centre) positions. The two players who went near to inclusion were forward John Fleming and centre Mark Taylor. From the moment the team was announced, they concentrated upon victory. This was a match that had to be won.

Similarly, in the Scottish camp, Nairn MacEwan worked hard with his men. It was almost a case of 'Scot versus Scot': Manager Russell Thomas claimed that possibly twenty-five of the New
180

Zealand party had some Scottish blood in their make-up.

Rain poured down upon the ground throughout the match, not the soft gentle rain normally associated with Auld Reekie, but really heavy stuff. The crowd was not unduly worried about the ground being heavy and the ball slippery; the cry would be 'Feet, Scotland, feet': a ball on the ground on a wet day is driven over the turf rather than carried; while the 'wheel' used to be a grand ploy. Few players enjoy going down on the ball before a Scottish foot rush; Danie Craven has often confessed to it being something of a nightmare! The light was very poor.

From the kick-off, the All Blacks were nervous. They had not beaten all four home countries before (the 'Invincibles' of 1924–25 did not meet Scotland because of a continuing dispute started in 1905 concerning commercialism). This time the All Blacks were in with a great chance, but deeply conscious of the risk that history might repeat itself. They were smarting under the criticism that as a side they were 'efficient but dull'. The weather offered little opportunity of it being otherwise in this match.

The match proved to be extremely exciting, if not particularly skilful in the difficult conditions. The All Blacks achieved their ambition of the Grand Slam, although clinching the match only in injury time. Scotland took an early lead of six points with the first try scored against the tourists since Munster, and converted it; but two errors by Andy Irvine outside his own line provided the All Blacks with scoring positions from which they collected a penalty goal, and a try (from a scrum) which was converted. This made it 9–6 to the All Blacks at the interval. There was everything to be played for in a second half with even less light than the first.

Another penalty goal put the All Blacks further ahead, but a dropped goal by Scotland pegged them at 12–9. This score remained until injury time, when the most exciting moment of the match occured. Scotland, with a remarkable last minute effort, bombarded the New Zealand line. They won a scrum on the right, and the ball moved left out to McGeechan. While Irvine joined the line, McGeechan swung out to drop for goal with his left foot. It would have earned the draw.

The All Blacks could not have complained at being thwarted, but their incredible tour luck held. Outside half Douglas Bruce flung himself across the flight of the ball speeding towards scoring the vital points. His body made contact; the ball flew back in the opposite direction, past McGeechan, into the open unguarded field. Centre Osborne booted up ahead, followed by fellow centre Bruce Robertson. Robertson in turn hacked on again, finally over the Scottish line. The Scots had no one back in defence, and no one could overtake Robertson to the touch down. It was a try for New Zealand (though few recognized the dashing counter-attackers in the dark!). McKechnie, a fine full-back on that day kicked the goal. Instead of 12–12 it was 18–9. That score is hardly a fair reflection on the day, but tenacity had carried New Zealand through, yet again.

New Zealand were fortunate in many ways because Referee John West was far from his best, being inconsistent. He refused to send an All Black offender from the field. After 24 minutes, as a lineout ended, lock Andy Haden floored Alistair McHarg with a k.o. punch. According to Four Home Union instructions, the offending player should have been sent off. Referee West did not fulfil the instructions; a penalty was awarded and Haden spoken to. The charmed life of the tourists continued controversially. Even if McHarg had infringed, no mitigating circumstances are allowed in the Laws of the Game. It is said, 'A player may not take the law into his own hands.' The fact that the act occurred in front of the Referee makes it all the more sad.

Mr West was not alone, however, in what appeared to be a decision to 'opt out' on the tour; referees from all four home countries were generally of the same mind. This is not a personal attack upon Mr West, whom I know well, but his action in being over-kind to the tourists was a highlight of refereeing throughout the tour. It made the All Blacks' record look more impressive than it was, and did little if any good for British rugby. British players asked, 'Why are there two sets of laws?' The following Monday, a player from Abertillery, punching an opponent from Tredegar, was sent from the field. Where was the justice? Andy Haden is no gentle giant!

Scotland did as well as they anticipated, and came very near to achieving their target. They were of course disappointed, believing that they had done enough to earn a draw. The tourists won enough possession to peg back the Scots, though, and Bruce kicked so well. Secondly, the sure hands and boot of McKechnie, the test cricketer, provided a secure last line of defence. Irvine, poor fellow, found the testing high kicks troublesome yet again.

Summary: Match 16

Saturday 9 December   Murrayfield, Edinburgh
Scotland 9 points (1 try, 1 penalty, 1 conversion)
New Zealand 18 points (2 tries, 2 penalties, 2 conversions)

TEAMS
Scotland: A. R. Irvine (Heriot's F.P.); K. W. Robertson (Melrose), J. M. Renwick (Hawick), A. G. Cranston (Hawick), B. H. Hay (Boroughmuir); I. R. McGeechan (Headingley) (capt.), A. J. M. Lawson (London Scottish); J. McLauchlan (Jordonhill), C. T. Deans (Hawick), R. F. Cunningham (Gala), A. J. Tomes (Hawick), A. F. McHarg (London Scottish), M. A. Biggar (London Scottish), D. G. Leslie (Gala) (sub: I. K. Lambie (Watsonians)), G. Dickson (Gala)
New Zealand: B. J. McKechnie; S. S. Wilson, B. J. Robertson, W. M. Osborne, B. G. Williams; O. D. Bruce, M. W. Donaldson; B. R. Johnstone, A. G. Dalton G. A. Knight, A. M. Haden, F. J. Oliver, L. M. Rutledge, G. N. K. Mourie (capt.), G. A. Seear

REFEREE: J. R. West (Ireland)

SCORERS
Scotland: Hay, 1 try; Irvine, 1 conversion; McGeechan, 1 dropped goal
New Zealand: Seear, Robertson, tries; McKechnie, 2 penalties, 2 conversions

Match 17: v. Bridgend

From Scotland, the All Blacks flew back to London, spent a day there, and travelled on to Porthcawl on the Monday in readiness for the penultimate match against Bridgend. Bridgend were celebrating their Centenary season, playing against a major touring team for the first time and looking forward to a bumper match. Alas, it was not to be! The weather turned sour, the match turned sour, and, as a result, the whole tour turned sour. Prop John

Ashworth stamped on J. P. R. Williams after four minutes' play. This, with Ashworth's appearance as substitute in the last match, destroyed all the goodwill. It indicated all too clearly the true attitude of the All Blacks to the tour.

The scene was set early for a lively match, with Bridgend wanting to win in their Centenary Year, and with Gleeson saying, 'We are determined to leave Wales unbeaten.' The young referee Laurie Prideaux was appointed for the match.

After four minutes' play, a ruck formed and wheeled round. As Ashworth passed J. P. R. Williams, who was lying three-quarters out of the ruck, nowhere near the ball, he stamped on Williams's face twice, driving a stud through the cheek. Williams got up, bleeding profusely, and left the field for attention after reorganizing his back division.

Before leaving London Airport on the Monday afterwards, Ashworth is reported as speaking without apology: 'I was not aware I was raking someone in the head. I went into the ruck and went over the top. I raked pretty vigorously [obviously] and was aware there was someone between me and the ball. I didn't know who it was at the time. I've not spoken to J. P. R. since [what a fine sporting attitude!], and have not seen the television film of the incident. The management have not reprimanded me for anything.'

Perhaps neither he nor the management cared or were interested in the foul play. Later, at London Airport, a rather riled Thomas and Gleeson had to admit that no action had been taken against Ashworth. Gleeson commented, 'We are not going back to that beautiful place, Bridgend, are we?' It was sarcasm at its worse, and more than that, arrogance. They would admit no guilt. If they had been the sportsmen they claimed they were, they would not have behaved as they did immediately after the match and in the days that followed before they boarded their aircraft.

While J. P. R. Williams was off the field, the All Blacks scored seven points. This was a decisive phase in the match. The first three points came from a penalty by Wilson from twenty-five yards' range. When Bridgend restarted, Kururangi, on the right wing, fielded deep in his own '25' and set off diagonally across field, slipping past several poor tackles. He made a run of nearly seventy yards before handing on to Taylor; with no J. P. R. in defence, he was over the line for a try. Wilson's kick at goal was wide, but it mattered little. The All Blacks had achieved a firm grip on the game during Bridgend's misfortunes.

Fenwick was short with a penalty attempt from forty yards, and Wilson kicked wide with another attempt, before J. P. R. returned with his face stitched and covered with plaster. Before the next score, Ashworth stamped on Bridgend centre, Lyndon Thomas, also lying away from the ball. His head was cut and we wondered at what madness had overtaken this errant player? Bruce was then late-tackled by Ian Williams. Wilson kicked a straight 47-yard penalty to make it 10–0. The All Blacks were more than comfortably placed, and the field became a morass. Hopes were raised for Bridgend as Fenwick kicked two penalty goals – the first for obstruction on wing Vivian Jenkins, the second for a lineout offence. It was 10–6 at the interval.

In the second half Wilson kicked his third penalty from 25 yards, making it 13–6; there appeared to be little doubt that the All Blacks would win. The game became more and more niggly. Wilson failed with three penalty attempts, and Fenwick with one.

Referee Laurie Prideaux appeared a little lost, and opted out of taking action on the 'punching and wrestling'. Gary Knight was seen punching, but claimed an opponent had pulled his hair! The game had so deteriorated that it had now become six of one and half a dozen of the other. It had all started with Ashworth's blatant attack on J. P. R., followed by poor refereeing. Near the end, the All Blacks scored a second try when, at a lineout near the Bridgend line, the home side unwisely tapped back. The loose ball was gathered by the alert Graham Mourie, who dashed over for an opportunist try that was not converted. A timid referee blew up three minutes early.

What was to have been the greatest celebration day in Bridgend's hundred years of service to the game ended as the saddest. Soaked spectators tramped away from the ground grumbling; few, if any, would have agreed to New Zealand coming back to Wales in 1980. They were asking, 'Is it really worth it for us, or for rugby?'

I visited the Bridgend dressing room, and was appalled by the sight of J. P. R. Williams's badly-damaged face. His father, Dr Peter Williams, told me then, 'If I had known this was going to happen, I would not have encouraged my four sons to play rugby.

I told Russell Thomas this in the stand after it happened.' He said this again at the after-match reception. Apparently it upset a lot of people on both sides. I would have said exactly the same thing, had it happened to one of my sons; the 'white-washing' that went on, especially by officials and the New Zealand management, merely served to damage the game further, already a game under severe fire from its genuine supporters and the world media for its newly-acquired violence. At the after-match function it was suggested that the majority of Welsh followers did not agree with Dr Williams. The truth is that they did so. When it was shown on television the next day, in slow motion, the wanton act aroused even more hostility.

I was able, on BBC television, to say how appalled I was by the act. The arrogance that followed on the Saturday merely confirmed my feelings. Ashworth was nominated as a replacement for the Barbarians match, an incredible folly on the part of the New Zealand management; the Barbarians 'alikadoos' were not impressed with such an approach. All were left wondering how far a New Zealand player could go before he was disciplined.

Summary: Match 17

Wednesday 13 December   Brewery Field, Bridgend
Bridgend 6 points (2 penalties)
New Zealand 17 points (2 tries, 3 penalties)

TEAMS
Bridgend: J. P. R. Williams (capt.); V. Jenkins, L. Thomas, S. P. Fenwick, I. Davies; I. Williams, G. Williams; I. Stephens, G. Davies, M. James, R. Evans, W. Howe, G. Jones, G. Williams, S. Ellis
New Zealand: R. Wilson; R. Kururangi, M. Taylor, W. M. Osborne, B. G. Williams; O. D. Bruce, D. S. Loveridge; J. C. Ashworth, J. Black, G. A. Knight, A. M. Haden, J. Loveday, W. Graham, G. N. K. Mourie (capt.), G. A. Seear

REFEREE: L. Prideaux (RFU)

SCORERS
Bridgend: Fenwick, 2 penalties
New Zealand: Taylor, Mourie, tries; Wilson, 3 penalties
186

Match 18: v. The Barbarians

The Barbarians trained on Thursday at Penarth and on Friday morning at Cardiff, receiving advice from Syd Millar, the only British coach to take a Lions team through a major tour unbeaten. It was a scratch side when it met at its Cardiff headquarters, and not much less when it took the field, but its spirit was right. Conditions were perfect, and the Arms Park was filled with a capacity crowd. The Barbarians lined up with all the All Blacks for the anthems and the play was keen, open and in good spirit.

It was 23 minutes before the All Blacks deservedly took the lead, with a try awarded to prop Brad Johnstone when a maul of forwards crashed over the Barbarians' line. McKechnie's conversion attempt sailed wide, and 15 minutes later the Barbarians levelled the scores after their own line had survived several fierce attacks and they had thrown away at least three chances. It was that sort of match, open and running, as rugby should be at all levels. In the fortieth minute of the first half, a penalty award at a lineout saw McKechnie kick the All Blacks back into the lead with a 26-yard goal. At half time the score was 7–4 to New Zealand.

At this stage, most spectators and critics were well satisfied with proceedings, although both sides had missed chances. The All-Black forwards had enjoyed the advantage during the first half, but Phil Bennett had done some noble work covering at the corner flags to prevent tries. The atmosphere was calm, if not throbbing with traditional enthusiasm, until the New Zealanders played what they seem to have thought was their trump card, but which proved to be the greatest mistake of their tour. Prop Brad Johnstone was seen to leave the field. Suddenly, galloping out of the tunnel came his replacement, No. 17; it was a few seconds before the great crowd realized who it was: none other than the stamper-in-chief John Ashworth. Booing greeted him. In defiance – or admiration – he raised both arms in the air to acknowledge the greeting, in the manner of Cassius Clay in his more ostentatious days! This was the final gesture of arrogance. From that moment, I lost almost all respect for the 1978 All Blacks. They had over-played their hand!

The Barbarians had lost their Irish loose head prop, Phillip Orr, after eight minutes, with a gashed hand. He told me afterwards, 'It was an accident, I had my hand on the ball!' Orr had been replaced by Barry Nelmes, the Cardiff captain, who thus made his fourth appearance against the tourists, equalling the record set up in 1935–36 by another England prop Douglas Kendrew, who appeared for Ulster, Combined Services, London Counties, and England. Nelmes appeared for Cardiff, South West Counties, Barbarians and England. His views on the tourists are interesting. When I asked him to evaluate the tour, he spoke fairly, as one would expect from a respected England forward, playing for and leading a senior Welsh Club. He said, 'They were an efficient side, excellent in defence. They had no great players, but they improved as a ball-winning unit as the tour progressed. They always played right up to the referee and got away with quite a lot of off-side play! Their captain, Graham Mourie, was clever, in that he gently questioned every referee's decision against the All Blacks. They were not easy to beat, because they knew what each other was doing. They were better at the end of the tour than at the start, and they changed their style after their defeat in Limerick. I do not think they will be remembered for anything special except their well-knit defence.'

Irvine set the tempo for the second half of the Barbarians match, with a drop at goal from a tapped penalty, but the ball sailed wide. A few minutes later the All Blacks were penalized at a ruck, and Bennett kicked an easy 15-yard goal to level the scores. Almost immediately the All Blacks hit back with a splendid run by Loveridge. Although he was tackled inside the Barbarians '25' with the ball going to ground, he was allowed to play it off the ground with his hands. It came back, and Rutledge charged over for a try that McKechnie could not convert. The lead of 11–7 for the All Blacks was soon increased to 15–7, when the All Blacks worked a blind-side move. Rives was rather slow getting to his man, and Bryan Williams slipped over for a try after working a clever scissors movement with Dunn. McKechnie was wide with the kick.

With 27 minutes remaining, one expected the All Blacks to romp home. A few minutes afterwards Bennett failed with a 35-yard penalty attempt that normally he would have kicked with ease, and then Hutchings kicked on instead of feeding Slemen outside him, wasting a try. But Bennett made a good save, and

Haden was palpably offside at a lineout, and Renwick crossed the All Blacks line only to have the ball knocked out of his hands as he was touching down. Was there no end to the good fortune of the tourists?

Then came a Barbarian try at long last. A short penalty ploy involved a dummy pass to the open side by Brynmor Williams, who then sent it out to Skrela on his left. Skrela sent Slemen galloping over, unmarked, near the left corner. Bennett kicked a superb conversion from near the touch-line. It was now 15–13.

The match was alight. Temporarily, the Ashworth business was forgotten. Irving attempted a long kick at penalty goal, all of sixty yards; his glorious high kick bounced on the All Blacks' cross-bar, back into the field of play. Then Haden pushed a catcher in the back before he had collected the ball, and Bennett kicked the goal, putting the Barbarians in the lead for the first time in the match, with seven minutes remaining for play. Mc-Kechnie failed with two more kicks at penalty goal. As full time passed into injury time, it looked as if the Barbarians would just do it.

We had forgotten the tourists' luck. Irvine caught a wide attempt at dropped goal by Osborne on the Barbarians goal line. He tackled as he touched down for a drop-out. Referee Sanson ordered a five-yard scrum. Back came a good heel to Loveridge. He fed Dunn, well clear of the spoilers, and Dunn dropped a neat goal to make it 16–15 to the All Blacks. Another injury-time escape.

The team left the field; there was some booing, and a feeble attempt to sing 'Now is the Hour'. The response was poor. The All Blacks had the poorest send-off for many a year.

The dinner was pleasant, but the speakers avoided some of the more vital issues. This may have been the thing to do for the dinner, but was it the best thing for the game? The Barbarians match had proved the most enjoyable of the tour from the pure rugby viewpoint, but a cloud hung over it, and there was always the luck that never deserted New Zealand.

The All Blacks record was seventeen wins in eighteen matches. Nevertheless, I wonder whether they will be remembered as well and as long as some of their predecessors.

Summary: Match 18

Saturday 16 December   Cardiff Arms Park
Barbarians 15 points (2 tries, 2 penalties, 1 conversion)
New Zealand 16 points (3 tries, 1 penalty, 1 dropped goal)

TEAMS

Barbarians: A. R. Irvine (Heriot's); H. E. Rees (Neath), R. N. Hutchings (Aberavon), J. M. Renwick (Hawick), M. A. C. Slemen (Liverpool); P. Bennett (Llanelli), D. B. Williams Newport); P. A. Orr (Old Wesley), P. J. Wheeler (Leicester), W. Dickinson (Richmond), W. B. Beaumont (Fylde), A. J. Martin (Aberavon), J-P. Rives (Toulouse), J-C. Skrela (Toulouse), D. L. Quinnell (Llanelli) (capt.)

New Zealand: B. J. McKechnie; S. S. Wilson, B. J. Robertson, W. M. Osborne, B. G. Williams; E. Dunn, D. S. Loveridge, B. R. Johnstone (sub: J. C. Ashworth), A. G. Dalton, G. A. Knight, A. M. Haden, F. J. Oliver, L. M. Rutledge, G. N. K. Mourie (capt.), J. K. Fleming

REFEREE: N. R. Sanson (Scotland)

SCORERS

Barbarians: Slemen, 2 tries; Bennett, 2 penalties, 1 conversion
New Zealand: Dunn, Johnstone, Williams, tries; McKechnie, 1 penalty; Dunn, 1 dropped goal

8

Goodbye to the Maestros!

In September, Gareth Owen Edwards, scrum-half and rugby player extraordinary, announced his retirement from the field. Rugby football was immediately poorer for his stepping down. Followers everywhere had applauded the man, who was much-loved, distinguished, modest and human, dangerous and supremely skilful. A player for all occasions, his is a personality of verve and purpose.

It was known that his retirement was imminent, and that his autobiography had been written but, nevertheless the announcement (less sentimental than it could have been) was tinged with sadness. How he will be missed, this dark-haired intense Welshman! Every schoolboy in Wales interested in Rugby who wishes to emulate a great player and copy his methods cannot do better than to study the films and television recordings of Gareth Edwards (and of Gerald Davies).

Edwards's career has been a remarkable achievement, and a triumph of the enthusiasm and resilience (apart from the matchless skills he possesses) that must rank him as one of the most outstanding of all-round players in the history of the game. He has moved relentlessly, through the years since his first cap at the age of 19, facing challenge after challenge, both within the borders of his beloved Wales and in Europe and the Southern Hemisphere.

Nothing has destroyed his love of the game, his pride in his own contribution to it, his modesty on every occasion, and his highly tuned sense of competition. There has been the occasional sad moment for him in defeat, but such moments have been few compared with those of triumph, with the smile of complete satisfaction. Rugby has been a challenge for him always, one to be met with good humour, and enjoyed. Despite his 31 years, there remains deep down a boy's love of playing a good game; he is one who has always sought perfection for himself and his team-mates, and his admission to the ranks of those who make professional personal appearances outside the game should not change him.

Watching rugby for nearly fifty years in many countries has provided me with the opportunity for close study and analysis of many outstanding players, including scrum-halves in abundance. Among the early names I watched when a schoolboy were the giant and legendary W. C. 'Wick' Powell, the 'miniature tiger' Tal Harris of Aberavon, Arthur John of Llanelli, Arthur Young of England, Mark Sugden of Ireland, Jimmy Nelson of Scotland and Danie Craven and Pierre de Villiers of South Africa; each was a hero in the position in those early days and one marvelled at the strength, skill and efficiency.

Powell had the long and bullet-like pass, especially in reverse, (though occasionally it was wayward), and was a hefty, stern giant of a man on the field, the first ninth forward in Welsh rugby. If one doubts this assessment, then ask those surviving wing forwards who played against him; none will give Powell a better reference than Wylie Breckenridge of Australia, the 1927-28 touring flanker.

Harris was a terrier; John a nippy, shrewd performer who died tragically young; Arthur Young was clever and tough for such a small man (who also died tragically young when on Army service in India). Sugden was tall, strong and immaculate, near to perfection in all his play and now one of the shewdest students of the game. Nelson was audacious, and Craven as strong as a high veld ox. de Villiers was dapper and clever and fine reader of the game.

Before them there was one outstanding scrum-half in the 'Golden Era', a man who was to Welsh rugby what Jimmy Wilde was to Welsh boxing, a 'Mighty Atom'; before Edwards, he was the greatest. He was Richard Morgan Owen of Swansea; his skill and shrewdness was such that a man of the quality of Tommy Vile could play but a few times as a challenger.

I also remember the recently deceased W. J. 'Bobby' Delahay, in the 1920s, before the advent of the big man, Wick Powell.

In the 1930s came the superb Haydn Tanner, whose first

appearance for Wales was made when a few months younger than Edwards, against the mighty 1935 All Blacks; it could not have been more memorable. He was a Gowerton schoolboy, and played inside the well-established Cliff Jones, Claude Davey, Wilfred Wooller and company with the cool skill and effectiveness of an expert in his twentieth international; it must still rank as the greatest of international debuts by any scrum-half. He played against many famous opponents: Bernard Gadney of England, George Morgan of Ireland, Ross Logan of Scotland, not to mention Joey Sadler of New Zealand and Danie Craven of South Africa before World War II and, later, Charles Saxton (New Zealand), Ernie Strathdee (Ireland) and Cyril Burke (Australia). Tanner played from 1935 to 1949 for Wales, and but for six years of the War could well have reached 50 appearances (although there were fewer international matches played during his career, as long tours were less frequent, and short tours never undertaken). He possessed most of the qualities that make for greatness, but lived in an era when squad training and coaching were haphazard affairs and never organized, and when selection, without the squad system, was a hit-or-miss affair.

With Owen and Edwards, Haydn Tanner forms the great triumvirate of Welsh scrum-halves; each differed in his approach, and played in different eras, yet each one of them was decisive, and had a marked influence upon the decades in which he appeared. Again, had their eras been transposed, they would have survived as great players with little adjustment. Genius in sport is adaptable.

So why should one regard Edwards as *the* greatest? Surely it cannot be for his record alone? Indeed, it is not (although the achievement in itself does guarantee him a place at the top). But, even if the powerful J. P. R. Williams, or another player, should overtake his record eventually, it will become progressively harder for his successors to achieve such a *consecutive* record. Of them, an attempt will require fitness, dedication, and the maintenance of form and enthusiasm.

Edwards had *all* the qualities of a top player; the strength of Powell, the shrewdness of Owen, the length of pass of Tanner and Willis, the punting ability of Rowlands, and the sleight of hand of Brace. Thus he becomes the prototype, as if moulded by the great ones of the past, eager to present the complete footballer. He was the *complete* footballer. That is why I have chosen to regard him as the greatest all-rounder the game has produced. Alun Thomas and Phil Bennett have played in almost every position behind the scrum with ease; Edwards could have been a flanker, a hooker or a prop as well, with his considerable strength and adaptability.

More important, he had the temperament to accompany his many skills, and the will to survive. He inspired a sense of purpose among his team-mates. (How much do Barry John and Phil Bennett, outstanding players in their own right, owe to him?)

For me, his hours of greatest perfection were in South Africa in 1974 as the controller-in-chief of the Lions side. South Africans wondered at his mastery and no better tribute can be paid to him than to say his absence made the difference between Test success and Test failure in New Zealand in 1977. (The All Blacks realized this all too well, however hard players like Brynmor Williams and Douglas Morgan tried.) Many argue that he did not enjoy the task of captaincy, and that he was inhibited by it. He, however, denies this emphatically; he admits that he was unhappy when he lost the post in the Welsh team, and regrets the fact he was never thus honoured by the Cardiff Club.

Gareth Edwards was 19 when he made his first appearance for Wales, on 1 April 1967 in Paris (a few months older than Haydn Tanner who was 18 years 11 months when he appeared in the 13–12 thriller against the All Blacks which was won by Wales).

Both Edwards and Tanner had enjoyed brilliant careers as schoolboys (at Millfield and Gowerton Grammar School respectively), and their calm and adaptability belied their age. They appeared to always have enough time in which to do everything, and they made it all look so easy. They both played for the Welsh Secondary Schools teams in their respective eras, and even in these junior representative matches revealed the skill and judgment of veterans.

They must rank as two of the greatest in the Welsh scene over the last fifty years, and certainly as the best two in their position. Edwards is perfectly built – one could even say 'constructed' – for his position; he is an expert gymnast, a more-than-useful soccer player, an athlete, and a practical joker of some quality; he is dominated and inspired by an unrivalled competitive spirit. Off the field he is a relaxed, emotional, high spirited, sensative, family-loving, proud, Welshman. Abroad, he is truly Welsh, a happy, young man, patient and understanding, a splendid mixer and rugby tourist.

Edwards has great charm, and the engaging smile of a true Welshman. You cannot dislike him. For rugby, he had natural genius; flair, accurate skills (through his career he worked hard to increase the length of his passing and kicking), and power. (His ferocious charge, with shoulder dropped, knocked down one, two, three, even four defenders in a row: he could crash through full-backs to score tries.)

But of all the weapons in his armoury, it was his long spin pass that was the most formidable and soul-destroying for his opponents. Barry John says of him: 'Gareth was difinitely *the* dominant scrum-half in world rugby. To have played with him for so long is such as undisputed honour for me – his magic touch was always present and his wizardry could cause no rivalry.'

'Playing rugby football is one thing, but to play with the most complete rugby footballer ever is another.' Phil Bennett (who shares with him, the world record international half-back partnership of 25 appearances) says of Edwards, 'It's simple – Gareth is just the greatest. He has so many exceptional qualities – like strength (I have seen him pick a forward up and hurl him into touch). Basically, he was so great because of his skills, yet the strength of the man is unbelievable.

'We enjoyed the best period of our long partnership in South Africa in 1974, when Gareth was magnificent. His long pass gave you time, and kept you away from opposing back rows. He would always protect you and was always the 'character' of every tour. He likes to talk a lot on the field; he is a fantastic story teller. I don't think we ever argued on the field. He's a pretty genuine guy and you need all the friends you've got out there on the field in an international match!'

When a schoolboy at Pontardawe, the man who did so much to mould his future career, Bill Samuel, drove him hard. Why? Samuel knew that he had under his care an exceptional sportsman, but that he had to be made to believe that life at the top would never be easy. He put discipline into the Edwards' mind. He put modesty into the Edwards' heart.

195

Because he set his own high standards, the rugby world never allowed him to forget them. He built an ogre he had to live with. Despite skills beyond compare in the game, occasionally – very occasionally – the ogre tormented him. But he could always put the ogre to flight with a brilliant try, a superb kick, an extra-long pass, or a try-saving tackle. Only then did he really smile, and allow himself the pleasure of a handspring. 'Rugby is to be enjoyed', he says, 'even in the heat of the toughest battle.'

Edwards knew that he had a personal standard of performance to maintain in the game even though he was an amateur, playing for the love of it. He achieved such greatness that when Frenchmen compared their new discovery, Jerome Gallion, with the master in 1978, it was a unique tribute to the Welsh player.

The 1978 season found him, at 30, no less enthusiastic. He trained hard and played consistently well for his club, together with his close friend Gerald Davies.

It was a surprise announcement, maybe, but a careful decision by Thomas Gerald Reames Davies, that he, one of the greatest wing-three-quarters of modern times, should retire in September shortly after Edwards had done so. The short, darting, dashing player had delighted thousands of followers worldwide before he laid aside his lightweight boots. His time in the game added a new dimension to wing-three-quarter play.

For those who had enjoyed his play (marvelling at its elusiveness), his retirement was a sad moment, and although not totally unexpected on the part of those who know him well, it came as a surprise because he had accepted the captaincy of the Cardiff Club in May, for the fourth successive time. He supervised early club training, but he delayed a decision to return to the side: it was this, perhaps, that was the key that he was then considering his future as it concerned his family, his career and his rugby.

At 34, ready to widen the aspects and scope of his professional career as an administrator, he announced his retirement suddenly, saying: 'I have no enthusiasm at the moment to start playing again, and so it is probably the right time to finish. I have always liked to make a decision about playing at the beginning of a new season and now I think this is the time for me to go. I have a book going, which I am writing myself, but there is nothing immediate about that, and it could take a bit of time.'

Rugbymen were caught momentarily unawares, and showed surprise. Davies had played an important part in Welsh rugby for a long time, and his announcement followed so quickly upon that of Edwards. However, whereas Edwards' retirement was less spectacular and lingering with speculation, that of Davies was sharp and sudden with a marked degree of spontaniety: it killed off any speculation and was done with the sharpness of many a brilliant try he had scored. Again, the break by Davies was unaccompanied by an agent and the ballyhoo of Sunday paper headlines, or even the publicity heralding a book. He left the game as modestly as he had played since appearing with distinction as a diminutive outside half at Queen Elizabeth Grammar School, Carmarthen.

On the field, Gerald Davies had style, grace and panache, and played with a face as serious as that of a matador. He had a sharp awareness, often made inconspicious by his gentle outward calm. Only occasionally would he lift his arms in exultation following a score by his side, or, when a pass failed to reach him or his centre turned inside to be trapped instead of giving him a chance to run for it, clasp his hands at the back of his head and turn away.

If given possession, he would set off prepared for the jink, the swerve, the side-step or the rabbit-like scamper. Once clear, he would hug the ball to his chest with his right arm, using the other arm as if it were a guiding sail for his slip stream, accelerating. Many adjectives have been used to describe his running, but I feel that his style was essentially modern – 'of the jet age'. For his five feet nine inches and eleven stones eight pounds, he was immensely strong in the hips and thighs before tapering down; it was this physical asset that gave him his power, pace, acceleration and elusiveness. Like a ballet dancer, he swivelled from the hips; this made his swerve deceptive. One particular try, for an International XV against Moseley on 27 November 1977 contained everything in his repetoire. It was the try of the match, and one of the best, if not the most important, of his career; it was of such quality as to mark Davies not only as one of the greatest of wings, but one of the most attractive players of all time.

He had not always been a wing, having played eleven times as a centre for Wales before the demands of injury on the Welsh tour of 1969 necessitated his moving out to the wing. He was, as one should have expected, an instant success, and he remained in the

Welsh side for another 35 matches. Even when he announced his retirement, there would have been still many more caps in Bill Clement's locker for the selectors to award to this brilliant rugby runner.

Davies was the senior player in the long era of Welsh success, although his cap tally was not quite that of Edwards (as a result of injury and his opting out for a full season to study and concentrate on his career). At all times he was a man of principle in the game, and he would not be moved easily. He was never afraid to stand and be counted for his personal beliefs; this was due as much to intelligent sensitivity as it was to native Welsh stubbornness. During the Irish dispute of 1972, he announced that he would not travel rather than hide behind any official Union decision; he declared himself not available for South African tours after his visit of 1968 with the Lions.

He belives in freedom of choice. Even as Captain of such an illustrious club as Cardiff – for three successive years – he remained independent. He talks fluently and seriously about rugby in discussion, preferring that to the folklore antics of some rugby players. He was never a carouser or an extrovert off the field on tour, preferring a glass of sherry or good wine, and intelligent conversation. Yet he was a good mixer (as one might expect from a family man), and he was ably supported in his second half of his career by his wife Cilla. Like Gareth Edwards, he is happily married with children; both have thus achieved fulfilment on and off the field, which has enabled them to continue their international careers successfully for a long period.

It has always been a pleasure to talk with these players, because both could, in few words, express the mood of a game and their approach to it. Rarely, if ever, did I hear them criticize a member of their own side. They would never allow any criticism within the dressing room to escape to the outside world. For Davies, the most disagreeable thing in the game was for players as individuals or a side to act outside the laws and ignore the spirit. In this he was adamant, and always prepared to back his beliefs in words and deeds.

I recall once popping into the Welsh dressing room, sometime after the end of the game, which had been a particularly hard match, in which Wales had succeeded. Davies was sitting on his own. He appeared sad and disillusioned. Eventually, he revealed he was sorry – not for himself, but for the game, and for an opposing player, one who had always been a friend at home and abroad. The player in question, in the opinion of Davies and many others, had opted out of the laws, and played against the spirit. Davies could hardly forgive this, even if it were done in pursuit of much-needed victory.

Davies would never condone his club side taking such action, and was upset when it happened in matches in which he played. He was never more upset than on the Welsh tour of Australia: 'There is no need for it. Rugby is a game to be enjoyed. It can be hard, but it is skill and enjoyment that must be uppermost in the minds of players. Teams must take the field to win, but to do so within the laws. Without this there can be no real satisfaction for player, official, or for spectator.' (In Australia, he had received many a kick in the head, despite the local claim that no Australian ever kicked an opponent; he had the stitches to prove it. Yet he does not harbour malice; he simply hopes that Australia will return to their running game.)

Recently, Davies was asked how he approached the game as a wing, and why he was successful. 'One acts instinctively', he replied, 'to each situation that arises. I prepare for myself ways of outwitting a particular opponent, and the real pleasure is in beating an opponent. That is what I liked best in the game!'

On modern rugby: 'Rugby is far different now from what it was when I first played for Wales in 1966; that is due to the squad training system. We used to get together for only one short training session before a match, and did not play to our full ability as a team or as individuals. By 1978, Wales took the field as a highly-skilled club side and played like one.'

He went on, however, to point out that for leading players the changes in twelve years had brought additional pressures: they are now more in the public eye. The squad system is demanding, tours are more frequent, and players have to give up much more of their leisure time. He questions the status and treatment of such players, and feels it leaves much to be desired. He believes that players on tour, who will be earning large profits for host unions, should receive only the best in the form of hotels, food and transport. Many players are not happy about the present situation. Players do earn big money for the game as a whole. They should not be paid to play, but they should be treated in a way which takes this into account.

Edwards feels the same way and asks for 'better treatment and better recognition'. I would agree with both of them.

Gerald Davies is a true West Walian, and Welsh-speaking; he was born in a village near Kidwelli, and educated first at Queen Elizabeth Grammar School, Carmarthen. (This was an excellent school of its kind, but has recently become incorporated in the comprehensive system, which development seems to have done considerable harm to rugby football at the Under-19 level in Wales.) From there, Davies went to Loughborough College, and qualified in physical education before graduating from Cambridge University, where he read English at Emmanuel College.

He played in three Intervarsity Matches, and was captain in his third year (1970). He then took a teaching post at Christ's Hospital at Horsham in Sussex. In 1974, he returned to Wales as a technical officer to the Sports Council for Wales.

Davies played for Cardiff before going to Cambridge, and then for the London Welsh while at Horsham. He rejoined Cardiff on his return to the City. The 1978-79 season would have been his fourth consecutive year as the Cardiff captain and although no major honours were achieved by the Club during his reign ('always the bridesmaid and never the bride'), and his approach to captaincy was sometimes criticized, he did instill a splendid spirit into the playing approach. Statistics do not really interest him; he is far more concerned with how *well* a team has played, and how much it has enjoyed its rugby. Neverthless he was extremely disappointed that in 1978 Cardiff just failed to win the *Western Mail* Club Championship and the WRU/Schweppes Cup. He admitted that it was 'a bitter pill to swallow'.

Davies made several tours abroad, including two with the British Lions: to South Africa in 1968, and to Australia and New Zealand in 1971. He was a great success on these tours, achieving world ranking as a wing, one of the best in this class. He played with distinction for the Barbarians against touring teams, and become the first-choice wing for any representative side.

In the course of his career, he suffered a few nasty injuries; one of the worst was a dislocated elbow late in the 1968 tour. In years following, he was worried by a recurrently troublesome hamstring injury. He would never play for club or country unless he considered himself one hundred per cent fit. It took an honest man to withdraw from an international match on the eve of a game that would have given him the Welsh three-quarter record in appearances, that against France in 1978. He did just that, and sat through the match wishing his deputy every success.

Davies did later achieve the coveted record in Australia. It was this tour, perhaps, which influenced him to cry, 'Enough!'

The game owes him much for the manner in which he has participated in it. He displayed a gentle modesty that hid a determination both to do well on the field for club or country, and to enjoy to the full the close association of a team game.

He has his own special views on the game and will retain them. One hopes that he will still contribute to it: he is needed. For those who watched him play, the memories of his try-scoring efforts and try-saving tackles will remain. Four tries at Napier in 1971, four tries at Pontypool in January 1978, a host of spectacular ones for Wales . . . many of these are recorded on film; these will keep alive the memory, the legend; if such a thing be needed of so magnificent a wing.

Both Edwards and Davies have played their last games for Wales; an era has ended. They will be greatly missed. No matter how many great players follow along the paths of rugby glory, they will never be forgotten. There will be no more long passes, dashes and determined tackles, no more superb tries (each scored 20 for Wales). But their spirit will ever be present at Cardiff Arms Park.

What splendid innings! Thank you Gareth and Gerald and goodbye, maestros, for the pleasure you have given to those who watched you in action.

The Playing Record of G. O. Edwards

53 Welsh Appearances:
  v. England: 1967-78
  v. Scotland: 1968-78
  v. Ireland: 1968-78
  v. France: 1967-78
  v. Australia: 1969, 1973, 1975
  v. New Zealand: 1967, 1969 (2), 1972
  v. South Africa: 1970
  Captain of Wales: 13 matches

10 Lions Appearances:
  v. New Zealand: 1971 (4)
  v. South Africa: 1968 (2), 1974 (4)

Partners:
B. John (23), P. Bennett (25, 1 sub), J. Bevan (4), D. Watkins (2)

Official Representative Match Record 1967-1978

	Pl.	Won	Dr.	Lost	
England	12	10	1	1	
Scotland	11	9	0	2	
Ireland	10	7	1	2	
France	12	6	2	4	
N Z	4	0	0	4	
Australia	3	3	0	0	
S A	1	0	1	0	
Lions	10	6	2	2	
Totals	63	41	7	15	70% success

9
The Future

Just before the year's end, Middlesex became the new county champions, defeating Northumberland at Twickenham 19–6 on 30 December.

Happy though the hard-fought county final may have been, all was not well in the game. The New Year hopes and good wishes were important not only for individuals but for the very game itself. 1978 had proved to be one of considerable change, not all for the better.

The standard of play fell away considerably at all levels; many famous players retired. Refereeing was much poorer than it should have been. The spirit of the game declined. These alarming factors were not the product of any single canker but of the changing attitudes to the game. By the year's end, there was growing concern, or more, about the game's future well-being. Few in high places were ready to admit that publicly, however.

I list in particular the following. They are not in order of danger – all are important. Certainly, the number one problem is the growing violence within the game at all levels and serious injuries to players caused as much by intent as by accident. Just before the year ended, Guy's Hospital Medical School published an invaluable survey on rugby injuries. One cannot fail to be disturbed by the finding that half of all the players engaged in the game suffer one or more injuries in a season which interrupt their playing.

After violence and serious injuries, I believe a problem is that too much rugby is played per season, especially in the British Isles; overseas tours, both long and short, are too frequent. The constant re-writing of the Laws leads to a decline in standards of refereeing due to the burden of so complex a set of Laws. There is also a poor system of selection. I regret growing lack of midfield flair and of rugby as a running and handling game; the grossly exaggerated importance of the penalty goal boosted by its frequency; the almost too rapid growth of the game throughout the world and its need of control. Keeping the game non-political is essential for its continued well-being.

The advent of big money in the game through increased commercialism and sponsorship may be of mixed benefit. There is great need to help South Africa now that she has fully accepted multi-racial rugby; there is need to improve and encourage schoolboy rugby so that potential players are not lost to the game; finally – perhaps most important – we need to guard the true spirit of the game.

How can one expect the true spirit of the game to be maintained when fine players at top level, like Chris Ralston and J. P. R. Williams, are badly injured? Only a return to the true spirit, protected by the Laws, can restore the game to its former standard, as an enjoyable and skilful game. Did John Ashworth enjoy stamping on the face of J. P. R. Williams at Bridgend? If he did not, he has shown remarkably little remorse. What is to become of a game of close physical contact, allegedly a manly game for character building, if violence is to be accepted? No man serves the game well if he does not complain of violence. The code of conduct must never condone violence.

A shadow of violence has lurked in the game since 1873, even before that, in the game's early forms; many has been the club with a 'rogue elephant' player. I have seen them, and have not always condemned them as heartily as I should have done. Club committees and coaches have overlooked their failings; some clubs have openly condoned the worst of actions. Countries have been guilty of this too; New Zealand apparently condoned violence at Bridgend. We live in a violent age but that is no excuse. Rugby is an amateur game where accidents alone are often serious enough to wreck careers, or even lives, of young players. Players even die as the result of accidents on the field of play. No player has ever been reported to have died from an act of violence, but I fear that if present developments continue, it may happen.

Much that happens is not reported in the media; many severe injuries may not be divulged to the world. What we hear through the media may be only the tip of an iceberg. I do not wish to be alarmist in approach, or suggest that rugby should be a game for 'sissies', but neither can it be a game of 'thuggery' where the violent player can seek protection even within the Laws.

The particular problem area is the ruck, maul or pile-up. If 'lack of technique' is offered as a defence, then I will have no part of it: injury at top level occurs just as frequently as at lower levels, and the former is where there should be the highest degree of technique.

The most dangerous offensive weapon on the field of play is not the fist favoured by the old-fashioned 'strong men'. It is the modern stud as worn in the light-weight footwear. More damage is caused each week by 'raking' (or as New Zealanders call it, 'Sprig massage'), than anything else. More muscle injuries may be due to the varying degree of fitness of players, the nature of the playing surface, and genuine bodily contact. Stamping and raking intentionally is without doubt 'malicious wounding'; I expect there will soon be prosecutions by players, supported by the clubs, for serious injuries caused by such acts.

The excuses, 'I was searching for the ball', or 'I could not distinguish between ball and head', are as pathetic as that of a mugger, pouncing on the unprotected. Law-makers should rectify the ruck, maul and pile-up, so as to eliminate the risk of serious injury. The question of studs, which became a vital issue in 1978 during the New Zealand tour, plus the detection and punishment of rough play and the dirty player, requires immediate and urgent attention.

I would accept a Law that allows the referee to give the non-offending side a try between the posts, plus a possible conversion, against the side of which a member was guilty of an action, in cases such as that of John Ashworth at Bridgend. If the referees can be helped by neutral touch judges in spotting such actions, so much the better. There would be more frequent detection, and no side would take kindly to a player forfeiting six points. Penalized sides would suspend such players, even if the referee did not wish to send them off. Referees, generally, did not help the game or their own cause in 1978.

The laxity in enforcement of the Laws did much harm to the principle of neutral referees. It was suggested that referees were seeking favour in selection as neutral referees for the 1979 French tour of New Zealand; that, if true, is an unhappy state of affairs, but is one that can never be proven. I favour the idea that it was all part of a 'be kind to the tourists' campaign, as well as the result of a system that provides referees with the incentive of an international match if they give a favourable impression in a provincial or club match in the ten days prior to an international.

Referees, naturally, will deny this vehemently, but it is bound to affect the approach sub-consciously; every referee wants to 'win a cap' in the form of an international match! The tendency is to watch the opposition and not the tourists, and while the opposition are rightly 'blown up' for their infringements, the tourists enjoy a charmed life. I have watched similar happenings overseas, where the Lions in their scarlet jerseys have been watched, but not the home sides. 1966 Lions manager, experienced player Desmond O'Brien, admitted to me, 'They penalize us correctly, but then, they only watch the red jerseys!' Clive Rowlands and John Dawes believed this to be true of the 1978 Welsh tour of Australia, as did Barry Nelmes of the 1975 tour by England in that country.

When referees did not bother to reprimand sides for rough play against the 1974 Lions in South Africa, the tourists adopted the '99 call', more a reflection upon the standard of refereeing, than the aggressive attitude of the Lions, the greatest British side of the century. Referees should never allow players to take the law into their own hands. John West of Ireland suffered criticism for partially condoning Andy Haden's k.o. punch in the Scotland–New Zealand match of 1978.

Refereeing the modern game is a difficult task, and a most thankless one. The increasing difficulty is closely linked with continual changes in the Laws, the greater sophistication of approach on the part of players, and a decline in the spirit of the game. There are few rewards for referees in any form; they tend to become more isolated at higher levels. They tend to split hairs in Law-interpretation. There is urgent need for the International Board to consider refereeing in detail during the present re-writing of the Laws of the Game.

I have known the three experts who form the Laws sub-committee, Hermas Evans (Wales) (chairman), Harry McKibbin (Ireland), and Dr Danie Craven (South Africa), since the War. I have the greatest faith in their ability. Mr Evans has just retired as a college principal. He has been deeply involved in the game for most of his life; Harry McKibbin is a legal expert, and Ireland and 1938 Lions centre; Danie Craven is one of the game's greatest figures and possibly its most knowledgeable student among its senior administrators.

Their task is a critical one, the most important in the game since the fateful International Board meeting of 1954 when the lineout was destroyed as a fair and just way of bringing the ball back into play after it entered touch. Since that year, in the quarter-century elapsed, there have followed many changes; some good, some bad. The need now is for simplification, easier interpretation, a reduction in the importance of the penalty goal, the elimination of the ruck (in the sense that the ball should either be played off the ground after a tackle by the hands, or revert to previous ruling of the tackled player getting up and playing it with the foot), a radical change at the lineout to bring a return of two-handed jumping, and the severest possible penalties for rough play (including the assistance of touch judges for referees in major matches).

During 1978, I have discussed the game's many and growing problems with a wide range of men of distinction, young and old: Lord Wakefield, Air Vice-Marshal Larry Lamb, John Dawes, Carwyn James, Ray Williams, Don Rutherford, Herbert Waddell, Gwynne Walters, Syd Millar, Gareth Edwards, Wilfred Wooller, Vivian Jenkins, Cliff Jones, John Reason, Kenneth Harris, David Frost, Denzil Lloyd, Wylie Beckenridge, Danie Craven, and others; they form a true cross-section of the game. I have also talked to senior officials of the Home Unions and the International Board, and to many national selectors. Their ideas vary, but they all seek to protect the game and its players; they seek an early return of the true spirit and flair.

James, an 'exile' in Italy for some time, wants urgently to see a return of natural flair all round, but especially so in midfield. Larry Lamb wants a *workable* code of Laws, and a return of self-discipline on the part of players. Waddell wants the spirit and comradeship and the amateurism as existed in the best days in the game. Williams and Rutherford seek a better understanding of the game and its principles in all grades. Walters keeps telling me, 'We have to do something about the ruck and pile-up and avoid unnecessary injuries.' Dawes, for all the criticism laid against him and his sides for the crash-ball approach, believes in the running game with full employment of the three-quarters; he has always coached it that way. Wakers seeks to revolutionize the lineout, and Cliff Jones campaigns for better communication with the media.

It has always been true of the game that we say, 'It is not as good as it was'. Perhaps this time, it is true, but it could be a great game still, if we can all work to get the spirit right. The first need for this to be achieved is to have a healthy respect for the un-protected player on the ground. Let us start from there; the game would lose none of its traditional hardness, but a great deal of its wanton and distasteful cruelty.

Coaching has come under fire during the 1978–79 season – or, as Ray Williams and Rutherford would argue, 'Bad coaching has been criticized!' The main attacks have come as a result of the decline in flair in British midfield play. One has to admit that criticism is justified, whether the deterioration is due to bad coaching, changes in the Laws, the approach of individual players, or even the lack of brilliant individualists such as Gareth Edwards and Phil Bennett. I do believe that coaching is as necessary as team and self-discipline, but there must not be too many set moves. Rugby is a faster game, overall, than it has ever been, mainly as a result of the emancipation of forward play.

Forwards are now very much a part of the fifteen-man game, but ignoring three-quarters produces 'ten-man rugby'. There should be no such thing, even if centres are neglected in attack. It is a fifteen-man game, and will remain so. If one studies the development of the game closely, it has always demanded that a good player should be fit, and be able to run, handle, kick, dodge, catch and tackle, *and*, at the same time, *think*!

The old joke about props not being able to run with the ball and think, has long since passed into oblivion. One should re-member that in 1903, at Swansea, against England, Welsh prop Jehoida Hodges went out on to the wing when Tommy Pearson had his ribs crushed by demon-tackler full-back, Gamlin. He scored three tries! This proud record was equalled by the Fijian prop, Walisoliso, against Wales at Cardiff in 1964. The Laws may have changed radically, over the years, but how much has individual performance changed?

The Law-makers state, correctly, 'We cannot play the game for the players, but we have to legislate against the Law-breakers, and the players must make the best of it!' That is why the spirit of approach and the standard of coaching, plus flair and attitude, are the vital factors for the future. One encouraging factor was the greatly improved standard of play, spirit and entertainment in the Intervarsity match of December. Oxford, a lighter and less experienced side despite a defeat, contributed much to the play; Cambridge, led by a player of international quality, scrum-half John Robbie of Ireland, produced the best standard of attainment and approach for many years.

It is true that standards are relative, but the *approach* should always be that of aiming at the highest standards. This latest Intervarsity match had much to commend it, despite the wet weather. Given the conditions, the attendance was excellent, encouraging for the game, both Universities, and for the sponsors, Bowring Ltd; they have helped unobtrusively in recent years, demanding comparatively little advertising, and showing an obvious enjoyment in ensuring the successful continuation of the historic fixture. The Bowring Bowl is a handsome trophy. University sport, generally, will benefit by the crowd support.

John Robbie, after a year of continuous injury bravely shouldered, must have done much to reclaim his place in the Irish national side, and a place on the summer tour to Australia. In the first match of the New Zealand tour, he performed most ably. He led an onslaught in the second half, the style of which, had it been copied by succeeding opponents, might have changed the touring team's record. With young men like Robbie ready to impose their character upon the game in the best possible way, there is always genuine hope for the future.

Mention of Bowring highlights the growing interest on the part of sponsors in Rugby Union Football. I expect this to increase in the years ahead. It needs to be rigidly controlled, especially in the face of unpleasant rumours that players are already paid for appearing in certain matches wearing certain makes of boots!

Some clubs have obtained sponsorship by the expedient of setting aside tradition, and changing the colours and patterns of their jerseys. However, I believe that firms like Schweppes, John Players, certain leading banks and oil firms, the Welsh Brewers, and others, intend to help the game without changing the face of it. But the competition between the makers of sports equipment and clothing hotted up considerably in 1978, and is likely to continue to do so in 1979. There is need for close analysis of future sponsorship on the part of the Home Unions.

One club, Pontypool, is being sponsored almost entirely by a local engineering firm, Sanders Valve, with the full approval of the Welsh Rugby Union. Other clubs may invite such help. Even Cardiff, most conservative of clubs, are now accepting sponsorship for individual matches.

Cup competitions, especially the national ones of England and Wales, are proving money-spinners. John Player Ltd and Schweppes Ltd will benefit in the long run for their sponsorship of these major events. However, the Unions must not become too money-conscious, even allowing that the cost of staging and administering the game has grown enormously in the last ten years.

The argument for more frequent long and short tours is partially the need of cash. But in recent years there have been too many tours. Four visits by the All Blacks in successive seasons is not ideal, and too-frequent tours strike at the very heart of the game, club rugby.

I believe the International Board should do everything possible to encourage South African rugby, but there should be a careful pruning of tours in the next decade. The effect upon club rugby does not produce an improvement in the standard of play. With an increased number of outgoing tours as well, it is obvious that the demands upon leading players today are far greater than they were twenty-five years ago.

Since the days of the 1950s, when three Lions sides (1950/55/59) really played for fun, in accordance with the highest ideals and with remarkable individual skill, the world game has become more sophisticated, even at school level. Whilst part of the reason may be the advent of coaching, this is not the main reason. Coaching has produced improved forward play and sterner contention overall for possession, but a greater sense of competition and nationalism had crept into the game.

The world attitude towards sport has changed considerably in the past twenty years, and will continue to do so. How then can Rugby Union Football remain aloof from the strong and often unsavoury influences that surround it? Rugby's administrators must be strong and realistic. I envisage the setting up of a permament secretariat by the International Board, for two purposes: to control the British-devised world game, and to ensure that its true amateur spirit of approach is maintained.

Much is being done by Rugby Union headquarters at Twickenham and Cardiff Arms Park to help the more isolated developing countries. All facets of the game have to be examined, discussed and helped. A better working knowledge of the Laws, and better refereeing, will ensure healthy development. Those countries behind the Iron Curtain must accept that rugby should not become a political battle ground, as have certain other sports. The English-speaking peoples and the French cannot ignore the game's rapid growth throughout the world. They must advise, guide and help. An active international secretariat would be the immediate answer. A meeting of the International Board once annually is not nearly enough to cope with the game's need.

The past twelve months have seen the departure from the international scene of several truly great players. Gareth Edwards, Mike Gibson, Gerald Davies, Sandy Carmichael, Phil Bennett, Terry Cobner and others have done much for the game as individuals and as team men. They will not be easily replaced on the field; I hope they will continue to serve the game in one way or another. They were really gifted players who yet possessed the game's traditional modesty. The departure of the stars leaves the stage wide open for the young challengers. It will not be easy for Jerome Gallion, Gareth Davies, Tony Ward, Terry Holmes, Paul Dodge, Keith Robertson, or others like. All must help regain the true spirit and flair of rugby football, and rid it of its wanton violence. Rugby should be as enjoyable for the players at the top as it is for those pounding away in the 'Extra B' XVs. It is a great game. It must go on with all the pride, skill, and, most of all, sportsmanship, that can be generated.

Index